The
Nut
Gourmet

Nourishing Nuts
for Every Occasion

Zel Allen

Book Publishing Company
Summertown, Tennessee

Cover design: Warren Jefferson
Cover and interior photos: Warren Jefferson
Interior design: Gwynelle Dismukes

Published in the United States by
Book Publishing Company
P.O. Box 99
Summertown, TN 38483
1-888-260-8458

Printed in the United States

ISBN-13 978-1-57067-191-3
ISBN-10 1-57067-191-5

15 14 13 12 11 10 09 08 07 06   9 8 7 6 5 4 3 2 1

Allen, Zel.
   The Nut gourmet / Zel Allen.
      p. cm.
   Includes bibliographical references and index.
   ISBN-13: 978-1-57067-191-3
   ISBN-10: 1-57067-191-5
   1. Cookery (Nuts) I. Title.

TX814.A45 2006
641.6'45--dc22   2006005414

Featured on the cover (counterclockwise from upper left):
26 Pecan Salad, p. 70, with Lemon Dill Sauce, p. 144
Wasabi Picstachio Vegetable Aspic, p. 80
Peanut Butter Carob Pie, p.192

Featured on back cover:
Almond, Mushroom and Spinach over Pasta with
   Savory Cashew Cream Sauce, p.100

Calculations for the nutritional analyses in this book are based on the average number of servings listed with the recipes and the average amount of an ingredient if a range is called for. Calculations are rounded up to the nearest gram. If two options for an ingredient are listed, the first one is used. Not included are fat used for frying (unless the amount is specified in the recipe), optional ingredients, or serving suggestions.

To my husband and dearest friend, Reuben,

whose partnership has enriched my life

and inspired many creative endeavors

through the years.

Contents

Acknowledgments

There are not enough words to express the appreciation I owe to my husband, Reuben. I am deeply indebted to him for the many creative suggestions, encouragement, and support he has given me in this endeavor. Always willing to taste that little something I just had to try out, he never let me down with honest evaluations that helped bring the final results to fruition. A former English and journalism teacher, he lassoed stray dangling participles and kept those sometimes funny phrases from stampeding my manuscript.

Of course, a great big thanks goes to my four wonderful children, Chuck, Bruce, Amy, and Gregg, who jokingly refer to my nutty creations as "science experiments," as they reach for another helping. I am indebted to my daughter, Amy, for her generous time in putting the nutritional data into nice, neat tables. Appreciation goes to Bruce, whose nurturing words and encouragement keep me inspired. A big thank-you hug goes to Chuck for encouraging me to include his fabulous recipe for the Sugarplum Spiced Walnuts. And to Gregg for his infinite knowledge of creative marketing ideas.

Appreciation goes to my exceptional neighbors Joan and Larry Harmell and Helen and Alex Muller, who have enthusiastically taste-tested many of the recipes in the book. With special affection I thank my friend and "little brother" Scott Sachs, who told me years ago, "I know you've got a book in you somewhere" and wasn't surprised when I told him the good news about actually getting published. As a fine chef and caterer, Scott was the one I turned to when I needed a solution for binding a runaway pie filling. Another thanks goes to Chef Dave Anderson, restaurateur of Madeline Bistro, who said the magic word "boil," a step that made the Down-Home Pecan Pie come to life.

A gracious thanks to Joe McSweyn, my OMD, who provided the idea for the Chocolate Peanut Butter Mousse. Humble appreciation goes to my friend Dr. Neal Pinckney who inspired the Nutty Buckwheat Pancakes recipe and went out of his way to offer help and encouragement. Thanks to cookbook author Nava Atlas for her generous offer to help publicize *The Nut Gourmet* on her Web site.

Appreciation goes to Doctors Neal Barnard, Jay Gordon, and Bill Harris for their generosity in contributing such positive endorsements on the book cover. Their validations mean a great deal to me.

A hearty thanks to the Internet readers of *Vegetarians in Paradise* who have written letters of thanks and encouragement over the seven years of its publication on the Web. My indebtedness goes to Kathy Seifert, director of Glendale Community College Community Services, for adding Cooking the Vegetarian Way to her class offerings. Teaching the cooking classes has given me the opportunity to test many of the recipes in the book. My heartfelt gratitude goes to Jeff and Sabrina Nelson of VegSource, whose generosity has made *Vegetarians in Paradise* and this book a possibility.

I am ever so grateful to Brenda Davis, RD, for the profound and enthusiastic support demonstrated in the exceptional foreword she contributed to *The Nut Gourmet*. Her knowledge as a registered dietitian provides assurance to anyone in doubt about the nutritional benefit of consuming nuts.

And to Jo Stepaniak, author and editor extraordinaire, goes my heartfelt gratitude for being my fairy godmother and creating divine sorcery with her magic cyber-wand. I am truly fortunate to have had Jo patiently guiding me through the editorial process. Clearly she has raised editing to an art. Her own books have a special place on my kitchen bookshelf and have been an inspiration and constant resource for me over the years. Now she has a very special place in my heart as well.

Deep appreciation goes to publishers Cynthia and Bob Holzapfel for having confidence in *The Nut Gourmet* and the willingness to publish it. I have had the good fortune to receive their heartwarming praise, and I am feeling very nurtured. Over the years they have produced a high-quality collection of vegetarian books that have been embraced by the vegetarian community. I am honored to have my book added to their list.

My gratitude goes to Warren Jefferson and his design team for the beautiful cover design and photos; Gwynelle Dismukes for adding spark to the book with an elegant layout design; Barb Bloomfield for her special touches with food styling; Anna Pope for making sure book copies travel to important destinations; Thomas Hupp for his PR expertise; and to everyone whose name I have yet to learn for giving their all to help make *The Nut Gourmet* an exceptional volume. I am truly in their debt.

Foreword

Many people view nuts as little more than fat-laden, salty snacks. Of course, they are absolutely right—when nuts are coated in partially hydrogenated oil, salt, sugar and/or chocolate. However, in their natural state, nuts are among the most underestimated nutritional power-houses in the diet.

No one can argue that nuts are a high-fat food, with 70–95 percent of their calories coming from fat. During the late 1980s to early '90s, fat was regarded as diet enemy number one, and all fats, regardless of the source, were thought to have negative consequences for human health. In the vegetarian world, very low-fat diets were embraced as the gold standard. Nuts and other high-fat plant foods were relegated to the doghouse. Fortunately, after many years of compelling scientific research, experts recognize that nuts are not evil villains but rather potent protectors, particularly where chronic diseases, such as heart disease, are concerned. Surprisingly, regular nut eaters are not at increased risk for overweight or obesity, and nuts have been very success-fully incorporated into weight-loss programs.

So what is it that makes nuts so beneficial? It could be the impressive level of powerful antioxi-dants they contain. For example, in a study that determined the ferric-reducing ability of plasma (FRAP) score (a measure of antioxidant potential or the ability of a food to quench damaging free radicals) of several common foods, walnuts shone with a score of 21, almost 10 points higher than the next highest scoring item, pomegranate, with a score of 11.3. Then again, it may be the amazing complement of disease-fighting phytochemicals, such as flavonoids (strong antioxi-dants that reduce the oxidation of LDL cholesterol) and polyphenolic compounds (e.g., ellagic acid, which protects against DNA damage and depresses tumor growth). Maybe it is the incred-ible array of trace minerals in nuts. Each variety of nut seems to offer its own unique comple-ment of these important nutrients. Almonds are rich in calcium and magnesium; cashews offer zinc, iron, and copper; hazelnuts and pecans are great sources of manganese; Brazil nuts are loaded with selenium; and pistachios provide potassium. These little gems are also sources of B vitamins, vitamin E, plant protein, and fiber. Of course, the cardioprotective effects of nuts could also be due to the arginine they provide. This amino acid is converted to nitric oxide in our bodies and acts as a potent vasodilator (something that causes blood vessels to relax or expand, improving blood flow). Could it be the healthful fats that make up most of the calories in nuts? While we once thought all fat was bad, we now know that certain fats are very healthful, and some are essential to life. Nuts are among the very best places to get fat. The fat in nuts is unsaturated (mainly monounsaturated), and when the fat in nuts replaces damaging fats in processed foods and animal products, positive health benefits are noted. Perhaps it is a combination of all of the above that makes nuts such a great addition to the diet. Whatever it is, there is no question that nuts have been pulled out of the doghouse and put up on a pedestal—right where they belong.

I have spent the greater part of my career assisting vegetarians and vegans in constructing diets that support excellent health throughout the life cycle. Two significant challenges are ensuring a balance of healthful fats and meeting needs for trace minerals. Including nuts in the daily diet goes a long way toward addressing both of these challenges. Nuts are rich in monounsaturated fat, and walnuts are rich in both essential fatty acids. Nuts are among our best sources of several trace minerals. The fat in nuts can help to maximize our absorption of some of our greatest protectors—fat soluble vitamins, certain minerals, and a wide variety of phytochemicals.

This book is a treasure—it is beautifully written, comprehensive, and entertaining. It provides accurate, detailed information about the value of nuts in the diet, numerous practical tips, helpful tables, and dozens of mouthwatering recipes. It is a delightful cookbook and a tremendous nutrition resource.

So go ahead, be a nut gourmet, a gourmet nut, or just a plain old nut . . . and welcome to the club.

Brenda Davis, RD

Introduction

Nuts are a wonder food that has sustained prehistoric cultures of hunter-gatherers, nomadic tribes, and native peoples through centuries of long, harsh winters. Though sustenance was of primary importance, people of ancient cultures simply enjoyed nuts because they were satisfying and flavorful. Today, with such a variety of nuts available year-round, you can create a unique cuisine that incorporates them into sauces, soups, spreads, sandwich fillings, entrées, salads, dressings, stuffings, smoothies, and desserts.

In addition to offering delightful, satisfying flavor, nuts provide darned good nutrition, supplying outstanding plant proteins, phytochemicals, essential fatty acids (good fats), great fiber, and energy-boosting carbohydrates. And what could be more convenient? Each nut comes wrapped in its own unique shell to protect its flavor and nutrients.

Rather than offering standard recipes that merely feature a sprinkling of nuts, this book incorporates nuts as an integral part of these recipes so they actually become the focal point of each dish. Perhaps savory Butternut Corn Cashew Soup (page 62) will beckon on some chilly autumn or winter evening. A perfect meal starter, the soup also serves as a satisfying main dish throughout the cold winter months. Possibly you'll want to prepare hearty Walnut Lentil Pie (page 44), the ideal entrée for guests who deserve something extra-special. Delight your sweet tooth by munching on Fruity Pecan Balls (page 210), which don't even require cooking.

Of important note is how best to make full use of this book. Planning an entire meal of nut-based recipes from the various sections of the book would result in overdoing a good thing. Instead, choose one special dish, like Sultan's Delight with Savory Pistachio Sauce (page 124), to enhance your meal that day. Next day, select another, perhaps Yam and Nut Butter Soup (page 61) or Creamy Cashew Basil Dressing (page 91), to round out your lunch or dinner.

For optimum health, none of the recipes contain salted, oil-roasted nuts. Unless otherwise indicated, all the recipes use only raw nuts.

Since no kitchen would be complete without a few tools to make cracking and chopping nuts easier, I have included a list of suggested gadgets and how best to use them (see page 33). Through the ages, nut lovers have developed resourceful methods that enable them to crack the toughest of nuts. This book offers some clever yet down-to-earth nut-cracking techniques, along with a sprinkling of fascinating facts about some extraordinary efforts that have been used to reach the nutmeats.

There's no guesswork to purchasing and storing nuts. These details can be found in Cracking the Code: Buying and Storing Nuts (page 21). In this brief section you'll become acquainted with the best seasons to purchase nuts and the advantages of buying nuts in the shell. You'll also learn why it's smart to purchase nuts in small quantities. For larger purchases, you'll learn how to safely store nuts for longer periods. Though oil-roasted and salted nuts offer satisfying taste, you'll discover why they may be harmful to your health.

The book reveals the health benefits you'll derive from enjoying nuts on a regular basis. Read about the many studies that uncovered surprising results about how nuts can help prevent heart disease. If you are a nut fancier like I am, you may be pleased to learn that it is not necessary to focus on any one particular kind of nut. Though each variety differs somewhat in nutritional content, all nuts are highly nutritious.

A number of handy tables offer the cook a quick reference to important information, such as nut measurement equivalents (page 37). For instance, when a recipe calls for two-thirds cup ground cashews, the table will show the equivalent is one-half cup whole cashews.

Several nutritional tables are included in the book as well (see Appendix, page 241). One shows the distribution of fatty acid composition of various tree nuts. For example, the table gives a percentage breakdown of the monounsaturated fat, polyunsaturated fat, saturated fat, and omega-3 fatty acids contained in each kind of nut and its oil. Two other tables list the vitamin and mineral content of nuts, while a separate table offers information regarding protein, fiber, and fat content.

The heart of the book is, of course, the gourmet recipe collection that opens the door to the exciting world of nut cuisine. You will quickly discover how nuts can contribute a wealth of zesty flavors in dishes that are the centerpiece of a meal. Each recipe has been tested many times over to ensure consistent success.

Reap the pleasures of crunchy almonds, buttery macadamias, or delicately sweet pecans. Reach for a handful of pungent walnuts or creamy pine nuts. Tempt yourself with fresh raw green pistachios or the sweet aroma of creamy cashews. Include some fleshy, flavorsome Brazil nuts or toothsome hazelnuts in a favorite recipe. Bring a bowlful of freshly roasted peanuts in the shell to the table. Celebrate the holiday season with a succulent dessert like Chestnut Mousse with Chocolate Truffle (page 212).

Once you've bought a pound or two of your favorite nuts, or splurged on new ones you are eager to try, you are ready for some kitchen pleasures with *The Nut Gourmet*. Take joy in the process of preparing these delicacies as well as enjoying the end result. Each dish you create will surely be enriched with that extra pinch of zeal you've lovingly added.

Go Nuts for Goodness Sake!

How often I've heard friends respond to my offer of nuts by saying, "Oh, no thank you, they're too fattening." In other instances, people who simply cannot stop eating them tell me, "I know nuts are bad for me, but I just love 'em." Many people are convinced that nuts are unhealthful because they are high in fat. What they fail to realize is the fats contained in nuts are actually beneficial. Along with their healthful mono- and polyunsaturated fats, nuts are a storehouse of vitamins, minerals, and phytochemicals that aid in lowering cholesterol and reducing the risk of heart attack. Nuts offer other benefits because they are a source of plant sterols, indoles, phenolic compounds, and bioflavonoids that have been shown to prevent some cancers.

Bolstering the case for including nuts in the diet, the United States Food and Drug Administration released a report in July 2003 giving nuts the thumbs-up. They announced product labels could now make health claims that consuming 1.5 ounces of nuts a day as part of a diet low in saturated fat and cholesterol was beneficial in reducing the risk of cardiovascular disease.

Nuts Are a Treasure Trove of Nutritious Properties

Too often people are so focused on the fat content of nuts they ignore other data listed on nutrition panels. For instance, the labeling confirms that nuts are a very low-sodium food and they contain no cholesterol. Nuts are an excellent source of plant protein and dietary fiber. One ounce of raw almonds provides 6 grams of protein plus 3 grams of fiber. That same quantity of raw peanuts provides 7 grams of protein and 2 grams of dietary fiber. Yet these amazing figures are pushed out of focus while attention is given to the high fat content of nuts, often made unhealthful by the addition of oils and salt "to make them taste better." In addition, this exceptional food contains a host of beneficial nutrients not listed on food labels, like vitamins, minerals, and phytochemicals. In their simple, natural state, nuts are a nutrient-dense food that has rich, satisfying flavor without the need for alteration or enhancement.

Even though all nuts have some nutritional components in common, each variety has some unique properties. Chestnuts, for example, are the only nuts that contain a measurable quantity of vitamin C. One ounce of boiled chestnuts contains 7.6 grams of vitamin C, while most other nuts contain none.

All nuts contain calcium, but almonds stand apart with 248 milligrams for 3.5 ounces. With 17.3 milligrams of copper for 3.5 ounces, hazelnuts are recognized for their high level of this mineral, which contributes to bone health and keeps blood vessels functioning optimally.

Iron and zinc, two minerals present only in small quantities in a plant-based diet, can be found in nuts. Cashews and pecans boast ample supplies of zinc, with 5.6 milligrams and 4.5 milligrams respectively for 3.5 ounces. One of the many important functions of zinc is its contribution to our sensory ability to taste.

Cashews contain exceptional quantities of iron, a mineral vital to the production of hemoglobin. Brazil nuts are the champions of selenium, an important antioxidant and detoxifier, while pistachios, chestnuts, and almonds contain a storehouse of potassium, which plays a major role in the regulation of our heartbeat.

Every variety of nuts offers fiber, but pistachios and almonds are at the top of the list. Credit almonds and filberts for their high content of vitamin E, an antiaging protector against free radical damage to our cells. Ranking just below beans, berries, artichokes, and apples, pecans offer the highest number of antioxidants in the nut family. Each variety of nut contains arginine, the amino acid that aids in forming nitric oxide to keep the blood vessels pliable for good blood flow. Peanuts and almonds supply us with the greatest quantity of arginine.

Nuts are exemplary citizens of the plant world and deserve a place on the daily breakfast, lunch, or dinner plate. Because data from recent studies unveiled the merit of nuts, health professionals now agree that a small daily serving of 1.5 ounces of nuts may reduce the risk of heart attack.

Put Oil-Roasted Nuts on the No-No List

Common sense tells us that nuts roasted in unhealthful oils and doused with salt are not a smart addition to anyone's diet. First, the oil used in roasting may be partially hydrogenated, a process that changes the chemical structure of the oil, turning it into a dangerous trans-fatty acid. Hydrogenated and partially hydrogenated fats are two to four times more troublesome in the bloodstream than saturated fat. Because trans-fatty acids tend to raise LDL cholesterol (the bad guys) and lower HDL cholesterol (the good guys), they are a factor leading to serious coronary artery disease. Frequently nuts are roasted in partially hydrogenated oils, turning healthful raw nuts into a product that poses a health risk. Medical experts warn that hydrogenated fats and excessive amounts of saturated fats in the diet contribute to atherosclerosis, a buildup of plaque in the arteries that raises the risk of heart attack.

Second, roasting nuts in oil adds unneeded calories. Consider that one tablespoon of any oil contains about 120 calories and approximately 14 grams of fat.

The third problem to the unhealthful combination is the amount of salt one can consume in a handful or two of salted nuts. The accepted level of salt intake that nutritionists agree upon is about one teaspoon (2300 mg) per day. At social gatherings, guests may easily exceed this amount by unconsciously reaching for one handful of salted nuts after another.

Nuts Promote Weight Loss

Because nuts are so full of nutrients, their fats, carbohydrates, and protein combine to bring rich, earthy flavor to the palate and provide a feeling of satiety when small amounts are added to the diet. Even the "little bit goes a long way" practice of consuming one or two ounces of nuts a day can promote weight loss when other dietary fats are reduced. Eaten in these small quantities, nuts can provide a healthful alternative to foods high in saturated fats and cholesterol such as meat, chicken, fish, eggs, and dairy products. Consider incorporating nuts into a salad, soup, vegetable stir-fry, or casserole with vegetables, legumes, and grains. You won't lose anything but a few pounds.

People used to eating fatty foods will find nuts an enjoyable substitute. Because nuts are high in mono- and polyunsaturated fats, yet low in saturated fat, dieters will find these small quantities of nuts a pleasurable replacement for their usual snack foods, such as potato or corn chips. It is important, however, that dieters' total calorie consumption be taken into consideration. One cannot lose weight by simply adding another high-fat food to an already fatty diet.

Nuts Contain Good Fats

The monounsaturated fats in cashews, almonds, peanuts, hazelnuts, macadamias, pistachios, and pecans, and the polyunsaturated fats in walnuts, are shown in many studies to reduce LDL cholesterol, resulting in a lower risk of heart attack. Studies have found that nuts are helpful in preventing some types of cancers, while other studies report that nuts reduce the risk of type 2 diabetes.

Amazing Health Benefits in a Nutshell

Recent health studies touting nuts as superfoods make it easy to boast about the benefits of eating them often. That wholesome little kernel tucked inside a nutshell contains a wealth of nutrients powerful enough to lower cholesterol, reduce the risk of heart attack, lower blood pressure in patients with hypertension, and produce weight loss. The phytochemicals found in nuts also have antioxidant and anti-inflammatory abilities capable of preventing some cancers. Nuts may even play a role in maintaining healthy sexual function in men.

In his book *Healthy Nuts*, Gene Spiller, a nutritional research scientist, cites a study conducted at the Seventh Day Adventist Hospital in Loma Linda, California, and published in the July 1992 issue of Archives of Internal Medicine. The results surprised researchers by revealing that people who ate 1.5 to 2 ounces of almonds four to five times a week had a much lower risk of heart attack than those who ate no nuts at all. Another unexpected outcome revealed that when the participants ate a daily snack of raw almonds, about 320 calories, they did not gain weight in spite of the high-fat content of nuts. Some researchers believe it may be the vitamin E plus other phytochemicals in nuts that offer the antioxidant potential to lower cholesterol. Leslie Klevay of the Human Nutrition Research Center of the United States Department of Agriculture feels the trace mineral copper contained in nuts may be crucial in preventing heart disease. The typical American diet is often lacking in copper. Nuts are one of the few categories of food that contain this important mineral. Other sources of copper include beans, lentils, whole wheat, seeds, and prunes.

In a six-year follow-up of the Loma Linda study conducted in 1974 and 1975, with an additional seven-year follow-up, the 34,000 participants filled out questionnaires that related to their dietary habits, exercise, and health status. Interestingly, the researchers had not focused on nuts at the outset of the study and only realized their benefits when comparing the data at the conclusion of their work.

Similar results were found in the Iowa Women's Health Study published in the *New England Journal of Medicine* in 1996. Larry Kushi, one of the directors of the study, stated, "The more frequently the women ate nuts, the lower their heart-disease risk. This was true even when the nut consumption was only a few times a week." The study, conducted at the University of Minnesota School of Public Health, enrolled 38,000 participants and followed them for several years.

Researchers feel the health benefits of nuts are connected more to the kind of fat that nuts contain rather than the overall amount of dietary fat that people consume. Cashews, almonds, peanuts, hazelnuts, macadamias, pistachios, and pecans are all high in monounsaturated fat. Walnuts contain a wealth of omega-3 fatty acids, which are polyunsaturated fats similar to the polyunsaturated fatty acids found in salmon. Though experts in the field of nutrition do not agree on the exact amount of healthful fats people ought to consume, they do concur that the mono- and polyunsaturated fats contained in whole foods such as nuts, seeds, and avocados are important components in a healthful diet. Nutrition gurus like Walter Willett, chairman of the Department of Nutrition at Harvard University, John Farquhar, professor of Medicine at Stanford University, and Gary Fraser, professor of Medicine and Epidemiology of Loma Linda University, all recognize the value of including nuts in the diet as part of maintaining good health.

A daily serving of three ounces of raw almonds took the spotlight in Gene Spiller's studies conducted at his Health Research and Studies Center in Palo Alto, California. In one study the participants consumed the almonds, some whole and some ground, as the main source of protein and fat in the diet. Almond oil was the only oil or fat permitted during the nine-week study. Within three weeks, the twenty-seven men and women who completed the study showed a 10 percent drop in blood cholesterol, with a 12 percent reduction in LDL, the bad cholesterol. These figures remained stable throughout the nine-week study, with no change in triglycerides and HDL, the good cholesterol. He also noted that there was no significant change in the body weight of the participants.

In the other study of four weeks duration, Dr. Spiller wanted to compare the almond study results with two other diets. Along with the three ounces of almonds, he used three ounces of olive oil, also a monounsaturated fat, as the source of fat, along with protein from cottage cheese and yogurt in one diet. In the other, he used cheese, a saturated fat, as the source of fat and protein. He also matched the amounts of fiber and protein in each of the diets to be consistent with those of the almond diet.

The diet using almonds as the source of protein and fat showed the greatest effect on lowering blood cholesterol. The participants consuming the cheese did not show lower cholesterol levels, while the diet using olive oil, cottage cheese, and yogurt showed only minor changes in lowering blood cholesterol.

As far back as 1970, David Kritchevsky, of the Wistar Institute in Philadelphia, compared animal protein to plant protein in an experiment to lower blood cholesterol in laboratory animals. The plant protein resulted in a lower cholesterol level than the animal protein. Dr. Kritchevsky then experimented with different ratios of two amino acids, arginine and lysine, to discover which ratio promotes better blood flow for patients with high cholesterol.

Nuts play an important role in the cholesterol picture because of their naturally high level of arginine. Researchers are discovering that arginine has a beneficial effect on lowering cholesterol due to its ability to synthesize nitric oxide (nitrogen and oxygen), a compound that relaxes and widens the blood vessel walls. Arginine and its ability to aid in coalescing nitric oxide may also be a factor in maintaining healthy sexual function in men. Credit goes to nuts with their high levels of arginine. Researchers believe arginine may even prevent deposits of cholesterol in the arteries and could be responsible for helping to lower blood pressure for patients with hypertension.

Eating nuts may actually prevent the formation of abnormal blood clots inside the blood vessels. Again, praise goes to arginine, which is more concentrated in nuts and other plant foods than in animal proteins. When comparing exact protein quantities of animal and plant foods, researchers found beef protein contains 300 to 450 milligrams of arginine, while milk protein contains about 250 milligrams. However, nuts, a plant protein, soar well above the animal proteins with 600 to 900 milligrams of arginine.

The ten-year Nurses' Health Study at the Harvard School of Public Health, which included more than 86,000 women, also showed similar positive results. Frequently including nuts in their diet, as much as five times a week, lowered their risk of heart attack. Frank Hu, lead researcher on the study, reported, "Even when we adjusted for factors like smoking, exercise, and consumption of fruits and vegetables, nuts showed up as a powerful defense against heart disease."

"Monounsaturated and polyunsaturated fats have been shown to lower LDLs, or so-called bad cholesterol," says Dr. Hu in the study published in the November 1998 issue of the *British Medical Journal*. Researchers also learned that those participants who ate nuts actually tended to weigh less than those who didn't eat nuts.

Including peanuts, peanut butter, peanut oil, and peanut flour in your diet may offer natural protection against some cancers. Though peanuts are actually legumes, they offer similar health benefits as nuts. Peanuts played a starring role in a study led by Atif Awad reported in 2000 in *Nutrition and Cancer*. The study identified a phytosterol, called betasitosterol, capable of inhibiting colon, breast, and prostate cancer growth.

In the forefront of a study conducted at the U.S. Department of Agriculture in Raleigh, North Carolina, in 2000, two ounces of peanuts were found to contain 160 micrograms of the phytochemical resveratrol. Several studies found this naturally occurring polyphenol may be beneficial to heart patients for its antioxidant and anti-inflammatory attributes. Resveratrol is also being studied for its possible anticancer activity. Almonds, berries, and grapes also contain resveratrol.

Macadamias were a prominent focus in a study by David Colquhoun at the University of Queensland in Australia in which they were found effective in lowering overall high cholesterol by

7 percent and lowering LDL cholesterol by 11 percent. Another researcher tested macadamias on subjects with normal cholesterol of about 200 milligrams and, again, macadamias, the native nuts of Australia, succeeded in lowering their cholesterol levels to about 191 milligrams.

Rui Jiang of Harvard School of Public Health in Boston found that eating five one-ounce servings of nuts each week reduces a woman's risk of developing type 2 diabetes by almost one-third. His results were published in the *Journal of the American Medical Association*, November 25, 2002.

Almonds were an important component in lowering cholesterol in a four-week Canadian study authored by David Jenkins et al., published in the *Journal of the American Medical Association*, July 23, 2003. The study compared three groups of people with high cholesterol. Two groups, the control group and the statin drug group, followed a vegetarian diet that was high in insoluble fiber and included soy and dairy products. The third group, the portfolio diet group, followed an almost completely plant-based diet with one ounce of almonds daily. The researchers reported that the portfolio diet, including almonds, soy protein, oat bran, olive oil, and soluble fiber, lowered blood lipids 28.6 percent, almost as well as the statin drugs (30.9 percent), and far exceeded the control group's results (8 percent).

Nuts are also credited for preventing gallstones. Researchers conducting the Health Professionals Follow-up Study published in 2004, involving 51,529 American male professionals, revealed that those who ate nuts frequently, about five times a week, cut their risk of gallstones by 30 percent compared to people who consumed nuts infrequently. Because regularly eating nuts lowers cholesterol, the nut eaters were able to prevent excess cholesterol from collecting in the gallbladder and crystallizing into gallstones. The January 2005 *Harvard Health Letter* explained that the good unsaturated fat in nuts lowers the bad LDL cholesterol, which in turn controls how much cholesterol enters the bile in the gallbladder. The high fiber content of nuts is also thought to prevent recirculation of bile acids in the intestines.

Study after study clearly indicates that the nut family plays an important role in offering natural protection against heart disease and some cancers and may prove effective in prolonging healthy sexual function in men. Though many of the studies were conducted with women participants, the researchers felt that men would receive the same benefits from consuming small quantities of nuts several times a week.

For many years people have perpetuated misconceptions, myths, and misinformation about the health benefits of nuts, but Mother Nature has known the truth all along. Perhaps now, with irrefutable medical and scientific acknowledgment, the nut family will be elevated to an esteemed place in the culinary world and get the respect it has always richly deserved.

Nuts in Moderation

Whenever I purchase a new cookbook, I am so inspired to cook I can hardly wait to plunge in and try the recipes. With a dizzying enthusiasm, I'll select dishes for an entire meal, including an appetizer, entrée, and dessert, and spend the entire day joyfully cooking.

Hopefully you'll find the recipes in this book equally compelling. However, if that same inescapable eagerness tempts you to do the same, I offer this note of caution. You will benefit most by choosing just one recipe a day. Consistently, researchers conducting nut studies concluded that by consuming nuts in small quantities, about 1.5 ounces, or a handful, a day, people gained the most health benefits. Too much of a good thing can become an unhealthful practice.

While most recipes in the book highlight nuts, a few dishes contain no nuts at all. These recipes act as accompaniments to ones containing nuts.

Welcome to the world of nuts with their wonderful flavors, textures, eye appeal, and health-enhancing benefits.

Calories Do Count

For those concerned about calories, notice that it doesn't take eating many nuts to put on pounds. As beneficial as nuts are, they are most nutritious when enjoyed in small quantities.

Like potato chips, nuts can also subconsciously entice the hand to reach into the nut bowl repeatedly. Be kind to your figure and stick with a handful or two each day for good nourishment.

Remember, too, that nuts are healthiest in their raw state or dry-roasted. When roasted in oil, nuts can add extra calories that mount up to extra pounds.

When measuring nuts by the cup, consider that nut pieces will weigh more and be higher in calories than whole nuts or halves. If this sounds confusing, consider that nut pieces compact more densely in the measuring cup than whole nuts or halves.

Cracking the Code:
Buying and Storing Nuts

Not all nuts are equal when it comes to purchasing and storing. Some require special attention when selecting, while others have unique storage needs.

The ideal time to purchase fresh nuts in the shell—such as walnuts, almonds, hazelnuts and pecans—is in early autumn, just after they have been harvested and are at their very freshest. Fresh chestnuts are imported, mainly from Italy and Asia, and are available from October through February.

All year long, packaged shelled nuts are available in grocery stores, natural food markets, gourmet nut shops, and high-end grocery stores. You may be one of the fortunate people who has nearby natural food markets selling a wide variety of nuts in bulk.

It's always best to purchase packaged nuts in stores where there is a quick turnover, to be assured that the supply is fresh. Because nuts are rich in healthful fat, they have a short shelf life of just a few months and are subject to rancidity. The Resources section (page 238) will help you locate dealers that sell a wide variety of nuts in bulk at reasonable prices and in high volume so you can be assured of freshness.

Once you bring your shelled nut purchases home, store them at room temperature for a short period, up to two months. Long exposure to light and air tends to hasten spoilage. If you plan to buy more than you can use in a short time, simply store them in airtight containers in the refrigerator where they will keep for nearly a year. Keep in mind, though, that any food kept for that length of time is no longer fresh and is bound to lose nutrients, flavor, and moisture.

If you make a large nut purchase, you can freeze the nuts in heavy-duty zipper-lock plastic bags or airtight containers for up to one year. The nuts can be in any form: whole, chopped, ground, diced, dry-roasted, or raw. Nuts that are processed with salt or oil should be frozen for only three months. Nut butters also freeze well and will keep for up to four months. Before using frozen nuts (whether shelled or in the shell), thaw them at room temperature for about three hours.

Nuts in their shells have a distinct advantage when it comes to storage. Most shells are naturally airtight, preventing oxygen from reaching the inside. When kept in a dry place away from direct heat, nuts in their shells can be stored at room temperature for several months.

Some grocers and natural food markets offer packaged shelled nuts in a variety of forms:

| raw unsalted | dry-roasted unsalted | oil-roasted unsalted |
| raw salted | dry-roasted salted | oil-roasted salted |

The most nutritious choice is nuts in their raw form with all of their natural goodness intact and nothing else added. Roasting nuts in oils that are often partially hydrogenated creates trans-fatty acids that contribute to an increase in cholesterol levels. Not only do trans fats raise the bad LDL cholesterol and lower the good HDL cholesterol, they also raise lipoprotein (a), a damaging form of LDL cholesterol. Trans fats can cause an increase in triglycerides and are considered twice as harmful as saturated fats. Oil-roasted nuts are also much higher in calories. Raw nuts are a whole food with nothing harmful added and nothing valuable removed or destroyed by heat processing.

Take special care to read the labels on cans of roasted nuts. Usually the ingredient list will include partially hydrogenated oils. Dry-roasted nuts do not contain added oils and do not have the added calories of oil-roasted nuts.

Peanuts

Although peanuts are frequently grouped with nuts, they are actually legumes. Some natural food markets sell raw peanuts in the shell as well as those that are already shelled. Asian markets may also have raw peanuts available. While they lack the pleasant flavor of roasted peanuts, raw peanuts make an excellent and nutritious addition to soups, stir-fries, and casserole dishes.

Though many peanut lovers eat them raw, peanuts may have more health benefits when cooked. According to the Food and Agriculture Organization of the United Nations, peanuts should be cooked either by roasting or boiling to destroy the substances that prevent us from using the protein inside the peanuts. Cooking peanuts also destroys aflatoxin, a poisonous mold known to be a human carcinogen. Peanut growers in the United States take precautions to avoid conditions that create aflatoxin, but Third World countries may have different standards. Roasted peanuts in the shell are readily available in almost any supermarket. For the best flavor, you can't beat freshly roasted peanuts in the shell. Many farmers' markets will feature a vendor roasting them right on the premises. To avoid overconsumption of salt, purchase unsalted peanuts.

Smart consumers are aware of the health benefits of natural peanut butter and prefer it over the processed varieties that are loaded with sugar, partially hydrogenated vegetable oils, and salt. The rich, nutty flavor of natural peanut butter, made only from roasted peanuts, is so pleasing it needs no enhancement.

Peanuts in the shell require a dry environment for storage. Always store peanuts in a porous bag, such as a paper bag or even a burlap sack. Keep them in an upper cupboard away from moisture.

It's important to keep them dry to avoid mold. Because good air circulation is important, never store them in a plastic bag or plastic container. Peanuts can keep for up to twelve months if stored properly.

Natural peanut butter, like all nut butters, has a shelf life of one year. Once opened and refrigerated, nut butters will keep fresh for up to one year. Natural peanut butter should be stirred well with a firm flatware knife to combine the peanut paste with the oil that has separated. Refrigeration will also help keep the oil from separating out again.

Walnuts

Walnuts are harvested in early autumn, usually September. By October the supermarkets begin receiving their autumn supplies and display them in bulk bins or packages throughout fall and winter. If stored in their shells, walnuts can keep at room temperature for six to eight months without spoiling. Shelled walnuts are usually sold in one-pound plastic packages and can be kept in the refrigerator for up to one year to prevent rancidity. For freezer storage, pack them in heavy-duty zipper-lock plastic bags and store them in the freezer for up to one year.

When shopping for walnuts in the shell, make sure they do not smell rancid. Shake the nut. If it rattles, the kernel is old and dried up. Look for shells that are undamaged and contain no cracks or wormholes.

Though it is a rarity to find black walnuts or butternuts for purchase in the West, they may be available along the U.S. East Coast. They are almost always sold in shelled form because the nuts are difficult to crack and the nutmeats are hard to extract. Packed in heavy-duty zipper-lock plastic bags and stored in the freezer, black walnuts and butternuts will keep for up to one year.

Pistachios

Most of the pistachios sold in the United States are grown in California and are sold either in the shell or already shelled. Pistachio shells are naturally beige in color. If you encounter pistachios with red shells, you can be sure they have been dyed and imported from countries surrounding the Mediterranean, especially Turkey and Iran. Although the red dye is intended to color only the shells, some may seep into the nuts as well. When purchasing pistachios, choose those with natural beige shells and avoid the unhealthful red dye that may cause allergic reactions like skin rashes, asthma, or hyperactivity. Some red food dyes are known to cause cancer in laboratory animals and humans.

Some might wonder why the red dye. The story goes back to the 1930s when pistachios were imported into the American market from Turkey and Iran. Because of inferior harvesting practices, the nuts arrived with mottled-looking, discolored, and generally unattractive shells that American sellers were hesitant to put on the market. (The Middle Eastern growers delayed removing the pistachio hulls after harvesting, which caused the shells to develop spots and discoloration.) A New Jersey businessman decided to dye them red to make them more appealing. They became so popular that all the importers began to dye pistachios red. In the 1970s, California growers began to harvest successful crops of beautiful pistachios with perfect tan shells (the growers removed the hulls promptly after harvesting to avoid discoloration) and out went most of the red-dyed pistachios. However, they are still available on a small scale.

If you plan to store a large quantity of pistachios, it's best to put them into heavy-duty zipper-lock plastic bags and freeze them. Frozen, they will keep for several months. For shorter storage you can refrigerate pistachios for four to six weeks.

If you simply enjoy nibbling on a handful or two of pistachios a day and are using them up quickly, you can store them for about a month in the cupboard at room temperature.

Chestnuts

Fresh chestnuts begin appearing in the produce section of most supermarkets in October, though they receive little attention until Thanksgiving. Traditionally, they are cooked and added to stuffings. Fresh chestnuts are available through March, though supermarkets usually will not carry them much after Christmas. Asian markets, however, will have them throughout the winter.

Store chestnuts in the shell in the refrigerator where they will keep for several months. Once cooked and shelled, they will only keep for three to four days in the refrigerator.

Cooked and shelled chestnuts can be purchased in jars in natural food markets and some specialty food stores. If unopened, jarred chestnuts will keep for a year or longer. If the chestnuts are too firm for your needs, simply put them into a saucepan with a little water, and steam them for 20 to 30 minutes, until fork-tender.

Chestnut purée is also available in jars, but since it is not a popular item, not many stores stock it. You may be able to special order it from a natural food market or specialty grocery.

Dried chestnuts are available in Asian markets, especially Chinese groceries. I've tried soaking them for eight to twelve hours and boiling them for up to three hours, and they still don't soften like fresh chestnuts. The real disappointment, though, is their strange taste. After several experiments, I confess that I simply gave up.

Even though fresh chestnuts are considerably more labor intensive, their distinctive flavor and creamy texture are so appealing, they truly warrant the extra work.

Crisping Nuts

If nuts stored over a long period lose their natural crispness, you can quickly revitalize them. Just preheat the oven to 250 to 300 degrees. Arrange the nuts on a baking sheet and place them in the oven for 6 to 9 minutes. Cool completely before storing.

Nut Butters

Natural nut butters that contain only raw or roasted nuts are found in natural food markets, some supermarkets, and specialty grocery stores. If you've never tasted the satisfying wholesomeness of almond butter, treat yourself to a jar, and spread it on your favorite whole grain toast. Perhaps you may prefer the delicate sweetness of cashew butter or a combination of cashew-macadamia butter.

Less common but equally delicious is hazelnut butter. In recent years a plethora of soynut butters have made their debut. Read labels carefully. Some may contain unhealthful ingredients, some are highly sweetened, and some even contain dairy products.

Nut butters that have been stored on the pantry or grocery shelf have a natural tendency to separate, sending their heavier solid portions to the bottom of the jar and the oils to the top. Simply blend them by stirring gently with a firm flatware knife. Lifting and twisting the knife also helps to emulsify the nut butter.

Unopened jars of nut butter can safely sit on the cupboard shelf for one year. Once opened, stir to reincorporate the oil, and store the jar in the refrigerator, where it will keep for up to one year.

Tips and Tricks

Perhaps the tempting sale price for bulk mixed nuts in the shell was too irresistible to pass up, and there you are with a bagful. Consider this chapter "the everything you need to know about handling nuts guide." Helpful hints for cracking, toasting, dry roasting, garnishing, seasoning, and blanching are packed into this tidy little corner. Brazil nuts and chestnuts require a few special tricks, which you'll find in this section. Here you'll also discover techniques on soaking and sprouting and using nuts as thickening agents; you may even come across a baking hint or two.

Cracking

MACADAMIAS: Shelled macadamias are readily available in stores; they are rarely sold in the shell. Be grateful for the convenience. If you've ever tried to crack a macadamia shell, you will surely admit, "It's a tough nut to crack." If you do purchase them in the shell, a firm blow with a hammer will crack them open. Also on the market are some very heavy-duty nutcrackers that work successfully for cracking the tough macadamia shells. Refer to the Resources section (page 238) for information on where to purchase special nutcrackers for macadamias.

CASHEWS: You'll discover that cashews are never sold in the shell but come packaged and ready to eat. The reason is the complex nature of the cashew itself. The cashew is actually a kernel encased within two layers of hard shell. Between the layers is a caustic substance that is corrosive enough to burn off warts. Commercial cashew growers usually roast the whole nut, a process that destroys the irritating substance and makes the shell brittle enough to crack. Because of this process, cashews are heat-treated before coming to market. Thus, even cashews that are labeled "raw" may not be acceptable to those who follow a strict raw food diet.

ALMONDS, HAZELNUTS, PECANS, AND WALNUTS: A simple nutcracker, or a fancy one if you choose, will do the job efficiently for almonds, hazelnuts (filberts), pecans, and walnuts. Then, one mustn't forget that old-fashioned, ultra-resourceful method of putting two nuts into the palm of the hand and squeezing like the devil. Well, it worked for my father and my Uncle Louie.

PISTACHIOS: Pistachios that are partially opened can easily be pulled apart with the fingers. Those that are completely closed can be tapped with a hammer or opened with a pair of pliers.

PEANUTS: For peanuts in the shell, hold one between the fingers of both hands, and apply a simple twist of the wrist while squeezing on the peanut. Works every time.

BRAZIL NUTS: Because Brazil nuts have an extremely tough shell, they pose a decided challenge to cracking. If you apply the nutcracker before processing the nuts, good luck. You can crack them open, but then removing the nutmeat will be your next task, and a task it is. Because they cling fast to the shell, you have to dig them out with a nutpick.

There are two easy methods that will make simple work of cracking open Brazil nuts. One is to drop them into a pot of boiling water and boil for 2 to 3 minutes. Drain off the water and cool them enough to be handled. Then apply the nutcracker. An alternative method is to preheat your oven to 400 degrees. Place the whole Brazil nuts in a shallow baking pan in a single layer and roast them for about 20 minutes. Remove them from the oven and allow them to cool before applying the nutcracker.

CHESTNUTS: Chestnuts reside on my favorite pedestal. There is a tendency for many people to avoid using fresh chestnuts because, admittedly, they are a bit of work. Here's the technique. Using a firm, sharp paring knife, make a crisscross cut on both the flat side and the domed side of each chestnut. Put the chestnuts into a large saucepan, and cover them with two inches of water. Cover and bring to a boil over high heat. Turn the heat down just slightly, and boil the chestnuts gently for about 20 minutes.

Now, prepare a cup of tea for yourself and sit down at the table with the pot of cooked chestnuts on a trivet. Have a bowl handy for the peeled chestnuts and another for the shells. Take out three or four chestnuts at a time and put them on a small dish or bowl in front of you. Cool them only slightly. They peel more easily when they are quite hot. Using your paring knife, take hold of the shell close to a crisscross cut, and remove the shell with a pulling motion. You will need to remove the brown inner skin, too. Be prepared for a little tug-of-war. Sometimes the inner skin is a bit stubborn. If it is too resistant, the chestnut may need to be cooked a few more minutes.

As the chestnuts cool, they become more difficult to peel. It's best not to fight with them. Just put the pot back on the burner and heat them up for a few minutes so you can finish the task with ease. The job can actually be fun if you can convince your family to participate in the peeling project.

Roasting is another method of heating the chestnuts so the peels can be removed. Pile the crisscross-cut chestnuts onto a baking sheet and roast them at 375 degrees for 15 to 20 minutes. Cool them slightly and peel away. Some chestnut aficionados suggest soaking the chestnuts for about 20 minutes before roasting, claiming it makes them easier to peel.

Still another method for heating chestnuts prior to peeling them begins with making a crisscross cut on the flat side. Then put them into a large, deep skillet with a small amount of oil, about one tablespoon for each pound of chestnuts in the shell. Turn the heat to high and cook them for 5 to 10 minutes, tossing the chestnuts continuously with a wooden spoon or shaking the pan to prevent the direct heat from burning them.

PINE NUTS: Pine nuts are often sold already shelled. In past years I used to purchase them in bulk in their shells. Cracking and eating them was usually a communal experience where a group of friends gathered around the table, dug into a bowl of "monkey nuts," and cracked them one at a time between our teeth. If you are fortunate enough to encounter pine nuts in their shells, you can enjoy the same pleasures while sparing the teeth. Supply the family with a few pairs of pliers and crack away.

Toasting

Toasting nuts is easy and quick. The simplest way I've discovered is to put a small quantity, up to 1 cup, of any variety of shelled nuts into a dry skillet. Turn the heat to high, stand faithfully over the pan with a wooden spoon, and stir continuously until the nuts begin to turn a golden color. If you prefer not to stir the nuts, you can shake the pan constantly. The process takes 2 to 3 minutes at most. If you have several things cooking at the same time and you take your eye off those nuts for just a hair of a minute, that's when they are likely to burn.

As soon as they reach that rich golden color, immediately transfer them to a dish to cool. If you leave them in the skillet, the residual heat will continue to toast them and quite possibly burn them.

For toasting larger quantities of nuts, consider dry roasting them in the oven.

Dry Roasting

Dry roasting nuts is easy and will bring you the same result as toasting. Simply preheat your oven to 350 degrees, spread the nuts on a baking sheet in a single layer, and roast them for 5 to 15 minutes. Their color will deepen and they'll develop a pleasant nutty aroma. The longer they roast, the more intense the flavor. Be careful not to over-roast them. Nuts have a tendency to burn easily, and may taste burnt before they actually look burnt. Do a taste test after the first 5 minutes. Timing will depend on the variety of nut.

If your oven runs a little hot, you can always set the temperature to 300 degrees and slow roast, testing after 10 minutes to determine the perfect timing for each nut. At this lower temperature, it may take up to 25 minutes to reach that perfect roasted flavor.

Peanuts are usually roasted in the shell for 15 to 20 minutes at 350 degrees. Begin testing for that ideal roasted flavor after 10 to 12 minutes.

Unless commercially roasted shelled nuts are labeled as having been dry-roasted, they are usually roasted in oil, often partially hydrogenated oils that contain trans fats. You can prepare oil-roasted nuts at home with vegetable oils, but nuts really don't need any added fat. Admittedly, they provide tasty eating, but they also add unnecessary calories and harmful trans fats, especially when heated for a long time at high temperatures. Cooking oils found in the supermarkets are almost always hydrogenated, and will add trans fats that raise LDL cholesterol (the bad cholesterol).

For crisper nuts, soak them in water for about 30 minutes. Then drain, pat dry, and roast them for about 30 minutes at 350 degrees, turning them every 10 to 12 minutes until they are crisp.

Garnishing

You can quickly enhance the presentation of almost anything you serve, from appetizers to desserts, with a sprinkling of nuts that have been chopped, slivered, sliced, coarsely ground, or finely ground. Sometimes a single whole or half nut will add the perfect touch. Try a sprinkling of toasted pine nuts or chopped salted peanuts to finish a dish just before serving.

For convenience, chop and/or slice a variety of nuts to keep on hand in the refrigerator. Store them in small zipper-lock plastic bags or little plastic containers for easy access. Time-savers like this can be a blessing when you're rushing around the kitchen preparing for guests.

Seasoning

Sometimes nuts can serve as flavor enhancers. Chopped salted peanuts are one example of nuts used as a seasoning. Though these are simply sprinkled over the top of a dish, they contribute to the overall flavor.

You can create your own seasoning mixtures by blending coarsely ground nuts with chopped fresh herbs like parsley, garlic, and dill weed. This combination is great as a soup garnish. I'm particularly fond of ground pecans mixed with minced fresh cilantro, mint, and basil as a garnish and taste enhancement on a salad of tossed baby greens.

Nuts as Thickening Agents

Finely ground nuts like cashews, almonds, hazelnuts, and pistachios can serve to thicken a sauce or gravy when added near the end of the cooking. Have the prepared ground nuts ready to add to sauces that are at a full boil. Then, using a wire whip, add the ground nuts, stirring continuously, and keep the sauce bubbling for a minute or two longer until the sauce reaches the desired thickness.

Pounding nuts into a thick paste with a mortar and pestle and adding the paste to thicken stews and soups is a centuries-old tradition that is still practiced among many European cultures and Native American tribes.

Blanching

Enjoy nuts fully dressed—that is, with their skins on. The skins provide an excellent source of fiber. With blanching, considerable fiber gets tossed into the wastebasket. As an example, one cup of whole almonds contains 15.5 grams of fiber, while a cup of blanched almonds provides only 9.7 grams. Though the blanched almonds still provide considerable fiber, nature intended us to benefit from the whole nut left completely intact.

There are those times, however, that call for blanching nuts such as almonds or hazelnuts to create an appealing garnish or to retain the light-colored appearance of the inner nut. To blanch, simply put the shelled nuts into a deep bowl and pour in enough boiling water to cover them. Allow them to stand for 3 to 5 minutes. Hazelnuts may need just a few more minutes in the "hot tub." Drain off the hot water and rinse the nuts in cold water. Then it's a one-nut-at-a-time peeling project.

An alternative method is to put 2 to 3 inches of water into a saucepan. Bring the water to a boil and add the shelled nuts. Boil them for 1 minute, then drain them in a strainer. This process loosens the skins.

FOR ALMONDS: Hold the broad end of the nut between your thumb and index or middle fingers and pinch. The skins should come off easily, with the nut sliding out from the pointed end. Too much pressure may send the naked little almonds flying across the room. After a few of these, you'll begin to judge just how much pressure to apply to the pinch.

FOR HAZELNUTS: The old-fashioned method was to use a small, firm paring knife and peel the skins off with a pulling motion. For an easier method, begin with roasting the nuts at 350 degrees for 10 to 12 minutes. Transfer them to a zipper-lock plastic bag, close it tightly, and allow the nuts to sweat for about 5 minutes. Finally, empty the nuts from the plastic bag onto a terrycloth towel, enclose them, and rub like the dickens. The skins should come off easily. If you still encounter nuts that stubbornly cling to their skins, resort to blanching them again.

Soaking

People often remark that they simply cannot digest nuts. You can easily enhance the digestibility of nuts by soaking them for 8 to 12 hours. It's quite amazing what a little water will do to bring about a positive change in the composition of nuts. Soaking removes the enzymes that inhibit the digestion and assimilation of nuts. Essentially, "predigestion" of the proteins, carbohydrates, and fats contained in the nuts takes place when they are soaked in water.

Nature provides natural safeguards called growth inhibitors that prevent nuts from readily sprouting; at the same time, these growth inhibitors make nuts harder for some people to digest. During the soaking process, the growth inhibitors are released into the water, making the nuts easier to digest. Soaking nuts also softens them, making them easier to break down for use in making nut milks, smoothies, and spreads. After soaking nuts, discard the soak water.

Whether to soak or not is a matter of personal preference. Generally, I enjoy nuts in their raw state. At times, however, I become the gourmet who yearns for the rich flavor of toasted nuts, while on other days I soak them to create a softer, creamier texture for smoothies or soups.

Sprouting

Raw nuts contain a germ capable of producing new life in the form of a sprout that will grow into a new plant. As a preliminary to sprouting, nuts are soaked for several hours, activating enzymes and metabolic processes in the germ. During the course of sprouting, proteins are broken down into amino acids, carbohydrates become simple sugars, and fats are turned into fatty acids. Vitamins and minerals may increase 300 to 1500 percent.

Ideally, raw peanuts in the shell are conducive to sprouting, while nuts such as almonds, cashews, walnuts, and pecans are not. These nuts may take several weeks to sprout under ideal conditions. While many sprouted seeds develop three- to five-inch stems topped with little nutritious green leaves, sprouted nuts will eventually become giant trees.

Making Nut Butter

Homemade nut butter is a joy to the palate and is easily prepared with a good-quality food processor and a spatula. To make raw nut butter, simply add raw nuts to the food processor, and process until the nuts release their oil and form a paste. Some nuts, like almonds, cashews, and hazelnuts, tend to be a bit drier and need a little additional oil, about 1 to 2 tablespoons of canola oil for every 2 cups of nuts, to help them break down into a paste. Process the nuts to the desired texture—creamy or crunchy. Be patient—the processing time varies for different nuts, but generally it takes 4 to 8 minutes. You may have to stop the machine several times, scrape down the sides of the work bowl, and redistribute the nuts to achieve an even texture.

For a richer flavor, oven roast the nuts on a baking sheet before processing them into nut butter (see page 28). Then toss them right into the food processor.

Take up the current vogue and season your nut butter with a variety of sweet or savory flavors. Creativity and nuance bring new taste thrills into the kitchen and allow home chefs to express ideas without restraint.

For savory flavors, add salt to taste, and use seasonings such as dehydrated onion or onion powder, garlic powder or roasted garlic, dried chiles or chili powder, parsley, rosemary, pepper, ginger, and even hickory smoke flavor. Commercial companies have combined a host of savory seasonings with peanut butter for a delightfully unique taste treat.

On the sweet side, experiment with adding dried fruits, evaporated cane juice, molasses, agave nectar, maple syrup, or date sugar. Add flavoring extracts such as vanilla, almond, coconut, lemon, mint, and fruity enhancers like raspberry or strawberry. Try adding zesty spices like ground cinnamon, allspice, nutmeg, or ginger. Chocolate syrup, shaved chocolate, and coarsely ground chocolate make great pairings with nut butters and blend well with spices like cinnamon. These are only a few suggestions to start the ideas flowing.

The Nutcracker's Toolbox

NUTCRACKER: There's nothing like an old-fashioned nutcracker for attacking nuts in the shell. When shopping around, you'll no doubt come across a number of ingenious contraptions that crack nuts with the most creative techniques you'll ever encounter. Some are quite efficient; some actually make the task more difficult; while still others are coffee table conversation pieces. After a few experiments with various nutcrackers, I've found that the old-fashioned, standard hand nutcracker works best. That's the one that's made of two metal rods attached at the top by a metal bar. With the nut placed between the notched portion of the metal rods, all you do is hold both rods in one hand supported by the other, and squeeze like the dickens.

HAMMER: Resourcefulness in the kitchen is a helpful attribute. When you're lacking any other kitchen tools, get out the old hammer and pound the nuts between two sheets of waxed paper, or better still, put the nuts in a zipper-lock plastic bag. The hammer is a must for cracking macadamia nuts in the shell and works just fine for coarsely crushing walnuts, almonds, hazelnuts, pecans, cashews, Brazil nuts, and peanuts. To coarsely crush already shelled nuts, put them in a zipper-lock plastic bag, seal it tightly, and set the plastic bag on a firm cutting board on top of the kitchen counter. Then pound the nuts with the hammer until you have the desired texture.

TRUCK: If you are fortunate enough to live in an area where you can purchase fresh black walnuts in the shell, you'll appreciate the expression "tough nut to crack." Black walnuts are so tough, in fact, that some people have resorted to placing the nuts on the ground and driving a truck back and forth over them in order to crack the shell.

NUTPICK: Reminiscent of a dental pick, this simple-looking item comes in very handy for digging out nuts that prefer to cling to their shells, such as Brazil nuts. It's also helpful for pulling out walnuts and pecans that are stubbornly lodged into their shells.

THE COFFEE TABLE CONVERSATION PIECE: I discovered that this contraption, which looks more like a torture device, actually works quite well in cracking the toughest of nuts, including macadamias. Perched on a flat wooden base is a metal rig with two cylindrical rods horizontally facing each other. One portion has threads so you can adjust for different size nuts that fit between the two cylinders. A long metal arm with a wooden handle swings the cylinders open and shut, and cracks the nut when you press downward with athletic might and a thunderous grunt.

Tools for Crushing, Chopping, Grinding, Dicing, and Grating

FOOD PROCESSOR: The food processor has been my indispensable, constant companion in the kitchen. The relationship I have with my food processor nearly borders on adoration. It puzzles me that past generations of great cooks produced divine creations without one. Modern technology has made many tasks easier. I'm all for using equipment to help cut down on the time it would take to cut, chop, dice, or purée foods that our mothers and grandmothers did by hand.

For working with nuts, use the food processor with the steel S blade inserted. It chops and grinds hard nuts like almonds, hazelnuts, and Brazil nuts with ease. With chopping in the food processor, you may notice the pieces are not uniform. Don't sweat it—pieces of various sizes add interesting texture to a dish.

When grinding hard nuts such as almonds, filberts, and Brazil nuts, the food processor will make an even, coarse meal. Cashews will become a fine meal, as will pecans and walnuts. Begin by pulse-chopping first to break down the nuts into smaller particles. Follow this step by pressing and holding down the switch until the desired texture is obtained.

BLENDER: For making smoothies, mousses, and parfaits that include nuts, the blender is the perfect machine. For preparing nut milks, the blender is indispensable. I recommend one with variable speeds. For incorporating nuts into a mixture, I begin with no more than 1 cup of ingredients on a low speed for 30 to 60 seconds, allowing the machine to break down the chunkier pieces. Then I add the remaining ingredients and increase the blender speed to medium for a few seconds before finally blending on high speed to produce the smoothest mixture.

ELECTRIC COFFEE GRINDER: What a bonus this little gadget is in the kitchen! It grinds nuts like cashews into a fine, powdery meal that I use to thicken sauces and soups. Since the grinder has a limited capacity, nuts must be ground in small batches. After a few experiments you'll be able to judge just how much to put in at one time.

Since I'm not a coffee drinker, my coffee grinder has never encountered a coffee bean. If you do grind coffee with this handy device, it's best to invest in a separate one for grinding nuts to avoid nuts with a coffee flavor or vice versa. In addition to nuts, the electric coffee grinder is ideal for grinding whole spices, such as cloves, allspice, and cinnamon. It also grinds dried legumes, such as lentils and green or yellow split peas, into a fine meal for thickening soups, sauces, or making legume pâtés.

ELECTRIC MINI-CHOPPER/GRINDER: Similar to the electric coffee grinder in its ability to turn whole nuts into a fine meal in a matter of seconds, this little device is inexpensive, versatile, small, and compact. Some mini-choppers have a little larger capacity than the coffee grinder and may grind one cup of whole nuts in only two batches.

HAND-CRANK NUT GRINDER OR NUT MILL: When you want coarsely ground nuts for a dessert topping or garnish on a savory dish, this little item does the deed. It's my favorite tool for grinding the walnuts used in my Walnut Stuffed Eggplant (page 120). Of course, you'll have to use hand power, but a little exercise in the kitchen is simply a bonus. If you haven't seen a nut mill before, the bottom portion has a glass or plastic container that screws onto a small hand crank section that holds a few nuts. Looking down from the top you'll see metal blades that turn as you crank the handle. Check out the housewares section of your favorite department store or visit a gourmet cook's shop to find the perfect nut mill. Some nut mills work with a twisting motion instead of a crank. Either will do the job.

HAND FOOD CHOPPER: This handy little device has a clear glass or plastic cylindrical container at the bottom to hold the nuts. At the very top is a plunger with a spring action. The bottom of the plunger is attached to a series of sharp cutting blades. You simply press down on the plunger that pushes the cutting blades down onto the nuts in the container. With a series of up and down pumping motions, you can chop to your heart's content. The nuts may not be evenly chopped, but for most dishes it really doesn't matter. The hand food chopper is usually available at kitchen shops or the housewares section of your local department store.

METAL GRATER: When that very special dish needs just the right garnish to add the finishing touch, consider a topping of shredded or grated whole or blanched almonds or Brazil nuts. Turn to your metal grater with both a coarse and fine section. Grating one nut at a time may seem time consuming, but only a few nuts are needed for an attractive garnish. Do plan ahead for shredding or grating Brazil nuts. They will shred more easily if you simmer them 3 to 5 minutes and dry them thoroughly before shredding. A note of caution is important when using a metal grater for small items like nuts. Each of the cutting edges of the grater is sharp. Remember to work carefully to avoid slicing a few fingers into your garnish.

GOOD-QUALITY KNIVES: If you invest in nothing else in kitchen equipment, you'll benefit many times over from the purchase of at least two good knives. A 7- or 8-inch chef's knife and a 5- or 6-inch utility knife are necessities in every kitchen. Add a 3.5-inch paring knife to your collection and you're almost set. Choose knives with a firm blade—you'll notice the benefits immediately.

A sharpening steel to keep the edge honed completes the basic knife needs. Ask a knowledgeable knife person in a cutlery shop to show you how to properly use the sharpening steel. There is a technique, and if done correctly, your knives will last a long time and remain sharp. You'll appreciate a nice sharp paring knife with a firm blade when peeling chestnuts for holiday cooking.

BY HAND: If you're new on the cooking scene and haven't yet acquired any kitchen machines or gadgets, you can always count on the meditative experience of chopping nuts by hand. Here is where your excellent knives will do the work for you … well, almost. Hand-chopping nuts of any quantity is still work that takes time.

For slicing almonds or Brazil nuts, a good sharp knife works best, short of purchasing them already sliced. For easier slicing, you may want to soak the nuts in water several hours ahead. Dry them thoroughly with kitchen towels before slicing.

ROLLING PIN: For creating crushed and coarsely ground textures, you can always put nuts, such as pecans or walnuts, between two sheets of waxed paper or into a zipper-lock plastic bag and apply pressure with a rolling pin as you move it back and forth. This is an old technique my mother used and probably her mother as well.

Nut Measurement Equivalents

Daily consumption of 1.5 ounces of nuts offers many health benefits. To measure this amount, use your hand as a convenient guide. For most nuts, one handful is approximately 1.5 ounces. Pistachios are a bit lighter, allowing you an extra half-handful. Brazil nuts are the opposite. Their heavier weight allows you only half a handful. One cup of shelled nuts is equal to approximately 4 ounces.

Unsweetened chestnuts that are cooked and peeled are available in jars during the holiday season. Look for them in specialty stores and natural food markets. A 15-ounce jar contains about 2½ cups.

Use the table on the next page to help you with converting nut measurements from whole nuts into their chopped or ground form. Nut sizes and weights vary somewhat, producing slightly different results when measuring a cup or two in preparation for a recipe. While it's not possible to offer exact measurements, don't worry about the one extra or one less tablespoon of nuts. In most recipes, it won't alter the final results.

Table 1.1 Nut measurement equivalents

Nut in Shell (1 pound)	Cups Shelled	Chopped, Ground, or Slivered
Almonds	3	3¾ cups slivered
	1	1⅛ cups chopped
	¼	⅓ cup + 2 tablespoons meal
Brazil nuts	3	—
	1	1¼ cups chopped
	¼	⅓ cup buttery meal
Cashews	1	Scant 1 cup chopped
	¼	⅓ cup meal
Chestnuts	3 to 3½	—
	1	1¼ cups chopped
Hazelnuts/Filberts	3½	—
	1	1 cup chopped
	¼	Scant ½ cup meal
Macadamia nuts	2½	—
	1	1 cup chopped
	¼	¼ cup buttery meal
Peanuts	2⅓	1⅓ cups peanut butter
	1	1 cup chopped
	¼	⅓ cup meal
Pecans	2¼	—
	1	1 cup chopped
	¼	¼ cup buttery meal
Pistachios	3½	—
	¼	⅓ cup meal
Walnuts, black	½	¾ cup chopped
Walnuts, English	4	—
	1	¾ cup chopped
	¼	¼ cup buttery meal

Appetizers

WHEN I THINK ABOUT SERVING APPETIZERS BEFORE DINNER,

I tend to focus on little tidbits as appetite teasers that won't spoil the guests' enthusiasm for the meal ahead. But then there are other occasions, like midday gatherings or savor-and-nibble parties, when appetizers call for heartier dishes.

Appetizer seasonings lean to the lustier side to stimulate the palate as well as conversation. When guests visit my home for the first time, I want them to know they are about to experience a unique meal. The appetizer is their first taste of what lies ahead.

Bringing guests who've never met to a comfort level sharing thoughts, jokes, or experiences is not difficult with just the right starter. A dish that has people dipping into a communal bowl works quickly to start them chatting, often evoking laughter, especially when two guests reach for the same carrot stick.

The perfect starter does not have to be an intricate preparation. For me, the main course determines how much time I will have to devote to the appetizer. Quite often it's a simple dip with zesty overtones, or an easy dish that blossoms with color.

In this section you'll find appetizers for any occasion, whether you're planning a predinner starter or a wine-and-nibble gathering.

Marinated Tofu Fingers
with Spicy Peanut Sauce

Yield: 10 tofu fingers

Marinated Tofu

1/3 cup plus 1 table-
spoon rice vinegar

1/3 cup light
brown sugar

1/2 teaspoon soy sauce

1/4 teaspoon crushed
red pepper flakes

1 pound extra-firm tofu,
cut into 10
thick fingers

Spicy Peanut Sauce

1/3 cup unsalted
chunky peanut butter

3 tablespoons freshly
squeezed lemon juice

3 tablespoons
maple syrup

1 tablespoon water

1/4 teaspoon salt

1/8 teaspoon hot sauce

MARINATED TOFU and a vibrant peanut sauce were destined to meet as a great starter, perfect for any occasion. Prepare the sauce and marinate the tofu a day ahead so all that's needed is a quick sizzle on the barbecue or a brief warming in the oven. In addition to a dipping sauce, the Spicy Peanut Sauce doubles as a tasty dressing for a salad or steamed vegetables.

TO MAKE the marinade, combine the vinegar, brown sugar, soy sauce, and crushed red pepper flakes in a 1-quart saucepan. Gently warm over medium heat until the sugar is dissolved. Pour into a shallow baking dish and add the tofu fingers. Marinate for 4 to 12 hours, turning several times.

Insert 10 wooden skewers deeply into the tofu fingers, and grill the fingers on the barbecue for about 5 minutes, turning frequently to avoid burning.

TO MAKE the peanut sauce, combine all the sauce ingredients in a bowl and stir with a wire whip until smooth and creamy. Serve the tofu fingers with the sauce on the side.

Baked Tofu Fingers: Preheat the oven to 400 degrees. Do not use the skewers. Arrange the tofu fingers on a lightly oiled baking sheet and bake them for about 20 minutes.

Per "finger": Calories 128, Protein 6g, Fat 6g, Carbohydrate 15g, Vitamin E .5mg

See photo facing page 96.

Yield: 8 to 10 servings

Tofu Pesto Torte

1 cup fresh spinach, stemmed, washed, and lightly packed

1 cup fresh basil leaves, washed and lightly packed

3 tablespoons extra-virgin olive oil

$\frac{1}{2}$ cup pine nuts

1 garlic clove

$\frac{1}{2}$ teaspoon salt

$\frac{2}{3}$ cup sun-dried tomatoes

12 ounces extra-firm tofu, rinsed and drained

6 ounces firm tofu, rinsed and drained

2 teaspoons freshly squeezed lemon juice

1 $\frac{1}{4}$ teaspoons salt

1 teaspoon rice vinegar

$\frac{1}{4}$ teaspoon dried oregano, crushed

$\frac{1}{4}$ teaspoon dried basil

Green leaf lettuce

1 small ripe Roma tomato, sliced

Basil sprigs

IMAGINE A TALL, CREAMY, pine nut-enriched torte that makes a presentation so appealing guests are often reluctant to dip into it. The pesto clings to its traditional Italian flavor, sans the Parmesan cheese, and offers exceptional eating pleasure. This dish is perfect to make ahead. Serve it with several spreading knives, whole wheat sourdough bread, mini rice cakes, rice crackers, or toasted pita wedges.

TO MAKE the pesto, combine the spinach, fresh basil, olive oil, pine nuts, garlic, and salt in the food processor and process until completely smooth. Transfer to a medium bowl and wash the processor work bowl.

Place the sun-dried tomatoes in a heatproof bowl and pour boiling water over them to cover. Let rest for 10 minutes to soften. Drain well. Using a kitchen scissors, snip the tomatoes into thin strips and set them aside.

Combine the extra-firm and firm tofu, lemon juice, salt, vinegar, oregano, and dried basil in the food processor and process until completely smooth.

Line a deep 4-cup bowl or mold with enough plastic wrap to drape over the sides. Spread one-third of the tofu mixture over the bottom of the bowl, then layer half the pesto, followed by half the sun-dried tomatoes. Next, layer half the remaining tofu mixture, the remainder of the pesto, and the remainder of the sun-dried tomatoes. Top the torte with the remainder of the tofu mixture. Fold the plastic wrap over the top to cover completely, and refrigerate the torte for 4 to 12 hours.

Just before serving, fold back the plastic wrap and unmold the torte onto an attractive serving dish. Surround the torte with leaf lettuce, and garnish with the tomato slices and a few sprigs of basil.

Per serving: Calories 56, Protein 2.5g, Fat 5g, Carbohydrate 2g, Vitamin E .3mg

Cashew Mushroom Bruschetta

Yield: 4 to 5 servings

QUICK, TASTY, AND SATISFYING are the three words busy home chefs want to see when selecting an appetizer recipe. After preparing the main course dishes for a dinner party, the host or hostess may not have time to create an intricate appetizer. This starter comes together quickly and works equally well for informal family gatherings and fussier dinner parties. Serve it in an attractive bowl, accompanied with toasted pita wedges.

½ pound sliced cremini or button mushrooms

2 tablespoons water

½ cup coarsely chopped cashews

3 ounces soft tofu

2 garlic cloves, minced

½ to 1 teaspoon freshly squeezed lemon juice

Salt and freshly ground pepper

Paprika

COMBINE the mushrooms and water in a deep 10-inch skillet and cook over high heat for about 2 minutes, or until softened.

Put the cashews, tofu, garlic, and lemon juice into the food processor and process about 1 minute, just long enough to break the cashews into smaller bits.

Add the cashew mixture to the mushrooms in the skillet and heat gently to warm through. Season to taste with salt, pepper, and a sprinkling of paprika.

Per serving: Calories 117, Protein 6g, Fat 8g, Carbohydrate 8g, Vitamin E .2mg

Cashew Stuffed Mushrooms

Yield: 10 servings

YOU CAN ALWAYS RELY on this easy, no-cook preparation to bring on the compliments. Serve this hors d'oeuvre at a potluck and watch it disappear almost instantly.

20 button mushrooms

¼ cup apple cider vinegar

¼ cup soy sauce

2 tablespoons water

¾ cup coarsely chopped cashews

4 green onions, coarsely chopped

½ cup chopped red bell pepper

½ cup chopped green bell pepper

2 to 3 heaping tablespoons capers, well drained

1 teaspoon soy sauce

Lettuce leaves

Cilantro leaves

Pine nuts

WASH the mushrooms and pat them dry. Using your thumb, press gently on the side of the stems to loosen and remove them. Set the stems aside.

Combine the apple cider vinegar, soy sauce, and water in a large bowl and add the mushrooms. Toss them until evenly coated. Marinate for 1 to 2 hours at room temperature, tossing occasionally.

Combine the mushroom stems, cashews, green onions, red and green bell peppers, capers, and soy sauce in the food processor. Process briefly, just until blended but still chunky.

Remove the mushrooms from the marinade and dry them with paper towels. Stuff the cavities with the cashew mixture.

Line a serving dish with lettuce leaves and arrange the stuffed mushrooms on top. Garnish by pressing the base of each tiny cilantro leaf into the center of the stuffing with a toothpick. For the finishing touch, push an upright pine nut into the center next to the cilantro leaf.

Per serving: Calories 83, Protein 4g, Fat 5 g, Carbohydrate 7g, Vitamin E .2mg

Mock Chopped Liver

I'M THOROUGHLY CONVINCED there's pure magic in the humble little lentil. Otherwise, how could two distinct dishes evolve from one recipe? First, there's a no-fail Mock Chopped Liver that tastes so convincingly like the real thing it may even fool an aficionado. It receives a warm welcome mounded on a lettuce-lined platter, garnished with sliced carrots and cucumbers, and served with whole grain crackers. Alternatively, serve it with a platter of lettuce leaves sliced in half crosswise for each guest to spoon on a generous serving and roll them up. If you put the same mixture into the oven, out will come Walnut Lentil Pie, a scrumptious entrée.

2½ cups water

½ cup dried lentils

¼ teaspoon salt

1¼ cups coarsely chopped walnuts

1 large carrot, coarsely shredded

1 cup chopped onions

¾ cup cooked brown rice

1 tablespoon plus ½ teaspoon red miso

1½ teaspoons soy sauce

Freshly ground pepper

COMBINE the water, lentils, and salt in an open 2-quart saucepan. Bring to a boil, turn the heat down to medium, and cook uncovered for 25 to 30 minutes, until the lentils are tender but still firm.

Grind the walnuts in the food processor until almost smooth. Add the shredded carrot, onions, brown rice, miso, soy sauce, and pepper to the walnuts in the processor. Drain and discard any excess liquid from the cooked lentils and add them to the processor. Process for 1 to 2 minutes, until smooth. Serve immediately or thoroughly chilled. Stored in a covered container in the refrigerator, Mock Chopped Liver will keep for three days.

Walnut Lentil Pie: Prepare Mock Chopped Liver as directed. Preheat the oven to 350 degrees, and lightly oil a 10-inch glass pie pan, 8-inch square glass baking dish, or a 9-inch springform pan. Spoon the mixture into the oiled dish and bake uncovered for 40 to 45 minutes. Cool 15 to 20 minutes. To serve, cut the pie into wedges or squares. Serve with Lemon Dill Silken Sauce (page 144). Yield: 4 to 6 servings

Double Recipe Walnut Lentil Pie: Preheat the oven to 375 degrees and lightly oil a 9-inch springform pan. Double the ingredient amounts and spoon the mixture into the prepared pan. Bake for 1 hour and 10 minutes, or until firm when the top is lightly tapped. Allow the pie to rest about 15 minutes to firm up before serving.

Per serving: Calories 180, Protein 7g, Fat 11g, Carbohydrate 16g, Vitamin E .1mg

Artichoke Party Dip

IMPRESS YOUR PARTY GUESTS with a succulent, flavorful hot dip that combines artichoke hearts, creamy tofu sauce, and crunchy pistachios. Prepare a platter of raw vegetables, serve a basket of assorted whole grain breads, and enjoy the dipping experience.

Yield: 6 to 8 servings as a party dip

4 to 5 servings as a lunch or dinner fondue

1 (13.5-ounce) can water-packed artichoke hearts

1 pound extra-firm tofu

1/2 cup vegan mayonnaise

2 tablespoons vegan Parmesan

2 large garlic cloves

1 tablespoon plus 1/4 teaspoon rice vinegar

1 tablespoon nutritional yeast flakes

1 tablespoon freshly squeezed lemon juice

1 1/4 teaspoons plus 1/8 teaspoon salt

1/2 teaspoon plus 1/8 teaspoon ground coriander

1/2 teaspoon plus 1/8 teaspoon dried dill weed

1/2 teaspoon onion powder

1/2 teaspoon evaporated cane juice

1/4 teaspoon freshly ground pepper

2 green onions, finely chopped

1 (4.6-ounce) can water chestnuts, drained and diced

1/2 cup pistachios

Paprika

PREHEAT the oven to 350 degrees. Drain the artichoke hearts, reserving 1/4 cup of the liquid. Discard the remainder of the artichoke liquid. Chop the artichoke hearts into 1/2-inch pieces and set aside.

Place the tofu, mayonnaise, Parmesan, garlic, rice vinegar, nutritional yeast, lemon juice, salt, coriander, dill weed, onion powder, evaporated cane juice, and pepper in the food processor. Add the reserved artichoke liquid and process until smooth and creamy. Transfer to a 2-quart baking dish and stir in the artichoke hearts, green onions, and water chestnuts, mixing well.

Set aside 2 tablespoons of the pistachios. Stir the remaining pistachios into the artichoke mixture. Sprinkle the top with the reserved pistachios and a dash or two of paprika. Bake for 30 minutes. Serve hot.

Per serving: Calories 271, Protein 12g, Fat 18g, Carbohydrate 16g, Vitamin E 1.1mg

Pistachio Pea Pâté

Yield: 1 cup

WITH A DELICATE SWEETNESS from raw pistachios and peas, this easy-to-assemble pâté always receives a warm welcome. It's light, nutritious, and thoroughly satisfying as a spread on crisp vegetable slices and leafy greens. Arrange the vegetables on a large platter, and give the pâté the spotlight by placing it in the center. Serve with spreading knives so guests can dress each vegetable with a dollop of pâté.

1 cup chopped zucchini

2 ounces pistachios (scant ½ cup)

½ cup frozen peas, thawed

1 teaspoon water

¼ teaspoon salt

Dash ground nutmeg

COMBINE the zucchini, pistachios, peas, water, and salt in the food processor and process until thick and creamy. Transfer to a serving bowl and sprinkle with nutmeg.

THE ANCIENT PISTACHIO, with its striking green nutmeats, holds prominence in tasty, historical desserts such as baklava, nougat, and Turkish delight, where it serves as a major ingredient. In biblical times, chopped pistachios were added to fruit compotes, puddings, and stuffings, while the nuts in their ground form added body and flavor to many savory sauces. Today pistachios are more familiar to Americans as a snack food, while in Iranian cooking the nuts are often added to rice dishes along with raisins or currants, herbs, and saffron.

Per serving (2 tablespoons): Calories 50, Protein 2g, Fat 3g, Carbohydrate 4g, Vitamin E .2mg

Hot Karachi Pea Dip

THE PLEASING COMBINATION of peas, spices, and pistachios creates the base of this Indian-inspired starter, while its uniqueness comes from the finishing splash of pomegranate syrup. Serve the dip with toasted whole grain pita wedges or whole grain crackers.

1 1/2 cups frozen peas, thawed

1/2 cup pistachios

5 tablespoons water

1 tablespoon freshly squeezed lemon juice

3/4 teaspoon salt

3/4 teaspoon curry powder

1/4 teaspoon cayenne

1 tablespoon pomegranate syrup

COMBINE the peas, pistachios, water, lemon juice, salt, curry powder, and cayenne in the food processor and process until creamy.

Transfer to a 1-quart saucepan and gently heat, stirring frequently, until thoroughly warmed but not boiling. Spoon into an attractive serving bowl and lightly drizzle the top with the pomegranate syrup.

IF PISTACHIOS COULD TALK, they would have intriguing accounts of their fascinating travels as they journeyed by camel caravans from Persia to China via the Silk Road.

Per serving: Calories 116, Protein 5g, Fat 6g, Carbohydrate 12g, Vitamin E .4mg

SQUEEZING PRECIOUS NUTRIENTS from the mighty nut is not a New Age discovery. In ancient China, revered milky beverages were extracted from pine nuts and hazelnuts as well as the soybean. Though dairy products were introduced and reintroduced into China many times, the Tang Dynasty, 618–907 AD, was the only reign to accept them. Before and after their rule, nut milks and soybean milk were exclusive to that region.

Breakfast Dishes

BREAKFAST, HMMM, I CAN'T REMEMBER WHEN I MISSED ONE.

While some of my friends start their day with nothing more than a cup of coffee and manage to survive until noon, I begin my day thinking about what's for breakfast. I simply can't ignore that inner voice summoning me to the kitchen to scramble up some tofu or stir up a pot of old-fashioned oatmeal and sip a cup of steaming hot herbal tea.

On weekends I might prepare Nutty Oatcakes (page 53) or Maple Dream Muffins (page 50), but on weekdays I prepare breakfasts that are simple yet hearty and full of fiber, such as cooked cereals.

Fruit is always on the morning menu, although it changes with the seasons. When stone fruits and melons reach the farmers' markets in summer, they are such a welcome change from the apples, pears, and citrus fruits I've been chopping and slicing all winter. A simple wedge of melon with its juicy sweetness makes a perfect breakfast when it's served with whole grain bread and something luscious to spread on top. Other times a juicy navel orange or half a sweet pink grapefruit satisfies.

Maple Dream Muffins

1 cup pitted prunes

$\frac{1}{3}$ cup plus
1 tablespoon water

1$\frac{1}{2}$ cups coarsely
chopped walnuts

1$\frac{1}{3}$ cups maple syrup

1 cup vanilla soymilk

1 teaspoon maple extract

1$\frac{1}{2}$ cups old-fashioned
rolled oats

$\frac{3}{4}$ cup all-purpose
whole wheat flour

$\frac{3}{4}$ cup whole wheat
pastry flour

1 tablespoon
ground cinnamon

2 teaspoons
baking powder

1 teaspoon baking soda

1 cup chopped dates

A FAMILY FAVORITE, these moist, spicy, and nutty muffins are an excellent choice to serve for brunch or breakfast on the run. They're so fully flavored they need no jam or other topping. If the recipe makes too many muffins for your needs, simply tuck a few into the freezer for a future occasion.

PREHEAT the oven to 350 degrees and line 18 standard-size muffin cups with paper baking cups. Combine the prunes and water in the blender and process until smooth. Measure $\frac{1}{2}$ cup of the prune purée for the recipe and set it aside. Refrigerate or freeze the remaining prune purée for a future recipe.

Toast the walnuts in a 10-inch nonstick skillet for 1 to 2 minutes over high heat, tossing continuously with a wooden spoon until lightly browned. Immediately transfer the walnuts to a dish to cool and set them aside.

Combine the reserved prune purée, maple syrup, soymilk, and maple extract in a small bowl.

Combine the rolled oats, all-purpose whole wheat flour, whole wheat pastry flour, cinnamon, baking powder, and baking soda in a large mixing bowl, and stir with a wire whip to distribute evenly. Make a well in the center of the dry ingredients and add the maple syrup mixture. Add the dates and 1$\frac{1}{4}$ cups of the walnuts and mix well.

Fill the muffin cups two-thirds full with batter and top with the remaining walnuts. Bake for 20 to 22 minutes, or until a toothpick inserted into the center of a muffin comes out dry. Serve warm or at room temperature.

Covered with plastic wrap or packed into zipper-lock plastic bags and stored in the refrigerator, leftover Maple Dream Muffins will keep for two days. To serve, warm them in a preheated 350 degree oven for 5 to 8 minutes. For longer storage, pack the muffins into heavy-duty zipper-lock plastic bags and freeze them for up to three months.

Notes: If you prefer, $\frac{1}{2}$ cup jarred prune purée may be used in place of the pitted prunes and water.

• If you do not have whole wheat pastry flour on hand, use an equal amount of all-purpose whole wheat flour. This will produce a slightly heavier muffin.

Baking Hint

To prevent nuts from sinking to the bottom of muffins or cakes, toss the nuts with flour so they are lightly coated before adding them to the batter.

Per muffin: Calories 204, Protein 3g, Fat 7g, Carbohydrate 36g, Vitamin E .2mg

Bannocks

COMPANY'S COMING FOR BRUNCH and you need just the right dish to delight the senses. This Scottish flat bread sweetened with brown sugar is perfect and makes an ideal breakfast or brunch any season of the year. Serve it with your favorite jam, apple butter, or pumpkin butter, or enjoy the bannocks with Date 'n' Raisin Tofu Spread (page 174), Apricot Cashew Butter (page 169), or Hazelnut and Fruit Spread (page 168). Add some veggie sausage, fresh fruit in season, a steaming herbal tea, and enjoy an exceptional breakfast treat.

6 cups quick-cooking rolled oats

²⁄₃ cup light brown sugar

¹⁄₂ cup currants or black raisins

¹⁄₂ cup coarsely ground walnuts or pecans

2 teaspoons salt

2 teaspoons ground cinnamon

1 teaspoon baking soda

¹⁄₂ teaspoon ground allspice

1¹⁄₂ cups boiling water

¹⁄₄ cup organic canola oil

PREHEAT the oven to 325 degrees and have ready a dry baking sheet. Combine 4 cups of the rolled oats with the brown sugar, currants, walnuts, salt, cinnamon, baking soda, and allspice in a large bowl. Add the boiling water and the canola oil and mix well. Set the dough aside for 5 minutes.

Sprinkle 1 cup of the remaining rolled oats on a smooth countertop or breadboard. Place the dough on top and briefly knead the rolled oats into the dough for about 1 minute.

Sprinkle ¹⁄₂ cup of the remaining rolled oats on the countertop. Using a rolling pin, partially roll out the dough. Sprinkle the remaining ¹⁄₂ cup rolled oats over the top of the dough and roll into a ¹⁄₄-inch-thick square.

Using a dull knife or a spatula, cut the dough into 15 to 20 pieces (squares, rectangles, or irregular shapes, about 2-inches square) and place them on the baking sheet. Bake for 6 minutes. Turn the pieces over and bake another 6 minutes. Serve warm or at room temperature.

Packed in zipper-lock plastic bags and stored in the refrigerator, leftover Bannocks will keep for one week. For longer storage, pack in heavy-duty zipper-lock plastic bags and freeze for up to three months.

Per serving: Calories 529, Protein 15g, Fat 14g, Carbohydrate 91g, Vitamin E 1 mg

Nutty Oatcakes

Yield: 2 to 3 servings

THESE LITTLE FLAT BREADS are especially pleasing with fruit butters or sweetened tofu spreads, such as Date 'n' Raisin Tofu Spread (page 174) or Apricot Cashew Butter (page 169). All varieties of nut butters, jams, and jellies are also ideal toppings. For a complete breakfast, serve these crisp breakfast gems with fresh fruit or a fruit salad and a cup of herbal tea. These tasty oatcakes offer an added bonus. Since they require no refrigeration and keep for at least two weeks at room temperature, they make excellent travel food.

1 ½ cups old-fashioned rolled oats

5 to 6 tablespoons water

⅓ cup coarsely ground walnuts

1 tablespoon organic canola oil

¼ teaspoon baking powder

¼ teaspoon salt

PREHEAT the oven to 350 degrees and have ready a dry baking sheet. Blend 1 cup of the rolled oats into a fine meal in two batches in the blender at high speed. Transfer the meal to a medium bowl.

Add the water, walnuts, canola oil, baking powder, and salt, and stir to distribute the ingredients evenly. If the dough is too dry, add an additional tablespoon of water to make a firm dough that holds together well enough to form a ball.

Sprinkle ¼ cup of the rolled oats on a board or countertop. Press the dough down to flatten it slightly and sprinkle the remaining oats over the top. Using a rolling pin, roll the dough into a circle about 8 inches in diameter. Cut the dough into 8 wedges and place them on the baking sheet.

Bake for 15 to 18 minutes. Turn the pieces over and bake another 4 to 5 minutes. Turn off the oven and leave the oven door open until the oatcakes cool, about 5 minutes. Serve them immediately, or cool completely and store them in a zipper-lock plastic bag at room temperature. For longer storage, pack them into heavy-duty zipper-lock plastic bags and freeze for up to three months.

Nutty Rye Cakes: Replace the rolled oats with an equal amount of whole grain rye cereal. Use only 5 tablespoons of water and increase the baking time about 5 minutes.

Per serving: Calories 336, Protein 10g, Fat 18g, Carbohydrate 35g, Vitamin E 1.4mg

Banana Pecan Pancakes

Yield: 4 to 5 servings
(36 to 40 small pancakes)

1 pound extra-firm tofu

³/₄ cup mashed ripe
bananas (about
2 bananas)

¹/₂ cup whole wheat
pastry flour

¹/₃ cup regular soymilk

3 tablespoons
evaporated cane juice

1 tablespoon freshly
squeezed lemon juice

1 teaspoon
vanilla extract

¹/₂ teaspoon
ground cinnamon

¹/₄ teaspoon
maple extract

Dash salt

2 tablespoons water

1 tablespoon
whole flaxseeds

²/₃ cup coarsely
chopped pecans

BREAKFAST OR BRUNCH becomes a special treat when nutty pancakes are on the menu. Serve them with maple syrup or your favorite topping, and round out the meal with a sauté of onions, peppers, and potatoes. Broiled or sliced tomatoes, fresh fruit salad, and some soy sausages or soy bacon make the breakfast a hearty extravaganza.

PREHEAT the oven to 400 degrees and line 3 large baking sheets with parchment paper.

Break the tofu into pieces and put them into the food processor. Add the bananas, flour, soymilk, evaporated cane juice, lemon juice, vanilla extract, ground cinnamon, maple extract, and salt. Process until well blended.

Combine the water and flaxseeds in the blender and blend on low speed for about 1 minute, until the mixture becomes thick and viscous (the consistency will be similar to thick oatmeal). Add to the tofu mixture in the food processor and process until well mixed.

Transfer to a large bowl and add the pecans, stirring well to distribute them evenly.

Drop the batter by heaping tablespoons onto the prepared baking sheets, putting 12 to 15 pancakes on each sheet. Keep the pancakes small, no larger than 2 inches in diameter, for easier turning. Flatten the pancakes slightly with a fork so they will bake evenly.

Place 2 of the baking sheets in the oven and bake for 12 minutes. Turn the pancakes with a spatula, reverse the baking sheets (move the upper baking sheet to the lower rack and the lower baking sheet to the upper rack), and bake 7 to 8 minutes longer. Place the finished pancakes on a serving dish and bake the remaining pancakes.

Per serving: Calories 330, Protein 14g, Fat 18g, Carbohydrate 34g, Vitamin E .7mg

Nutty Buckwheat Pancakes
with Dried Plum Sauce

Yield: about 4 servings
(18 to 20 pancakes)

1 cup buckwheat flour

1 cup all-purpose
whole wheat flour

1 cup walnuts, ground
to a coarse meal

1/4 cup evaporated
cane juice

1 teaspoon
ground cinnamon

1 teaspoon
baking powder

Dash salt

2 1/3 cups plus
2 tablespoons water

1/2 cup prune purée
(homemade, page 58,
or jarred)

2 teaspoons
vanilla extract

1 tablespoon
whole flaxseeds

Dried Plum Sauce
(page 58)

NO NEED TO FEEL pangs of guilt when indulging the family with pancakes made from wholesome grains like buckwheat and whole wheat. This recipe adds fiber and cuts calories by using prune purée in place of oil or margarine.

COMBINE the buckwheat flour, whole wheat flour, ground walnuts, evaporated cane juice, cinnamon, baking powder, and salt in a large bowl.

Combine 2 1/3 cups of the water, the prune purée, and vanilla extract in a medium bowl.

Combine the remaining 2 tablespoons water and the flaxseeds in the blender and blend on low speed for about 1 minute, until thick and viscous (the consistency will be similar to thick oatmeal).

Stir the prune mixture into the flour mixture and mix well with a wire whip. Add the flaxseed mixture, and stir until thoroughly incorporated.

Lightly oil a nonstick griddle and heat it over medium-high. When the griddle is hot, spoon the batter onto the surface, forming pancakes that are 3 to 4 inches in diameter. When the tops of the pancakes develop bubbles, about 1 minute, turn them over and cook 1 minute longer, or until golden brown.

Transfer to a serving dish and serve with Dried Plum Sauce.

Note: As an alternative to binding the pancakes with flaxseeds and water, combine 1 tablespoon powdered egg replacer beaten with 1/4 cup water and add to the wet ingredients.

Per serving (without sauce): Calories 370, Protein 9g, Fat 20g, Carbohydrate 43g, Vitamin E .3mg

Nutty Granola

A GREAT MORNING starter packed with nutritious ingredients, this earthy granola offers tantalizing taste, plenty of crunch, and zero hunger pangs until lunch. The recipe makes an extra-large quantity so you'll have plenty on hand.

8 cups old-fashioned rolled oats

3 cups barley flakes

1 1/3 cups oat bran

3/4 cup millet

2 cups unsweetened shredded dried coconut

1 cup sunflower seeds

1 cup coarsely chopped walnuts

1 cup coarsely chopped hazelnuts

1 cup coarsely chopped cashews

1 cup coarsely chopped Brazil nuts

1/2 cup roasted peanuts

1/4 cup carob powder (optional)

PREHEAT the oven to 325 degrees and have ready 4 baking sheets about 10 x 15 inches (jelly-roll pans are best). Plan to bake the granola in two ovens or in two batches.

In a giant mixing bowl, combine the oats, barley, oat bran, and millet, and toss them together with a large wooden spoon.

Add the coconut, sunflower seeds, walnuts, hazelnuts, cashews, Brazil nuts, peanuts, carob powder, if using, cinnamon, and allspice and mix well. Combine the maple syrup, brown rice syrup, canola oil, and vanilla extract in a small mixing bowl. Stir well and add to the grain and nut mixture, tossing well to distribute all the ingredients evenly.

Divide the mixture equally among the 4 baking pans and bake 2 pans (on separate racks) for 10 minutes. Remove from the oven, stir with a large spatula, and return to the oven for 10 minutes longer. Bake the remaining 2 pans.

1 tablespoon plus
1 teaspoon ground
cinnamon

1 teaspoon
ground allspice

1 1/2 cups maple syrup

1 cup brown rice syrup

2/3 cup organic
canola oil

2 teaspoons vanilla
extract

2 cups chopped dates

1 1/2 cups black raisins

1 1/2 cups
golden raisins

Cool the granola completely and transfer it to the giant mixing bowl. Add the dates and raisins and stir well to distribute them evenly. Store the granola in heavy-duty zipper-lock plastic bags or in airtight containers. Nutty Granola keeps well at room temperature or in the refrigerator for one month. For longer storage, pack it in heavy-duty zipper-lock plastic bags and freeze for up to three months.

THE PLANTERS PEANUT COMPANY began in the early 1900s. It was in 1916 that their mascot, Mr. Peanut, who stands tall with top hat, monocle, and cane, made his debut. Mr. Peanut was the winning entry in a contest the company's owner, Amedeo Obici, offered to school children.

In 1921, scientist George Washington Carver was given ten minutes to tell Congress about peanuts. His presentation so fascinated everyone that his ten-minute talk stretched into an hour and a half. His birthplace, Diamond Grove, Missouri, is now a national monument. Carver developed 325 products from peanuts.

Per serving (3/4 cup): Calories 444, Protein 9g, Fat 22g, Carbohydrate 57g, Vitamin E 2.6mg

Dried Plum Sauce

Yield: about 1¼ cups

½ teaspoon
vanilla extract

⅓ cup plus
1 tablespoon prune
purée (homemade,
below, or jarred)

⅓ cup water

¼ cup evaporated
cane juice

COMBINE all the ingredients in the blender and process until smooth. Thin to the desired consistency with additional water, if needed. Transfer the sauce to an attractive serving bowl and provide a ladle for serving.

Prune Purée

Yield: ¾ cup plus
1 tablespoon

1 cup pitted prunes

⅓ cup plus
1 tablespoon water

COMBINE the prunes and water in the blender or food processor and process until completely smooth.

Per serving (Plum Sauce): Calories 58, Protein 0g, Fat 0g, Carbohydrate 15g, Vitamin E .2mg

Soups

A STEAMING KETTLE OF SAVORY SOUP BRIMMING WITH BEANS AND VEGETABLES

and richly seasoned with herbs and spices is a hearty meal in itself. As a starter to a hearty entrée, a light broth with vegetables, such as Chayote Cashew Bisque (page 64), offers the ideal cup of soup.

In winter, that bowl of hot soup satisfies like nothing else. When the weather has us shivering, we can warm up quickly by adding spices that bring heat to the body—like ginger, garlic, cinnamon, cloves, allspice, cardamom, and pepper. One of my family's favorites, Butternut Corn Cashew Soup (page 62), possesses all the qualities that make a cool weather soup satisfying—it's thick, chunky, and full of body and great flavor.

In summer we make a complete adjustment in our thinking about soup. Sweet, cooling fruit soups can be welcome starters or even light lunches. Chilled raw vegetable soups with pungent seasonings, like Mango Macadamia Soup (page 66), are a delight. Cooked vegetable soups served hot or cold are equally refreshing.

Between seasons, look for the new produce items that come to market and lend a fresh spark to your soups. Vary the vegetables to keep the kettle interesting, and add an uncommon ingredient, either a pungent herb, a sassy spice, or an unusual variety of fruit or vegetable, to make the soup just a little mysterious.

Quite often nuts, either chopped, coarsely ground, or turned into a nut meal, can give that kettle of soup an extraordinary character. African Peanut Soup (page 60) combines many of the qualities that make a soup pungent, sassy, spicy, and nutty.

African Peanut Soup

RICHLY FLAVORED with peanuts and lightly spiced with a seasoning combination that hints of far away places, this hearty soup just might entice you to make an entire meal of it. This is one of my very favorite easy, no-fail recipes.

2 pounds ripe Roma tomatoes, chopped

2 onions, chopped

6 garlic cloves, coarsely chopped

2 tablespoons extra-virgin olive oil

5 cups water

1 (8-ounce) can tomato sauce

1/2 cup fresh mint leaves, minced

1 tablespoon chili powder

2 teaspoons ground cumin

1 3/4 teaspoons salt

1/8 teaspoon crushed red pepper flakes

2 cups finely chopped Swiss chard or spinach

3/4 cup unsalted chunky peanut butter

1/4 cup crushed roasted peanuts

COMBINE the tomatoes, onions, garlic, and olive oil in a large stockpot and cook and stir over high heat for about 5 minutes, or until the tomatoes are softened and the onions are transparent. Turn the heat down to a simmer.

Add the water, tomato sauce, 3 tablespoons of the mint leaves, chili powder, cumin, salt, and red pepper flakes and simmer for 10 to 12 minutes.

Add the Swiss chard and peanut butter and cook 3 to 4 minutes, stirring constantly to distribute the peanut butter. The soup will thicken slightly.

To serve, spoon the soup into bowls and garnish with a pinch or two of the remaining mint leaves and the crushed peanuts.

Soymilk: Regular or Unsweetened?

Regular soymilk adds that perfect touch of sweetness to dishes that would benefit from the extra flavor boost. If you prefer less sweetness or are aiming for a savory flavor, use unsweetened soymilk.

Per serving: Calories 328, Protein 12g, Fat 24g, Carbohydrate 22g, Vitamin E 3.4mg

Yam and Nut Butter Soup

Yield: 6 servings as an entrée; 12 to 14 servings as an appetizer

1 onion, chopped

$^1/_2$ cup water

1 teaspoon ground cumin

1 teaspoon ground coriander

1 garlic clove, minced

$^1/_2$ teaspoon salt

$^1/_4$ teaspoon freshly ground pepper

4 cups regular soymilk

3 cups peeled and chopped yams

$^1/_4$ cup unsalted peanut butter (creamy or chunky)

$^1/_4$ cup cashew butter

$^1/_2$ teaspoon salt

$^1/_8$ teaspoon crushed red pepper flakes

$^1/_2$ cup canned corn, drained

Paprika

THIS KETTLE, enriched with not one but two nut butters, can fall into two categories: an appetite teaser that will serve twelve to fourteen guests, or a wholesome entrée for six hearty appetites. Offer guests a small starter by serving the soup in attractive teacups. As a main dish, begin with a salad and serve a generous portion of soup along with whole grain bread.

COMBINE the onion, water, cumin, coriander, garlic, salt, and pepper in a 6-quart stockpot. Cook and stir over high heat, uncovered, for about 5 minutes, or until the onion is tender.

Lower the heat to medium-high and add the soymilk and yams. Cook and stir for about 10 minutes, or until the yams are softened. Transfer to the blender and process in batches until smooth and creamy. Return the soup to the stockpot, leaving about 1$^1/_2$ cups in the blender.

Add the nut butters, salt, and crushed red pepper flakes to the blender and process until creamy. Add to the stockpot and gently warm through.

Carefully spoon the soup into teacups, small dessert bowls, or soup bowls, and garnish with a spoonful or two of the corn and a dash of paprika.

Note: If the soup is a little too thick for your liking, simply thin it with a small amount of extra soymilk and adjust the seasonings.

Per serving (entrée): Calories 310, Protein 13g, Fat 14g, Carbohydrate 37g, Vitamin E 3.3mg

Butternut Corn Cashew Soup

1 large butternut squash
(about 2½ pounds)

1 cup raw or unsalted
dry-roasted cashews

3 ears sweet corn,
cooked, or 2 (15-ounce)
cans corn, drained

2 onions, finely chopped

2 large carrots, peeled
and finely chopped

2 celery stalks,
finely chopped

⅓ cup water

2 garlic cloves, crushed

1 teaspoon salt

¼ teaspoon
ground nutmeg

Freshly ground pepper

2 to 4 cups water

2 tablespoons minced
fresh herbs
(dill, basil, or parsley)

¼ cup pomegranate
seeds (optional)

FOR A HEARTY one-dish meal, enrich this soup with cashews and fresh corn. Brimming with creamy butternut squash, it's a gustatory delight. Although butternut squash is available year-round, its flavor is best in autumn.

PREHEAT the oven to 400 degrees. Place the whole butternut squash on a dry baking sheet and bake for 1 hour, or until soft to the touch.

Grind the cashews into a course meal in the food processor, or process them in an electric mini-chopper/grinder or coffee grinder for a fine meal, depending on your texture preference. Set aside.

With a sharp knife, cut the corn kernels off the cobs and set the kernels aside.

Combine the onions, carrots, celery, water, and garlic in a large stockpot. Bring to a boil over high heat, then lower the heat to medium-high. Cook for about 5 minutes, or until the vegetables are soft and transparent, adding more water if needed. Add the corn along with the salt, nutmeg, and pepper.

When the squash is cool enough to handle, cut it in half lengthwise and discard the seeds. Scoop out the flesh and process it in the food processor or blender until smooth. Add to the stockpot along with the ground cashews.

Stir in enough of the water to reach the desired consistency. Simmer for 5 to 10 minutes to blend the flavors. Adjust the seasonings, if needed.

Ladle into soup bowls. Garnish with the fresh herbs and pomegranate seeds, if using.

Note: To give the soup a more dominant corn flavor, use the drained liquid from the canned corn in place of some of the water.

Per serving: Calories 341, Protein 10g, Fat 12g, Carbohydrate 54g, Vitamin E .6mg

Fresh Chestnut Soup

Yield: 6 to 8 servings

3$\frac{1}{4}$ cups water

2 large carrots, peeled and chopped

1 large onion, chopped

2 celery stalks, diced

$\frac{1}{2}$ serrano or jalapeño chile, minced

2 quarts unsweetened soymilk

2 tablespoons plus 1 teaspoon nutritional yeast flakes

2 teaspoons salt

$\frac{1}{4}$ teaspoon plus $\frac{1}{8}$ teaspoon ground nutmeg

$\frac{1}{4}$ teaspoon dried tarragon

3 tablespoons cornstarch

1$\frac{1}{4}$ pounds fresh chestnuts in the shell, cooked and peeled (see page 27), or 1 (15-ounce) jar

2 tablespoons chopped fresh chives

WHILE THIS UNIQUE, tantalizing soup is cooking, it sends waves of beckoning aromas so irresistible it just may become a holiday tradition at your house. For the best flavor, prepare the soup a day ahead, giving it plenty of time for the seasonings to fully develop. To reheat the soup, warm it gently over medium heat and stir frequently to avoid burning.

COMBINE 1$\frac{1}{2}$ cups of the water with the carrots, onion, celery, and chile in a large, deep skillet. Cook and stir over high heat for about 5 minutes, or until soft. Set aside.

Combine the soymilk, nutritional yeast, salt, nutmeg, and tarragon in a large stockpot and bring to a simmer over medium-high heat.

Combine $\frac{1}{4}$ cup of the water with the cornstarch in a small cup or bowl and stir to make a thin paste. Add to the simmering soymilk and stir for 1 minute until it is well dissolved and the soup is slightly thickened. Remove from the heat.

Combine three-quarters of the cooked vegetable mixture, three-quarters of the prepared chestnuts, and the remaining 1$\frac{1}{2}$ cups water in the food processor and process until smooth. Add to the soup along with the remaining cooked vegetables.

Chop the remaining chestnuts and add them to the soup. Heat gently to warm through and blend the flavors. Garnish each bowl with a sprinkling of the chives and serve.

Measuring chestnuts

- A 15-ounce jar of cooked, peeled chestnuts contains about 2$\frac{1}{2}$ cups.

- One pound of fresh chestnuts in the shell will make 2$\frac{1}{2}$ cups peeled cooked chestnuts.

Per serving: Calories 321, Protein 15g, Fat 5g, Carbohydrate 53g, Vitamin E .2mg

Chayote Cashew Bisque

Yield: 4 to 5 servings

FEATHER LIGHT, this delightful bisque brings an unexpected surprise with the very first spoonful. The chayote squash delivers a delicate sweetness that lends an ideal balance to a savory meal.

2 chayote squashes
(about 1 pound)

1 cup water

1 sweet apple

1/2 cup cashews

2 cups vanilla soymilk

3/4 teaspoon salt

1 teaspoon maple syrup
(optional)

1/4 cup soy sour cream

Paprika

PEEL the chayote squashes with a vegetable peeler. Cut each one in half, remove the seed, and cut the flesh into coarse chunks. Place in a 6-quart saucepan and add the water. Cover and bring to a boil over high heat. Turn the heat down to low and steam for about 25 minutes, or until the squashes are fork-tender.

While the squash is cooking, core the apple but do not peel it. Cut the apple into chunks and put half of them into the blender. Set the rest aside.

Grind the cashews into a fine meal in an electric mini-chopper/grinder or coffee grinder and set aside.

When the squash is tender, put half into the blender with the apples, including all of the liquid in the saucepan, and blend until smooth. With the machine running, add the remaining squash and reserved apple chunks and blend until completely smooth. Return the mixture to the saucepan.

Add the soymilk and salt and bring to a boil over medium-high heat. When it reaches a boil, add the ground cashews and cook for 1 to 2 minutes longer, until slightly thickened.

Add the optional maple syrup for extra sweetness. Garnish each bowl with a dollop of the soy sour cream and a sprinkling of paprika.

Per serving: Calories 216, Protein 7g, Fat 11g, Carbohydrate 23g, Vitamin E .4mg

64   The Nut Gourmet

Pumpkin Soup

PUMPKINS are not only for carving. They create the base for a soup so velvety light and creamy you'll find it doesn't dull the taste buds for the rest of the meal. Ground cashews provide the thickening and join with root vegetables to contribute a pleasing sweetness. This recipe makes enough to enjoy leftovers the next day.

1 pumpkin (about 5 pounds), peeled and cut into 2-inch chunks

6 1/4 cups water

3 large carrots, peeled and cut into 1/2-inch chunks

1 parsnip, peeled and cut into 1/2-inch chunks

1 small sweet potato, peeled and cut into small chunks

1/2 teaspoon salt

2 onions, coarsely chopped

1 teaspoon extra-virgin olive oil

1 cup finely ground cashews

1 tablespoon plus 2 teaspoons maple syrup

1/2 teaspoon salt

1/2 teaspoon ground nutmeg

1/4 teaspoon ground cinnamon

1/4 teaspoon ground ginger

2 green onions, finely chopped

COMBINE the pumpkin, 6 cups of the water, carrots, parsnip, sweet potato, and salt in a large stockpot. Cover and bring to a boil over high heat. Turn the heat down to medium and simmer for 20 to 25 minutes, or until the vegetables are soft.

Combine the onions, remaining 1/4 cup water, and olive oil in a skillet and cook and stir for 6 to 8 minutes until soft, adding more water if needed.

Process the cooked pumpkin, vegetables, and onions in batches in the blender until smooth. Return the soup to the stockpot, and add more water if the soup is too thick.

Bring to a simmer over medium heat, and add the cashews, maple syrup, salt, nutmeg, cinnamon, and ginger. Gently simmer for about 5 minutes to blend the flavors. Adjust the seasonings if needed. Garnish each bowl with a generous sprinkling of the chopped green onions and serve.

Per serving: Calories 277, Protein 9g, Fat 11g, Carbohydrate 43g, Vitamin E 4mg

Mango Macadamia Soup

COLD SOUPS can't be beat for a light summer lunch or as a cool starter at dinnertime. When it's simply too hot to cook, don't. Let the blender become your partner in the kitchen, and enjoy the sweet flavors and freshness of a fruity vegetable soup that refuses to come near the stove. If macadamia nuts are unavailable, you can easily count on cashews or pine nuts to take their place.

1 large ripe mango

1 large carrot, peeled and chopped

1 yellow or orange bell pepper, chopped

1 cup water

1 large ripe Roma tomato, chopped

$1/2$ cup macadamia nuts

Juice of 1 lemon or lime (2 to 3 tablespoons)

$1/2$ teaspoon grated fresh ginger

$1/4$ teaspoon salt

COMBINE all the ingredients in the blender and process until as smooth or chunky as desired. Serve immediately or thoroughly chilled.

How to Peel a Mango

Wash the mango. Stand it up vertically and slice off the flesh from the elongated pit on each side of the fruit. Cut off any extra mango flesh that is clinging to the pit.

Once the fruit is cut from the pit, there are three ways to remove the flesh from the peel. One method is to scoop out the flesh with a spoon.

Another is to lay each cut half mango on the cutting board, and slice it into strips. Then use a sharp paring knife, held horizontally, to slice the flesh from the peel.

A third approach creates mango chunks or diced pieces. Lay the cut half mango on the cutting board and use a sharp paring knife to make several vertical and several horizontal cuts into the flesh, about $1/4$ to $1/2$ inch apart. Do not cut through the skin. Then hold the knife horizontally and slice the base of the flesh off the skin.

Per serving: Calories 248, Protein 3g, Fat 17g, Carbohydrate 25g, Vitamin E 1.3mg

Sunny Carrot Cashew Soup

WHEN SUMMER temperatures rise, give the stove a rest. Just a whirl in the blender is all it takes to produce this tasty raw soup that looks as sunny as its name implies.

3 large carrots, peeled and cut into coarse chunks

2 cups water

1 sweet apple (Pink Lady, Fuji, or Gala), cored and cut into chunks

1/2 yellow bell pepper, cut into chunks

1/2 cup freshly squeezed orange juice

1/2 cup cashews

2 tablespoons chopped onion (about 1 slice)

Salt

2 tablespoons finely diced raw beet (about 1 slice), or 2 tablespoons diced red bell pepper

1/3 to 1/2 cup Lemon Dill Silken Sauce (page 144)

COMBINE the carrots, water, apple, bell pepper, orange juice, cashews, onion, and salt to taste in the blender. Process on low speed for a few seconds. Then switch to high speed and blend for 1 full minute, until fairly smooth.

Garnish each bowl with some of the diced beets and a spoonful of Lemon Dill Silken Sauce. Pass the remainder of the sauce at the table.

Per serving: Calories 260, Protein 9g, Fat 13g, Carbohydrate 31g, Vitamin E 1mg

Mushroom Soup in the Raw

HAVE YOUR SPOON ready for a delightfully refreshing, mushroom lover's cold soup that can be prepared in minutes. If portobellos are not available, cremini or button mushrooms are excellent stand-ins.

2 large ripe tomatoes, coarsely chopped

1 large portobello mushroom, coarsely chopped

1 cup water

½ cup coarsely chopped pecans

1 to 2 tablespoons freshly squeezed lime juice

¾ teaspoon salt

¼ teaspoon ground cumin

¼ teaspoon ground cinnamon

⅛ teaspoon ground nutmeg

Freshly ground pepper

¼ ripe avocado, diced

¼ cup Lemon Dill Silken Sauce (page 144)

COMBINE the tomatoes, mushroom, water, pecans, lime juice, salt, cumin, cinnamon, nutmeg, and pepper in the blender and process for 1 to 2 minutes, until smooth and creamy. Pour into serving bowls.

Garnish each bowl with some of the diced avocado and a dollop of Lemon Dill Silken Sauce. Serve immediately or thoroughly chilled.

THE QUIET LITTLE PECAN, delicately sweet and so rich tasting, is as American as, well, pecan pie! There's no doubt about it—the pecan tree, which is kin to the hickory and walnut family, was growing wild in the United States long before any newcomers arrived here. Because the flavorful, convoluted nut doesn't grow naturally in any other part of the world, one would think the United States had an exclusive contract with Mother Nature and the wild pecan.

Per serving: Calories 199, Protein 5g, Fat 17g, Carbohydrate 11g, Vitamin E 1.7mg

Salads

SALADS WITH EXTRAORDINARY CHARACTER LITERALLY BLOSSOM

on the platter and clamor for attention. How can anyone resist crisp, crunchy greens embellished with colorful fruits and vegetables and accented with pungent accoutrements like kalamata olives, toasted nuts, hearts of palm, or artichoke hearts.

Some extraordinary salads become the main course for a light meal, such as Cool Quinoa Salad (page 75). Other salads that are equally special are more suited to a first course, such as the very dramatic 26 Pecan Salad (page 70). Mediterranean Salad (page 76) is perfect party fare, while others, like Red Baron Salad I (page 78) or Sweet Potato Waldorf Salad (page 77), add the ideal complement to the meal as a side dish.

For simple, everyday salads as a prelude to the entrée, I love to combine a variety of greens for their color and earthy flavors. Sometimes a chopped leaf or two of ruffled fresh mustard greens or a couple frilly kale leaves, finely shredded, make a salad bloom. In winter, the lush deep green of raw collards makes a pleasant addition to the salad bowl and lends a surprisingly sweet flavor, unlike their lusty bite when cooked. Collards grown in late spring and summer tend to snarl with a touch of bitterness. That's when I complement the sharpness with something sweet, like chopped apples or a handful of raisins.

In addition, I can't resist adding what many people call sinkers—those vividly colored chunks of crunchy veggies like radishes, bell peppers, cucumbers, carrots, celery, kohlrabi, turnips, and snap peas that often fall to the bottom of the bowl. A quick toss brings them to the surface where they show off their tempting array of colors.

On some days salads are the featured dish for our evening meal. For those dinners I practically empty the vegetable bin and toss in last night's leftovers as well. I make sure to include stick-to-the-ribs staples like legumes, whole grains, nuts, and seeds. Then I get to work creating a standout dressing that elevates a simple salad.

26 Pecan Salad

Yield: 4 to 5 servings

See photo facing page 97

WHILE EXACTLY twenty-six pecans may seem an odd thing to feature in a salad, when caramelized and served as a garnish, they're the perfect topping for this innovative dish, elegant enough for special occasions. The success of this salad relies on advance preparation of the balsamic vinegar reduction, the caramelized pecans, and the marinated tofu. When these items are prepared a day ahead, the salad can be assembled quickly.

Balsamic Vinegar Reduction

½ cup balsamic vinegar

Nuts

2 tablespoons maple syrup

26 pecan halves (½ cup)

Marinade

¼ cup soy sauce

1 tablespoon umeboshi vinegar or wine vinegar

½ pound firm or extra-firm tofu

TO MAKE the balsamic vinegar reduction, pour the balsamic vinegar into a very small saucepan. Simmer uncovered over medium-high heat for 12 to 15 minutes, until reduced by half (about ¼ cup). The vinegar will become slightly thickened. To test for the right consistency, use a spoon to scoop up some of the liquid and see how it pours back into the saucepan. It should appear to have thickened slightly and pour like a thin ribbon. Cool and store the reduction in the refrigerator. The reduction will thicken further when chilled.

TO CARAMELIZE the pecans, pour the maple syrup into an 8- or 10-inch non-stick skillet, and bring it to a boil over high heat. When it is bubbling, add the pecans and toss them with a wooden spoon to coat them completely. Stir for 1 to 2 minutes, or until all the liquid is absorbed. Remove from the heat and immediately pour the coated pecans into a dish to cool. When completely cool, break apart the pecans that have stuck together.

TO MAKE a marinade for the tofu, combine the soy sauce and umeboshi vinegar in a small plastic container with a lid. Crumble the tofu into the marinade, and stir to coat it evenly. Refrigerate it for 2 to 8 hours, tossing occasionally.

Salad

12 snap peas or snow peas, trimmed and cut in half lengthwise

1 red bell pepper, cut into 1-inch julienne

1 apple, chopped

1/2 head Boston lettuce, torn

4 leaves frilly kale, finely shredded

1/2 yellow or orange bell pepper, cut into 1-inch julienne

1/2 cup currants or black raisins

5 radishes, sliced

3 tablespoons extra-virgin olive oil

TO ASSEMBLE the salad, combine the snap peas, red bell pepper, apple, lettuce, kale, yellow bell pepper, currants, radishes, and olive oil in a large bowl and toss well. Sprinkle the marinated tofu over the top. Drizzle the balsamic vinegar reduction over the tofu. Top the salad with the caramelized pecans and serve.

Notes: Be careful not to overcook the balsamic vinegar. The reduction can become so thick it will solidify when refrigerated.

• For individual servings, combine the snap peas, red bell pepper, apple, lettuce, kale, yellow bell pepper, currants, radishes, and olive oil in a large bowl and toss until the vegetables and fruit are evenly coated with the oil. Spoon onto individual salad plates. Top each serving with a portion of the marinated tofu. Drizzle the balsamic vinegar reduction over the tofu, and garnish with the caramelized pecans.

Per serving: Calories 249, Protein 9g, Fat 16g, Carbohydrate 23g, Vitamin E 2mg

Chestnut and Cranberry Fanfare

Yield: 6 servings

THIS AUTUMN FRUIT medley stands out because it combines both the sweet and tart fruits of the harvest season that most people tend to eat separately. If you haven't been introduced to fresh chestnuts, you'll discover their sweet flavor and starchy texture is quite alluring. If time does not permit the luxury of working with fresh chestnuts, check out the natural food markets or gourmet shops for cooked, peeled, unsweetened chestnuts in a can or jar.

1¼ pounds fresh chestnuts in the shell, cooked and peeled (see page 27), or 1 (15-ounce) jar

2 large ripe Fuyu persimmons, diced

2 ripe bananas, cut in half lengthwise and sliced crosswise

¾ cup raisins

⅔ cup fresh cranberries, chopped

1 (5- to 7-inch) strip lemon or orange zest

PLACE the chestnuts in a bowl and break them into pieces. Add the persimmons, bananas, raisins, and cranberries, and toss to distribute the fruits evenly. Transfer to an attractive serving bowl. Curl a portion of the strip of lemon zest and arrange it artfully on top of the fruit salad.

WELL BEFORE THE PILGRIMS ARRIVED on the Eastern shores, the American chestnut tree stood as a mighty monument, many over one hundred feet tall, their trunks measuring five feet or more in diameter. Chestnut trees formed the forests that grew from Maine to Florida. Spreading westward they were found in Michigan down to the Alleghenies. There's an old saying that the chestnut forests were so thick a squirrel could jump from chestnut tree to chestnut tree from Georgia to New York without ever touching the ground.

American chestnut trees provided sustenance to humans and animals in numerous ways. Chestnuts were a dietary staple of the American Indians, who taught the Pilgrims how to prepare them and incorporate them into stews or grind them into flour for bread.

Per serving: Calories 227, Protein 3g, Fat 2g, Carbohydrate 53g, Vitamin E .3mg

Green Mango Salad

SUMMER'S INTENSE HEAT always sends me in search of cooling foods, those with a high water content and a touch of sweetness for an energy boost. I created this Southeast Asian salad after thoroughly enjoying the Thai restaurant version. Enjoy it as a first course or as a side dish.

2 unripe mangoes, peeled (see page 66) and cut into 1 x $\frac{1}{4}$-inch slivers

$\frac{1}{2}$ cup purple onions, sliced vertically

$\frac{1}{2}$ cup diced jicama

$\frac{1}{2}$ cup chopped unsalted roasted peanuts

$\frac{1}{4}$ red bell pepper, cut into 1-inch julienne

3 green onions (green part only), slivered into 1-inch lengths

2 tablespoons organic canola oil

2 tablespoons rice vinegar

$\frac{1}{2}$ to 1 jalapeño chile, minced, or dash cayenne

1 $\frac{1}{2}$ tablespoons evaporated cane juice

1 tablespoon sesame oil

1 tablespoon freshly squeezed lime juice

2 teaspoons minced fresh mint leaves

$\frac{1}{4}$ to $\frac{1}{2}$ teaspoon salt

5 to 6 butter lettuce leaves

Chopped fresh cilantro leaves

COMBINE the mangoes, onions, jicama, peanuts, red bell pepper, green onions, canola oil, vinegar, chile, evaporated cane juice, sesame oil, lime juice, mint, and salt in a large mixing bowl and toss well to distribute the ingredients evenly. Refrigerate for 3 to 8 hours to fully marinate the mangoes.

Place a lettuce leaf on each plate and spoon the mango salad into the leaf. Garnish with a sprinkling of chopped cilantro leaves and serve.

Per serving: Calories 217, Protein 4g, Fat 15g, Carbohydrate 22g, Vitamin E 3mg

Just Peachy Pine Nut Salad

Yield: 6 servings

PRESENT THIS SALAD when sweet stone fruits come into season. This combo packs the pungency of basil, the bite of onion, the creamy flavor of pine nuts, and the sweetness of peaches into a beautiful salad presentation. If you're aiming for a make-ahead prep, just add the peaches and dressing right before serving.

5 to 6 large ripe peaches, sliced

4 to 6 large romaine lettuce leaves, torn into bite-size pieces

1 small sweet red or white onion, thinly sliced vertically

1 cup basil leaves, lightly packed and coarsely chopped

½ red bell pepper, chopped

⅓ to ½ cup Poppy Seed Dressing (page 92)

½ cup pine nuts, toasted (see page 28)

COMBINE the peaches, lettuce, onion, basil, and bell pepper in a large bowl. Add the Poppy Seed Dressing and toss to coat well. Arrange the salad on an attractive serving platter. Garnish with the toasted pine nuts and serve.

Note: Any summer stone fruits would work in this salad in place of the peaches, as long as they are sweet. Even more appealing is a mixture of fruits. Peaches and nectarines, for example, are a tasty combination.

Per serving: Calories 135, Protein 3g, Fat 9g, Carbohydrate 14g, Vitamin E .1mg

Cool Quinoa Salad

Yield: 7 to 8 servings

4 cups water

2 cups quinoa

1 1/2 teaspoons salt

2 broccoli crowns, cut into small florets

1 1/2 cups frozen peas, thawed

1 (15-ounce) can black beans, rinsed and drained

1 sweet onion, thinly sliced vertically

1 red bell pepper, diced

1 cup toasted pecan halves (see page 28) or coarsely chopped pecans

2/3 cup chopped fresh dill weed

3 to 4 tablespoons organic canola oil

2 to 4 tablespoons freshly squeezed lime juice

2 tablespoons low-sodium soy sauce

Salt and freshly ground pepper

AN IDEAL SALAD for a hearty family meal or the buffet table, this medley of quinoa, broccoli, black beans, and fresh dill counts on toasted pecans to add the finishing touch. Serve it warm, immediately after preparation, or chill it and serve later.

COMBINE the water, quinoa, and salt in a 4-quart saucepan, cover, and bring to a boil over high heat. Turn the heat down to low, and steam for 15 to 20 minutes. Remove from the heat and let stand, covered, for 10 minutes. Cool until just warm, then transfer to a large bowl.

Fill a 4- or 6-quart saucepan two-thirds full with water and bring to a boil. Add the broccoli florets, and when the water returns to a boil, blanch the broccoli for 1 minute. Drain in a strainer and rinse under cold water. Add the florets to the bowl with the cooked quinoa.

Add the remaining ingredients and season with salt and pepper. Serve immediately or thoroughly chilled.

Per serving: Calories 432, Protein 14g, Fat 20g, Carbohydrate 52g, Vitamin E 2mg

Mediterranean Salad

Yield: 40 to 60 servings

FOR AN ATTRACTIVE party salad that serves a large crowd, rely on this tasty, easy-to-assemble combo that proudly announces its Mediterranean origins. For the best results, begin preparing this salad two days before serving.

2 pounds button mushrooms

1 1/4 cups extra-virgin olive oil

3/4 cup freshly squeezed lemon juice

1/2 cup water

1/4 cup balsamic vinegar

6 to 8 garlic cloves, minced

1 1/2 teaspoons salt

1 (62-ounce) jar marinated artichokes, with liquid

3 (6-ounce) cans black olives, drained

1 (1-pound) jar capers, drained

1 (1-pound) can or jar hearts of palm, sliced 1/4 inch thick

1 1/4 cups pine nuts

1 (8-ounce) jar stuffed green olives, drained

1/2 small head cauliflower, cut into miniature florets

4 carrots, peeled and thinly sliced

1 head red leaf lettuce

1/4 bunch parsley

1 ripe tomato

TWO DAYS before serving the salad, cut the mushrooms in half, or quarters if they are very large, and put them into a large, deep bowl or large jar. Combine the olive oil, lemon juice, water, vinegar, garlic, and salt in a large bowl or jar and pour over the mushrooms. Stir well, cover, and refrigerate, stirring 2 or 3 times during the day.

The next day add the artichokes and their liquid, the black olives, capers, hearts of palm, pine nuts, green olives, cauliflower, and carrots. Toss well to coat with the marinade. Marinate in the refrigerator for 24 hours.

Line a large, attractive bowl with the red leaf lettuce and transfer the salad to it. To garnish, place the parsley at the edge of the bowl. Make a tomato rose (see page 77), and nestle it in the bed of parsley.

Per serving: Calories 124, Protein 3g, Fat 10g, Carbohydrate 8g, Vitamin E 1.5mg

Sweet Potato Waldorf Salad

Yield: 2 to 3 servings

THE ADDITION OF the sweet potato and toasted pine nuts makes this simple salad an exceptional side dish or a hearty lunch. Because the natural flavors blend so well, there's little need for exotic seasonings. A basket of whole grain bread makes the ideal accompaniment.

1 sweet potato, peeled and sliced into 1/2-inch-thick rounds

1 sweet red apple, diced

1 ripe pear, diced

1 celery stalk, chopped

1/2 cup pine nuts, toasted (see page 28)

2 to 3 tablespoons vegan mayonnaise

1 tablespoon chopped fresh chives

STEAM the sweet potato for 7 to 8 minutes, until soft. Remove from the steamer and cool. Cut into bite-size pieces and put in a medium bowl. Add the apple, pear, celery, pine nuts, and mayonnaise, and toss well to distribute the mayonnaise evenly. Garnish with the chives and serve.

Making a Tomato Rose

It's easy to make a tomato rose using a serrated knife. Carefully peel the skin of the tomato in one long strip, beginning at the base of the tomato. Form a rose by rolling the tomato peel with the inner portion of the skin facing outward. Secure the flower with a toothpick, if needed. Party guests are always impressed with a colorful garnish that looks more difficult to make than it really is.

Per serving: Calories 426, Protein 6g, Fat 33g, Carbohydrate 31g, Vitamin E 3mg

Red Baron Salad I

BEET RED AND DRESSED in a shiny sauce, this salad is a showstopper with green pistachio accents. Unlike most salads, whose freshness depends on same-day preparation, this creation can be made a day ahead and still retain its exceptional flavor.

5 romaine lettuce leaves, torn

2 carrots, peeled and coarsely shredded

1 large or 2 small beets, peeled and coarsely shredded

1 large sweet red apple, cored and diced

1³⁄₄ cups shredded red cabbage

¹⁄₂ cup plus 2 tablespoons pistachios

1¹⁄₄ cups Mango Lime Dressing (page 87)

ARRANGE the lettuce on a large platter. Combine the carrots, beet, apple, red cabbage, and ¹⁄₂ cup of the pistachios in a large bowl and toss well to distribute the ingredients evenly. Add the dressing and toss well. Spoon over the lettuce and garnish with the remaining 2 tablespoons pistachios. Stored in a covered container in the refrigerator, leftover Red Baron Salad I will keep for about three days.

THE BRIGHT GREEN COLORING of the pistachio is completely natural. A deep green color is an indicator of the highest quality nut and brings the best prices. Lesser valued are those that range from yellow to light green.

Per serving: Calories 311, Protein 10g, Fat 17g, Carbohydrate 35g, Vitamin E 1.4mg

Red Baron Salad II

Yield: 5 to 6 servings

A SLIGHT VARIATION on a theme can often produce pleasantly diverse results. While Red Baron Salad I is bathed in a sweet mango dressing, this version speaks out with the assertive pungency of cider vinegar. An easy, make-ahead salad, it holds up well for a couple days in the refrigerator.

3 large carrots, peeled and coarsely shredded

2 large or 4 small beets, peeled and coarsely shredded

1 large sweet red apple, diced

3 to 3$^1/_2$ cups shredded red cabbage

$^1/_2$ cup black or golden raisins

$^1/_2$ cup pistachios

3 to 4 tablespoons organic canola oil

3 to 4 tablespoons apple cider vinegar

Salt and freshly ground pepper

Lettuce leaves (optional)

COMBINE the carrots, beets, apple, cabbage, raisins, pistachios, oil, vinegar, salt, and pepper in a large bowl and toss well. Serve the salad nestled in lettuce leaves as individual side dishes, or transfer it to a large serving bowl to bring to the table.

A PICTURESQUE TALE that originated in the Middle East describes two lovers in a romantic setting in a beautiful grove of pistachio trees. They meet on a moonlit night, sit under the trees, which just happen to have reached perfect maturity, and listen to the sound of the little pistachio shells bursting open. Blessings of good fortune, happiness, and abundance then befall them.

Per serving: Calories 271, Protein 5g, Fat 15g, Carbohydrate 33g, Vitamin E 2mg

Wasabi Pistachio Vegetable Aspic

Yields: 6 to 8 servings

See photo facing page 144.

DROP-DEAD GORGEOUS is an expression that usually refers to an attractive woman. Though it's difficult to imagine an aspic can compare in beauty, this one comes pretty close, with its kaleidoscope of colorful vegetables and green pistachio accents. Rather than animal-based gelatin, this recipe uses agar, a sea vegetable, to gel the aspic.

1 stick (0.25 ounces/7g) agar

2¼ cups water

2½ cups chopped napa or green cabbage (about 3 leaves)

1 cup coarsely shredded carrots

1 cup diced celery

1 cup diced red bell pepper

½ cup diced yellow bell pepper

¼ cup diced zucchini

10 pitted black olives, sliced

BREAK the agar stick into chunks and put them into a medium saucepan. Pour the water over the chunks and let soak for 30 minutes. The agar tends to float; just push it into the water with a spoon.

While the agar is soaking, combine the cabbage, carrots, celery, red and yellow bell peppers, zucchini, olives, pistachios, and capers in a large bowl.

After the agar is well soaked, bring it to a boil over high heat, stirring frequently. Boil for about 2 minutes, or until the agar dissolves completely. Remove from the heat and add the lemon juice, evaporated cane juice, salt, and wasabi paste. Stir well to dissolve all the ingredients.

Pour the agar mixture into the bowl with the vegetables and stir well until evenly combined. Spoon into a 5- or 6-cup mold and chill for 5 to 12 hours.

½ cup pistachios

2 tablespoons capers,
well drained

¼ cup plus
2 tablespoons freshly
squeezed lemon juice

2 tablespoons plus
2 teaspoons evaporated
cane juice

1 teaspoon salt

½ teaspoon
wasabi paste

1 cilantro, mint,
or basil sprig

To unmold, fill the kitchen sink with about three inches of hot water. Dip the chilled mold into the water up to its neck, and count to twelve slowly. Give the mold a gentle shake to loosen it and invert it onto a large platter. Garnish with the cilantro sprig.

Note: For an alternative presentation, spoon the mixture into a shallow 3-quart mold and chill thoroughly before unmolding. To serve as an appealing first course, present wedges of the aspic on lettuce-lined dishes and spoon a dollop of Lemon Dill Silken Sauce (page 144) over the top. Alternatively, serve the sauce on the side.

THE QUEEN OF SHEBA was convinced that pistachios were a powerful aphrodisiac and ordered the pistachio harvest of the best trees grown in Assyria to be used for her and her royal guests only.

Per serving: Calories 113, Protein 3g, Fat 6g, Carbohydrate 14g, Vitamin E .3mg

Perfect Purple Potato Salad

Yield: 4 to 5 servings

AN OLD-FASHIONED FAVORITE, potato salad changes its character and comes to the party wearing a bright purple outfit. Until recently, purple potatoes were only available in specialty markets or at farmers' markets. Today they are a regular item in most large supermarkets or can be special-ordered by the produce manager. In addition to their dramatic color, the Peruvian purples are sweeter than white potatoes. If purple potatoes are unavailable, substitute Yukon gold, white rose, or red rose potatoes. Russets are not suitable for potato salad because they are too dry and mealy. I save them for baking.

1 1/2 to 2 pounds Peruvian purple potatoes, cut into bite-size chunks

4 tablespoons extra-virgin olive oil

2 tablespoons apple cider vinegar

1 cup chopped celery

2/3 cup pistachios

1/2 red bell pepper, diced

1/2 cup diced Japanese or English cucumbers

1/2 cup diced sweet onions

2 tablespoons freshly squeezed lemon juice

1 tablespoon minced Anaheim or other mild chile

1 tablespoon minced fresh chives

1 tablespoon minced fresh thyme

1 tablespoon minced fresh parsley

1 tablespoon minced fresh oregano

1/2 teaspoon salt

Freshly ground pepper

PUT the potato chunks into a 4-quart saucepan with enough water to cover and a dash or two of salt. Cover and bring to a boil over high heat. Turn the heat down to medium and cook for 5 to 7 minutes, or until the potatoes are just fork-tender.

Drain the water and transfer the potatoes to a large mixing bowl. Add 2 tablespoons of the olive oil to the hot potatoes. Add the vinegar and mix well. Add the remaining ingredients and toss well to distribute the seasonings evenly. Adjust the seasonings if needed. Serve immediately or thoroughly chilled.

Per serving: Calories 403, Protein 9g, Fat 22g, Carbohydrate 47g, Vitamin E 2mg

Salad Dressings

DISCOVER THE GREAT VERSATILITY OF DRESSINGS WITH INNOVATIVE INGREDIENTS
that breathe zesty life into a salad. Quite often I choose the dressing first, then decide which salad ingredients would best complement it. Fresh ingredients from the fruit and vegetable bin create a good base, while the thickening is attributed to the wonderful world of raw nuts.

Rather than thinking of salad dressings only to pour over greens, experiment with incorporating them into other dishes. Here are some suggestions:

MARINADES: Some of the dressings in this section lend themselves to savory marinades for tofu, tempeh, vegetable patties, soy analogs, and even crudités served as an appetizer. Try marinating with Triple Citrus Dressing (page 93) or Strawberry Pine Nut Dressing (page 84).

SANDWICH SPREAD: Thicker dressings, such as New Moon Silk Dressing (page 89), make an ideal flavor base for spreading on bread for sandwiches.

PARTY DIPS: Break out of the old mold. Rather than the usual standbys you've always served, enjoy party dips with some new flavors. Explore Tomato Cashew Dressing (page 86) as a dip for crisp vegetables or cubes of extra-firm tofu.

TOPPING SAUCES: When you're looking for something a little different to flavor up a baked potato or steamed brown rice, prepare Macadamia Sun-Dried Tomato Dressing (page 90) or Cashew Lime Dressing (page 85).

SWEET SAUCE: For dunking or adding a topping, Mango Lime Dressing (page 87) is pure magic, while Tangerine Macadamia Dressing (page 88) lends a delightful Southeast Asian flavor.

Strawberry Pine Nut Dressing

WHEN STRAWBERRY SEASON comes along, include this dressing as one of the many ways to enjoy this succulent fruit. To lighten up on the calories, consider making the oil-free variation.

1 pint fresh strawberries

$^1/_2$ cup organic canola oil

$^1/_3$ cup water

$^1/_2$ cup pine nuts

2 tablespoons balsamic vinegar

1 $^1/_4$ teaspoons salt

1 large garlic clove

$^1/_4$ teaspoon dry mustard

$^1/_8$ teaspoon freshly ground pepper

WASH and stem the strawberries and set 6 berries aside. Cut the remaining strawberries in half and put them into the blender. Add the remaining ingredients and blend on high speed for 1 minute, until smooth and creamy.

Add the 6 reserved berries and pulse briefly to give the dressing a little texture. Pour into a small bowl and serve with a ladle. Stored in a covered container in the refrigerator, Strawberry Pine Nut Dressing will keep for four to five days.

Oil-Free Strawberry Pine Nut Dressing: Omit the canola oil and add 2 tablespoons light brown sugar. Yield: 2$^1/_2$ cups

Per serving (2 tablespoons): Calories 68, Protein 1g, Fat 7g, Carbohydrate 1g, Vitamin E 1mg

Cashew Lime Dressing

Yield: 1¾ cups

A HARMONIOUS BLEND of salty and tangy flavors coupled with a pleasing creamy texture, this dressing adds character and a nutty pizazz to any salad.

½ cup cashews

½ cup freshly squeezed lime juice

½ cup organic canola oil

½ cup water

2 garlic cloves

1½ teaspoons salt

¼ teaspoon freshly ground pepper

GRIND the cashews to a fine powder in small batches in an electric mini-chopper/grinder or coffee grinder.

Combine the remaining ingredients in the blender, add the ground cashews, and blend on low speed for a few seconds. Switch to high speed and blend for 1 full minute until the dressing turns white and creamy. Using a funnel, transfer the dressing to a narrow-neck bottle or similar container for easier serving. Stored in a covered container in the refrigerator, Cashew Lime Dressing will keep for one week. Shake well before serving.

Oil-Free Cashew Lime Dressing: Omit the canola oil, increase the water to 1 cup, and add ¼ teaspoon guar gum or xanthan gum. This version is best made a day ahead to allow the guar gum or xanthan gum to thicken the dressing.

Per serving (2 tablespoons): Calories 103, Protein 1g, Fat 10g, Carbohydrate 2g, Vitamin E 1.4mg

Tomato Cashew Dressing

Yield: 3½ cups

BY TURNING FRESH TOMATOES into a creamy dressing enriched with cashews, you can make any salad blossom with flavor all year long. But in summer, when tomatoes are at their peak, the dressing takes on a vibrant, yet delicate, sweetness. Home gardeners have an advantage—their homegrown tomatoes are far tastier than any supermarket varieties and contribute to making an extraordinary dressing.

½ cup cashews

½ cup organic canola oil

1 pound ripe tomatoes, coarsely chopped

¼ cup freshly squeezed lime juice

2 to 3 garlic cloves

1 to 2 tablespoons rice vinegar

1½ teaspoons salt

COMBINE the cashews and canola oil in the blender. Start on low speed for a few seconds, then switch to high speed. Blend for 1 minute, until creamy and smooth. Alternatively, begin by grinding the cashews to a fine meal in an electric mini-chopper/grinder or coffee grinder. Then add the cashew meal to the blender.

Add the remaining ingredients and blend on low speed for a few seconds. Switch to high speed and blend until creamy. Blend a shorter time if you prefer a dressing with a chunky texture. Using a funnel, transfer the dressing to a narrow-neck bottle or similar container for easier serving. Serve at once or thoroughly chilled. Stored in the refrigerator, Tomato Cashew Dressing will keep for four to five days.

Per serving (2 tablespoons): Calories 55, Protein 1g, Fat 5g, Carbohydrate 2g, Vitamin E .7mg

Mango Lime Dressing

Yield: 1³⁄₄ cups

RELY ON NATURE to come through with naturally sweet fruits that bathe a salad in luxurious flavors. This dressing pairs especially well with Red Baron Salad I (page 78) or salads that contain a sprinkling of fresh fruits or sweet vegetables like carrots, jicama, or beets.

1 large or 2 small ripe mangoes

8 pitted dates

¹⁄₂ cup water

2 tablespoons freshly squeezed lime juice

¹⁄₄ teaspoon ground cinnamon

COMBINE all the ingredients in the blender and process until smooth. Pour into a small bowl and serve with a ladle. Stored in the refrigerator, Mango Lime Dressing will keep for one week.

Note: If your mangoes are on the tart side, add more dates to sweeten.

Per serving (2 tablespoons): Calories 28, Protein 0g, Fat 1g, Carbohydrate 7g, Vitamin E 0mg

Tangerine Macadamia Dressing

Yield: 1⅓ cups

WINTER THROUGH SPRINGTIME, when tangerines are in season and at their sweetest and juiciest, is the ideal time to prepare this salad dressing. When available, honey tangerines are a good choice for their ultra-sweetness. Freshly squeezed sweet orange juice makes an excellent substitute and is more readily available throughout the year. Don't rule out tart oranges or tangerines. Both offer great flavor, though they do change the character of the recipe by giving it a sharp pungency. To sweeten, add maple syrup or agave nectar.

½ cup macadamia nuts

1 cup chopped tangerines (about 3 tangerines)

2 tablespoons plus one teaspoon seasoned rice vinegar

2 tablespoons water

2 tablespoons peeled and chopped fresh ginger

1 garlic clove

½ teaspoon salt

¼ teaspoon freshly ground pepper

GRIND the macadamia nuts into a creamy meal in an electric mini-chopper/grinder or coffee grinder. Transfer to the blender.

Add the remaining ingredients and blend until smooth and creamy. Using a funnel, transfer the dressing to a narrow-neck bottle or similar container for easier serving. Serve at once or thoroughly chilled. Stored in a covered container in the refrigerator, Tangerine Macadamia Dressing will keep for one week.

Per serving (2 tablespoons): Calories 79, Protein 1g, Fat 6g, Carbohydrate 6g, Vitamin E .1mg

New Moon Silk Dressing

Yield: 3 cups

FOR THOSE WHO GRAVITATE to thick, creamy salad dressings, this recipe may very likely become a new favorite.

1 (12-ounce) box soft silken tofu

$1/2$ cup organic canola oil

$1/2$ cup pistachios

$1/4$ cup apple cider vinegar

$1/4$ cup freshly squeezed lemon juice

$1/4$ cup water

2 teaspoons soy sauce

$1 1/4$ teaspoons salt

1 garlic clove, minced

$1/4$ teaspoon freshly ground pepper

COMBINE the tofu, $1/4$ cup of the canola oil, and the pistachios in the blender. Start the machine on low speed and process until the pistachios are well ground and the mixture is smooth.

Add the remaining $1/4$ cup canola oil, vinegar, lemon juice, water, soy sauce, salt, garlic, and pepper, and blend until smooth and creamy, beginning on low speed for a few seconds, then switching to high speed. Blend on high speed for 1 full minute. Pour into a small bowl and serve with a ladle. Stored in a covered container in the refrigerator, New Moon Silk Dressing will keep for one week.

SEE IF YOU CAN PASS the pistachio test: Share some pistachios with that someone special you love deeply and see if the nuts enhance your amorous feelings. In the ancient days, people of the Middle East thought of pistachios as a liaison to love.

Per serving (2 tablespoons): Calories 63, Protein 1g, Fat 6g, Carbohydrate 2g, Vitamin E .9mg

Macadamia Sun-Dried Tomato Dressing

Yield: 2²/₃ cups

Yield: 2⅔ cups

MACADAMIAS INFUSE this dressing with a rich creaminess. The distinct tang of sun-dried tomatoes, the silky texture from the soymilk, and the tartness of the lemon juice all unite to turn a salad into a very pleasurable dining experience.

10 sun-dried tomatoes

¹/₂ cup boiling water

¹/₂ cup macadamia nuts

1 cup plus 2 tablespoons regular soymilk

3 tablespoons freshly squeezed lemon juice

2 teaspoons apple cider vinegar

1 teaspoon salt

¹/₄ teaspoon freshly ground pepper

PUT the sun-dried tomatoes into a small bowl and pour the boiling water over them. Soak them for about 5 minutes, or until softened. Transfer the tomatoes and the soak water to the blender.

Grind the macadamia nuts into a fine meal in an electric mini-chopper/grinder or coffee grinder. Add the ground nuts to the blender along with the soymilk, lemon juice, vinegar, salt, and pepper. Blend on low speed for a few seconds. Switch to high speed and blend for 1 minute, until smooth and creamy. Using a funnel, transfer the dressing to a narrow-neck bottle or similar container for easier serving. Serve immediately or thoroughly chilled. Stored in a covered container in the refrigerator, Macadamia Sun-Dried Tomato Dressing will keep for one week. Shake well before serving.

Per serving (2 tablespoons): Calories 32, Protein 1g, Fat 3g, Carbohydrate 2g, Vitamin E 0mg

Creamy Cashew Basil Dressing

Yield: about 1 1/2 cups

FRESH BASIL contributes sass to this thick, creamy blend of flavors, and brings out the best in a bowl of greens.

1/2 cup coarsely chopped cashews

1/2 cup fresh basil leaves, lightly packed

1/2 cup freshly squeezed lemon juice

1/2 cup water

1/4 cup nutritional yeast flakes

2 large garlic cloves

1 tablespoon salt-free herbal seasoning

1/2 teaspoon salt

1/4 teaspoon guar gum or xanthan gum

GRIND the cashews into a fine meal in small batches in an electric mini-chopper/grinder or coffee grinder. Transfer to the blender and add the remaining ingredients. Process for about 1 minute, until smooth and creamy. Pour into a bowl and serve with a ladle. Stored in a covered container in the refrigerator, Creamy Cashew Basil Dressing will keep for one week.

Per serving (2 tablespoons): Calories 47, Protein 2g, Fat 3g, Carbohydrate 4g, Vitamin E .1mg

Poppy Seed Dressing

Yield: 1¹/₂ cups

A SWEET DRESSING is the perfect partner to Just Peachy Pine Nut Salad (page 74) or a salad that has fruity ingredients or a preponderance of sweet vegetables like carrots, jicama, or sweet peppers. This dressing also balances salty ingredients like kalamata olives, hearts of palm, or marinated tofu.

¹/₂ cup organic canola oil

¹/₃ cup apple cider vinegar

¹/₄ cup freshly squeezed lemon juice

¹/₄ cup water

2 tablespoons plus 1 teaspoon light brown sugar

2 tablespoons dry mustard

2 tablespoons poppy seeds

¹/₂ teaspoon salt

¹/₄ teaspoon freshly ground pepper

¹/₄ teaspoon paprika

COMBINE all the ingredients in a 1-quart jar and shake well. Using a funnel, transfer the dressing to a narrow-neck bottle or similar container for easier serving. Stored in a covered container in the refrigerator, Poppy Seed Dressing will keep for two weeks.

Per serving (2 tablespoons): Calories 94, Protein 0g, Fat 10g, Carbohydrate 3g, Vitamin E 1.6mg

Triple Citrus Dressing

Yield: 2 cups

WITH CITRUS FRUITS readily available year round, this dressing doesn't have to wait for a special season to share its bright, zesty flavors.

½ cup cashews

1 cup freshly squeezed orange juice

⅓ cup freshly squeezed lime juice

⅓ cup freshly squeezed lemon juice

¼ cup water

2 tablespoons apple cider vinegar

1 garlic clove, minced

1 teaspoon salt

½ teaspoon freshly ground pepper

½ teaspoon guar gum or xanthan gum

GRIND the cashews to a fine meal in an electric mini-chopper/grinder or coffee grinder and transfer to the blender. Add the remaining ingredients and blend, starting on low speed. Switch to high speed and blend for 1 full minute, until smooth and creamy. Using a funnel, transfer the dressing to a narrow-neck bottle or similar container for easier serving. Serve immediately or thoroughly chilled. Stored in a covered container in the refrigerator, Triple Citrus Dressing will keep for one week.

Per serving (2 tablespoons): Calories 35, Protein 1g, Fat 2g, Carbohydrate 4g, Vitamin E .1mg

THE NATIVE AMERICAN INDIANS relied on pecans and hickory nuts for their nutty beverages. They prepared pecan milk by pounding the nuts with a mortar and pestle before adding water and stirring the mixture into a nourishing beverage. Pecan milk was an ideal energy food for infants as well as the elders because it was so easy to digest.

Main Dishes

"I'm ready for big food!" He had it right. The main dish is "big food." Even the term "main dish" creates expectations of something bigger than the appetizer, bigger than the salad, and bigger than the soup. After all, it's the main dish.

The recipes in this section are a medley of dishes for everyday eating pleasure, such as Walnut Stuffed Eggplant (page 120), and some extraordinary entrées for special occasions, like Curried Christmas Timbales with Bell Pepper Relish (page 104)—all dishes that satisfy the great expectation for "big food."

Because nuts are so rich in healthful fatty acids, they provide an entrée with a wealth of flavor and the great mouthfeel one expects from a tantalizing centerpiece dish. Some of the entrées, such as Pistachio Fondue (page 106) or Almond, Mushroom, and Spinach over Pasta with Savory Cashew Cream Sauce (page 100), incorporate nuts that are ground into a fine meal to serve as a thickening agent for sauces or gravies.

Other dishes employ coarsely ground nuts that provide pleasing texture, such as Almond Nutloaf (page 98) and Mushroom Cashew Walnut Patties (page 97). Sesame Nut Patties (page 96) also incorporate coarsely ground nuts and offer an entrée with nutrient density as well as rich flavor and texture. In some dishes, like Stuffed Artichokes (page 114), whole nuts are given the starring role.

If you don't have the specific variety of nut called for in the recipe, don't let that discourage you from making that dish. Simply substitute whatever nut you do have. The flavor or texture may vary slightly, but you'll most likely be presenting your family or your guests a tasty, wholesome meal that has a unique flair. Vegans and vegetarians are familiar with savory dishes that contain nuts, but meat eaters rarely encounter nuts in the main course and may find it refreshing.

The recipes in this section feature diversity to offer sumptuous nutty dishes for every occasion from hurried midweek dinners to lavish, impress-the-boss creations.

Sesame Nut Patties

3¼ cups water, plus more as needed

1 cup wild rice

1 teaspoon salt

1 cup coarsely chopped walnuts

⅔ cup cashews

⅓ cup pistachios

1 tablespoon psyllium husks

1 tablespoon plus 1 teaspoon soy sauce

¾ teaspoon chili powder

½ teaspoon dried oregano

¼ teaspoon ground nutmeg

¼ teaspoon dried thyme

½ cup hulled sesame seeds

SANDWICH LOVERS will appreciate these unique and flavorful patties. Cook the wild rice a day ahead and the patties will practically make themselves. Then measure and set aside the cooked rice needed for this recipe. The leftover rice can be used in a salad or reheated for another meal. These sassy little patties are stout enough to stand on their own, or they can be served with a steamed vegetable and salad for a well-rounded meal.

LIGHTLY oil a large baking sheet and set it aside. Combine 3 cups of the water with the wild rice and salt in a 2-quart saucepan. Cover and bring to a boil over high heat. Turn the heat down to medium-low and steam for 50 to 60 minutes, or until the rice is tender. Measure 2 cups of cooked wild rice for the recipe and set it aside. (Store the remaining cooked rice in the refrigerator to use for another recipe.)

Grind the walnuts, cashews, and pistachios to a coarse meal in the food processor, and leave them in the processor.

Combine ¼ cup of the water and the psyllium husks in a small cup or bowl and stir well to moisten. Set aside for 1 minute to thicken, then add to the processor with the nuts.

Add the soy sauce, chili powder, oregano, nutmeg, and thyme to the processor. Process briefly until all the ingredients are well combined. Add 1 to 3 tablespoons of water if the mixture is too dry to hold together.

Form the mixture into patties about 3 inches in diameter. Sprinkle the sesame seeds on a dish and press both sides of each patty into the seeds. Arrange the patties on the prepared baking sheet.

Broil the patties 3 inches from the heat source for 2 to 5 minutes, until golden brown. Watch closely so they don't burn. Turn the patties over with a metal spatula and broil 1 to 2 minutes on the second side.

Per patty: Calories 233, Protein 7g, Fat 18g, Carbohydrate 15g, Vitamin E .3mg

Tofu Pesto Torte, page 41

Mushroom Cashew Walnut Patties

Yield: 10 to 12 (3-inch) patties

PATTIES AND BURGERS are hearty centerpiece items that pair easily with almost any vegetables, grains, or legumes. You can also serve them as a filling for a whole grain pita sandwich along with your favorite trimmings. Because the recipe uses cooked rice, it's a great way to use up leftovers.

8.5 ounces button, cremini, or portobello mushrooms, finely chopped (about 4 cups)

2 cups cooked short-grain or sweet brown rice

$1/2$ cup coarsely ground walnuts

$1/2$ cup coarsely ground cashews

1 garlic clove, minced

$1/2$ teaspoon salt

$1/4$ teaspoon freshly ground pepper

$1/4$ cup water

1 tablespoon psyllium husks

COMBINE the mushrooms, brown rice, walnuts, cashews, garlic, salt, and pepper in a large mixing bowl and mix well.

Combine the water and psyllium husks in a small bowl or cup, stir, and let rest 1 minute to thicken into a paste. Add the paste to the rice mixture and mix thoroughly to distribute the psyllium evenly.

Heat a thin layer of canola oil in a large nonstick skillet over high heat until just hot enough for a drop of water to sizzle.

Form the mushroom mixture into 3-inch patties, place them in the hot oil, and flatten them slightly with a spatula. Brown for 1 to 2 minutes on each side, or until crisp. Line a plate with paper towels. Transfer the patties to the plate to blot off excess oil before serving.

Note: To enhance the presentation of these tasty patties, spoon a dollop of Lemon Dill Silken Sauce (page 144) onto the center of each patty and dust them with paprika or a sprinkling of fresh herbs just before serving.

Per patty: Calories 117, Protein 3g, Fat 7g, Carbohydrate 12g, Vitamin E .1mg

26 Pecan Salad, page 70 with Lemon Dill Silken Sauce, page 144

Almond Nutloaf

A SPECIAL-OCCASION entrée is usually a little fussier than an everyday family-style dish, but I'm betting on no regrets once you've tasted this scrumptious nut-loaf that's especially attractive when baked in a springform pan.

2 onions

1 pound russet potatoes, unpeeled

1 garlic clove, coarsely chopped

2¼ teaspoons salt

2 cups whole almonds

⅓ cup walnuts

⅓ cup pecans

PREHEAT the oven to 375 degrees and lightly oil a 9-inch springform pan or an 8 x 8-inch glass baking dish. Line the bottom of the pan with parchment paper (for easier cleanup) and set it aside.

Cut the onions in half. Coarsely chop one of the halves and set it aside. Cut the remaining onions into chunks and pulse-chop them in the food processor until minced. Transfer the minced onions to a large bowl and set them aside.

Scrub the potatoes, cut them into coarse chunks, and put them into a 2-quart saucepan. Add the coarsely chopped garlic, the coarsely chopped onions, ½ teaspoon of the salt, and water to cover. Cover and bring to a boil over high heat. Turn the heat down slightly and simmer for 10 minutes, or until the potatoes are fork-tender. Drain the potatoes in a colander and transfer them to a large bowl. Mash the potatoes with a fork and add them to the bowl with the reserved minced onions.

Finely grind the almonds in the food processor. Add them to the bowl with the potatoes and onions.

Process the walnuts and pecans in the food processor until they are ground but still retain a little crunchy texture. Add them to the potatoes and onions.

1 ripe tomato, diced

⅓ cup plus
1 tablespoon water

¼ cup plus
1 tablespoon nutritional
yeast flakes

2 garlic cloves, minced

½ teaspoon
ground nutmeg

¼ teaspoon dried basil

¼ teaspoon
dried thyme

¼ teaspoon
dried marjoram

¼ teaspoon freshly
ground pepper

⅛ teaspoon vegan
Worcestershire sauce

Dash cayenne (optional)

1 large ripe tomato,
sliced

Add the diced tomato, water, nutritional yeast, minced garlic, remaining 1¾ teaspoons salt, nutmeg, basil, thyme, marjoram, pepper, Worcestershire sauce, and optional cayenne to the bowl. Mix well until all the ingredients are thoroughly combined. Spoon into the prepared pan, pressing with the back of a spoon or your hands to compact the mixture.

Arrange the tomato slices over the top and bake for 50 to 60 minutes. Remove from the oven and let stand for 15 minutes. Use a flatware knife to loosen the edges of the loaf, then release the springform sides and cut the loaf into wedges or squares and serve.

Per serving: Calories 427, Protein 15g, Fat 30g, Carbohydrate 32g, Vitamin E 11.8mg

Almond, Mushroom, and Spinach over Pasta
with Savory Cashew Cream Sauce

See photo facing page 145.

Yield: 4 servings

2¼ cups Savory Cashew Cream Sauce (page 141)

½ cup whole almonds

1½ cups chopped onions

¾ pound cremini or button mushrooms, sliced

2 large carrots, peeled and coarsely shredded

2 tablespoons water

1 tablespoon extra-virgin olive oil

2 garlic cloves, crushed

4 cups chopped spinach (about 1 bunch)

1 tablespoon freshly squeezed lemon juice

Salt and freshly ground pepper

8 ounces whole grain penne or curly pasta

½ cup diced red bell pepper

2 tablespoons minced fresh parsley

THE CRUNCHY TEXTURE of almonds adds a special spark to this unique pasta and vegetable presentation. But the highlight of this recipe is the savory sauce that turns the spotlight on the cashews.

PREPARE the Savory Cashew Cream Sauce, remove from the heat, and set it aside. Put the almonds in a zipper-lock plastic bag, coarsely chop them with a hammer, and set them aside. Alternatively, chop the almonds on a cutting board using a heavy-duty chef's knife.

Combine the onions, mushrooms, carrots, water, olive oil, and garlic in a large skillet and cook and stir for 5 to 7 minutes, or until the vegetables are tender.

Add the spinach and lemon juice and cook for 1 to 2 minutes longer. Season lightly with salt and pepper. Add the chopped almonds, toss well to distribute them evenly, and remove from the heat.

Cook the pasta until tender following the package directions. Drain. After the pasta is cooked, warm the Savory Cashew Cream Sauce and reheat the vegetables briefly.

To serve, put a helping of pasta on each plate. Spoon a generous amount of vegetables over the pasta, and top with the creamy sauce. Garnish with the red bell pepper and parsley.

Per serving: Calories 520, Protein 22g, Fat 28g, Carbohydrate 52g, Vitamin E 7mg

Fesenjen

HERE'S A VEGAN VERSION of a Persian dish that is traditionally made with chicken or duck and served with rice. Its stand-out feature is the lively sweet-tart sauce that employs walnuts and pomegranate syrup. Tofu stands in for the chicken and adds a pleasant tooth to the dish, which pairs well with steamed brown rice, bulgur wheat, or barley.

1 pound extra-firm tofu

2 tablespoons soy sauce

2 onions, coarsely chopped

1 tablespoon extra-virgin olive oil

$1/2$ teaspoon turmeric

2 cups coarsely chopped walnuts

$1 1/2$ cups plus 2 tablespoons water

$2 1/2$ tablespoons freshly squeezed lemon juice

2 tablespoons plus 2 teaspoons pomegranate syrup

2 tablespoons evaporated cane juice

$3/4$ teaspoon salt

2 tablespoons cornstarch

$1/2$ cup diced red bell pepper

RINSE and drain the tofu and cut it into $1/2$-inch cubes. Combine the tofu and soy sauce in a large, deep skillet, and cook over high heat, stirring frequently to brown the cubes on all sides. Transfer the tofu to a medium bowl and set aside.

Add the onions, olive oil, and turmeric to the same skillet and cook over high heat for about 5 minutes, or until the onions are softened and lightly browned. Transfer to the bowl with the tofu.

Put the walnuts into the food processor and pulverize them until almost the consistency of nut butter. Transfer to the same skillet and add $1 1/2$ cups of the water, the lemon juice, pomegranate syrup, evaporated cane juice, and salt. Cook over high heat for about 2 minutes, stirring constantly.

Combine the cornstarch and remaining 2 tablespoons water in a small cup or bowl and stir well to create a runny paste. Add to the bubbling walnut sauce a little at a time, stirring constantly until thickened.

Add the reserved tofu and onions and heat to warm through. Transfer to an attractive serving bowl and garnish with the red bell pepper.

Per serving: Calories 568, Protein 21g, Fat 42g, Carbohydrate 35g, Vitamin E .7mg

Curried Tofu Terrine

½ cup coarsely ground walnuts, toasted (see page 28)

3 green onions, minced

2 white rose or red rose potatoes, unpeeled and coarsely shredded

3 carrots, peeled and coarsely shredded

1 small onion, coarsely shredded

½ cup water

Salt and freshly ground pepper

1 pound extra-firm tofu

1 tablespoon plus 1 teaspoon rice vinegar

1 tablespoon plus 1 teaspoon freshly squeezed lemon juice

1½ teaspoons curry powder

1¼ teaspoons salt

¼ teaspoon freshly ground pepper

3 to 4 arugula leaves

A COMMON COMPLAINT vegetarians hear from nonvegetarians is that tofu is bland and can't be made to taste good. Surprise those doubters with this delicious terrine. Steamed green vegetables and black beans seasoned with garlic and lemon juice make an appealing accompaniment.

PREHEAT the oven to 375 degrees and oil a 9 x 5-inch metal or glass loaf pan. Line the bottom of the pan with parchment paper and oil the parchment. Sprinkle the walnuts and one-third of the green onions on the bottom of the loaf pan, and set it aside.

To make the filling, combine the potatoes, two-thirds of the carrots, onion, and water in a large skillet or wok and cook and stir over high heat for 15 to 20 minutes, or until the vegetables are tender. Stir frequently to prevent the vegetables from sticking to the pan. Season lightly with salt and pepper.

While the filling is cooking, combine the tofu, remaining green onions, vinegar, lemon juice, curry powder, salt, and pepper in the food processor and process until smooth. Press half the tofu mixture into the prepared loaf pan over the walnuts.

Spread the carrot and potato filling over the tofu, spreading it to the edges. Top with the remaining tofu, spreading it to the edges of the loaf pan. Bake for 30 minutes. Remove from the oven and let stand at room temperature for 10 minutes.

Run a flatware knife around all four edges of the loaf pan. Unmold the terrine onto an oval or rectangular platter and remove the parchment paper. Garnish the platter with the arugula leaves and remaining shredded carrots. Cut thick slices of the terrine with a serrated knife, and use a spatula to serve.

Notes: For advance preparation, make the terrine a day ahead and reheat it in a preheated 350 degree oven for 15 to 20 minutes.

• For a special finishing touch, serve the terrine with Lemon Dill Silken Sauce (page 144).

Per serving: Calories 172, Protein 10g, Fat 10g, Carbohydrate 15g, Vitamin E .1mg

Pineapple Boat's A-Comin'

Yield: 4 servings

1 large ripe pineapple
(3 to 4 pounds)

1 broccoli crown

1/2 pound asparagus,
green beans, or zuc-
chini, cut into 1-inch
lengths (about 2 cups)

1/2 red bell pepper, diced

1/3 cup whole raw or
roasted peanuts

1/2 to 1 jalapeño chile

2 garlic cloves, minced

1 (1-inch) piece fresh
ginger, peeled and grated

1/4 cup water

2 teaspoons organic
canola oil

3 cups cooked
short-grain brown rice

1 to 2 tablespoons
rice vinegar

1 to 2 tablespoons
soy sauce

2 large green onions,
chopped

1/3 cup coarsely
chopped unsalted
roasted peanuts

A STUFFED PINEAPPLE filled with a bountiful medley of rice, pineapple, and colorful vegetables makes a first-rate presentation any time of year.

PREHEAT the oven to 375 degrees and have ready a large baking sheet and an 8-inch square baking dish.

Wash the pineapple. With a firm, sharp knife cut the pineapple in half lengthwise, cutting through the green tops as well. Using a curved, serrated grapefruit knife, remove the pineapple flesh, leaving a 1/2-inch shell. Chop the pineapple flesh into 1-inch chunks and put them into a bowl. Set the chunks and the pineapple shells aside.

Coarsely chop the broccoli crown and place it into a large bowl along with the asparagus, red bell pepper, whole peanuts, chile, garlic, and ginger.

Heat the water and 1 teaspoon of the canola oil in a large, deep skillet. Add the vegetable mixture and cook and stir over high heat for about 3 minutes. Transfer to a dish or bowl.

Add the rice to the skillet and moisten it with the rice vinegar, soy sauce, and remaining 1 teaspoon canola oil. Add a little water if the mixture seems too dry.

Add the pineapple chunks, vegetables, and chopped green onions and mix well. Adjust the seasonings by adding more rice vinegar and soy sauce, if needed.

Stuff the mixture into the pineapple shells and place them on the baking sheet. Put any remaining stuffing into the baking dish. Top the pineapple and stuffing mixture with the chopped peanuts.

Cover the pineapples with aluminum foil, shiny side down, and bake for 20 to 25 minutes. Remove from the oven and cut each pineapple section in half.

Per serving: Calories 406, Protein 14g, Fat 16g, Carbohydrate 57g, Vitamin E 3.2mg

Curried Christmas Timbales
with Bell Pepper Relish

Yield: 6 servings

Timbales

¹⁄₂ cup Brazil nuts or whole almonds

1 pound firm tofu, rinsed and drained

1 tablespoon plus ¹⁄₂ teaspoon rice vinegar

1 tablespoon freshly squeezed lemon juice

2 garlic cloves

1¹⁄₂ teaspoons curry powder

1¹⁄₂ teaspoons salt

³⁄₄ teaspoon ground coriander

¹⁄₂ teaspoon onion powder

¹⁄₂ teaspoon turmeric

¹⁄₄ teaspoon plus ¹⁄₈ teaspoon freshly ground pepper

¹⁄₄ teaspoon dry mustard

PREPARE AN ALL-OUT SHOWSTOPPER that has both savory and visual appeal for special occasions like Christmas. Arrange these golden timbales in a circle on a large platter and fill the center with steamed vegetables. Spoon the Bell Pepper Relish over the tops of the timbales and around the outer edges of the platter. To ease the holiday stress, prepare these a day ahead (see note next page).

TO MAKE the timbales, preheat the oven to 350 degrees and line a 6-section, nonstick standard-size muffin pan with paper baking cups. Grind the Brazil nuts into a coarse, chunky meal in the food processor.

Add the tofu, vinegar, lemon juice, garlic, curry powder, salt, coriander, onion powder, turmeric, pepper, and dry mustard to the nuts in the food processor and process until moist, creamy, and well blended. If the mixture is too dry or crumbly, add 1 to 2 teaspoons of water to moisten, then process again thoroughly.

Fill the muffin cups with the tofu mixture. Pack it down to fill any air spaces, and smooth the tops. Bake the timbales for 30 minutes. Remove from the oven and cool for 15 to 20 minutes. Invert the muffin pan to release the timbales, and remove the muffin papers.

Bell Pepper Relish

1 red bell pepper, chopped

1 green bell pepper, chopped

1 cup chopped onions

1/4 cup black raisins

2 tablespoons pistachios

1 tablespoon extra-virgin olive oil

1 tablespoon water

Dash cayenne

Dash hot sauce

Salt and freshly ground pepper

TO MAKE the relish, combine the peppers, onions, raisins, pistachios, olive oil, water, and cayenne in a large, deep skillet. Cook and stir over high heat for about 10 minutes, or until the peppers and onions are almost browned. Add the hot sauce and season lightly with salt and pepper.

Note: For advance preparation, make the timbales a day ahead and reheat them in a preheated 350 degree oven for 12 to 15 minutes.

DURING THE MIDDLE AGES, Italian sweets consisted of honey-coated fruits, flowers, almonds, and seeds that were flavored with spices to aid the digestion after consuming large quantities of foods that were not very fresh. During the 1400s the French aristocracy distributed draggeoirs, which later became dragee, little comfit boxes of spiced, sugar-coated almonds that were given to wedding guests as favors. The coated almonds, called "chamber spices," were taken medicinally at bedtime to alleviate flatulence.

Per serving: Calories 211, Protein 10g, Fat 15g, Carbohydrate 14g, Vitamin E 1.1mg

Pistachio Fondue

Yield: 3 to 4 servings

A QUICK MEAL, a family dinner, or a company dish, this surprisingly light fondue also doubles well as a sauce for grains, baked potatoes, steamed artichokes, or baked tofu, and makes a great topping for vegetable casseroles. Serve the fondue in small bowls and accompany it with platters of steamed and raw vegetables for dipping.

1 cup pistachios

2½ cups unsweetened soymilk

2 tablespoons nutritional yeast flakes

1¼ teaspoons salt

Dash cayenne

Freshly ground pepper

GRIND the pistachios to a fine meal in several batches in an electric mini-chopper/grinder or coffee grinder. Transfer to a small bowl and set aside.

Combine the soymilk, nutritional yeast, salt, cayenne, and pepper in a 2-quart saucepan. Bring to a boil over medium-high heat. Watch carefully so the mixture doesn't boil over.

Add the ground pistachios to the bubbling mixture a little at a time, stirring with a wire whip for about 2 minutes, or until thickened. If necessary, lower the heat slightly to prevent burning.

Remove from the heat and let rest for 15 to 20 minutes to thicken further. Gently warm on medium heat, if needed. Stored in a covered container in the refrigerator, Pistachio Fondue will keep for up to five days.

Note: The fondue tends to thicken when refrigerated. Thin it to the desired consistency with unsweetened soymilk.

Per serving: Calories 348, Protein 18g, Fat 22g, Carbohydrate 23g, Vitamin E 3.5mg

Stuffed Tomato
with Almond Veggie Pâté and Mango Sauce

Yield: 3 servings

Stuffed Tomato

3 large lettuce leaves

3 large ripe tomatoes

Almond Veggie Pâté

2 large carrots, peeled and coarsely chopped

1 large bok choy leaf, or 1 whole baby bok choy, coarsely chopped

1/2 cup almond meal

2 tablespoons freshly squeezed lemon juice

1/2 teaspoon salt

1/4 teaspoon cayenne

Mango Sauce

1 ripe mango

3 tablespoons freshly squeezed lemon juice

2 tablespoons pine nuts

1/8 teaspoon salt

1 tablespoon maple syrup (optional)

FOR A TASTY light lunch or dinner, prepare this nutty vegetable pâté and spoon it into a wedge-cut tomato that opens to resemble the petals of a flower. Topped with a pine-nut-laced mango sauce, this delectable double-nutty treat can be prepared in minutes.

LINE 3 plates with a leaf of the lettuce. To prepare the tomatoes, cut each tomato into 8 wedges, leaving them attached at the base of the tomato to form a flower. Place the tomatoes on the lettuce leaves and set them aside.

TO MAKE the pâté, put the carrots, bok choy, almond meal, lemon juice, salt, and cayenne into the food processor and process until smooth or chunky, as desired. Spoon the mixture into the tomato flowers.

TO MAKE the sauce, combine the mango, lemon juice, pine nuts, salt, and the optional maple syrup in the blender and process until smooth.

Top the almond veggie pâté with a dollop of the sauce, and serve the remaining sauce on the side.

Per serving: Calories 303, Protein 19g, Fat 12g, Carbohydrate 38g, Vitamin E .5mg

Yield: 4 to 5 servings as an
entrée; 8 servings
as an appetizer

Spinach Tofu Torte

THIS SPECIAL-OCCASION DISH combines vegan pepperoni, spinach, and tofu in a beautiful two-layer torte filled with pistachios and artichoke hearts. It's my first choice when I want to offer an entrée that marries great flavor with a gourmet presentation.

1 large bunch fresh spinach (about 6 cups lightly packed leaves), washed and dried in a salad spinner

1 pound extra-firm tofu, rinsed and drained

1 (4.2-ounce) package vegan pepperoni, diced

1 tablespoon freshly squeezed lemon juice

1 large garlic clove

1 teaspoon salt

1 teaspoon water, if needed

PREHEAT the oven to 375 degrees and oil a 9-inch springform pan. Line the bottom of the pan with parchment paper (for easier cleanup).

To make the torte, put half the spinach into the food processor and pulse-chop, adding the remaining spinach a little at a time until all the spinach is finely chopped. Stop the machine occasionally to scrape down the sides of the work bowl and redistribute the spinach.

Add the tofu, pepperoni, lemon juice, garlic, and salt to the spinach in the food processor and process until all the ingredients are well incorporated. Add the water if the mixture seems dry. Spread half the mixture into the prepared springform pan, spreading it to the edges.

1 (13.75-ounce) can water-packed artichoke hearts, drained and chopped

½ cup pistachios

Parsley sprigs

Cherry tomatoes

For the filling, sprinkle the chopped artichoke hearts and pistachios over the tofu mixture, and top with the remaining tofu mixture, spreading it evenly to the edges.

Bake for 40 minutes or until firm when lightly pressed near the center. The top may develop small crevices when it is fully baked. Remove from the oven and let stand for 10 minutes. Carefully run a flatware knife around the edges to loosen the torte, and remove the springform collar. Place the springform base with the torte on an attractive serving platter and garnish with parsley sprigs and cherry tomatoes.

Spinach Tofu Torte with Veggie Bacon: Omit the veggie pepperoni and add 1 (6-ounce) package veggie bacon, diced.

Spinach Tofu Torte with Kalamata Olives: Add 8 to 10 diced kalamata olives to the artichoke filling.

Spinach, Tofu, and Black Olive Torte: Omit the artichoke hearts and add ⅔ cup sliced black olives to the filling.

Spinach, Tofu, and Mushroom Torte: Omit the artichoke hearts and add ½ pound coarsely chopped and sautéed shiitake or cremini mushrooms to the filling.

Per serving (entrée): Calories 295, Protein 26g, Fat 13g, Carbohydrate 19g, Vitamin E 2mg

Wild Rice, Chestnut, and Pecan
Stuffed Squashes

Yield: 8 to 10 servings

FIT FOR A ROYAL BANQUET, these elegant stuffed squashes provide a festive entrée for a holiday season menu. Accompany them with the traditional trimmings like cranberry sauce, sweet potatoes, roasted vegetables, and pumpkin pie. The recipe will be easier to assemble if you prepare the chestnuts the day before. As a time-saver, consider purchasing cooked, peeled chestnuts in a jar.

$3\frac{1}{4}$ cups water

1 cup wild rice

1 teaspoon salt

4 or 5 small winter squashes (see note next page)

Organic canola oil, as needed

3 celery stalks, finely chopped

1 small onion, finely chopped

5 garlic cloves, crushed

1 tablespoon extra-virgin olive oil

PREHEAT the oven to 400 degrees and have ready 1 or 2 baking sheets. Combine 3 cups of the water, the wild rice, and salt in a 2-quart saucepan. Cover and bring to a boil over high heat. Turn the heat down to medium-low, and cook for 45 to 55 minutes, or until the rice is tender.

Wash the squashes, cut them in half with a firm chef's knife, scoop out the seeds, and brush the cavities with canola oil. Arrange the squashes on the baking sheets, cut side down, and bake them for 30 minutes.

To make the stuffing, combine the celery, onion, remaining $\frac{1}{4}$ cup water, garlic, and olive oil in a large skillet. Cook and stir for 5 to 6 minutes, or until soft and transparent. Transfer to a large bowl along with the chestnuts.

Toast the bread until it is dry. Cut it into small cubes and add them to the bowl with the chestnuts. Add the cooked wild rice, mushrooms, pecans, salt, thyme, oregano, poultry seasoning, and pepper and mix well. Adjust the seasonings, if needed.

1 1/4 cups peeled cooked chestnuts (see page 27), or 1 (15-ounce) jar

4 slices whole grain bread

1/2 pound button or cremini mushrooms, chopped

2/3 cup coarsely chopped pecans, toasted (see page 28)

3/4 teaspoon salt

1/2 teaspoon dried thyme

1/2 teaspoon dried oregano

1/2 teaspoon poultry seasoning

Freshly ground pepper

1/2 cup chopped fresh parsley

Remove the squashes from the oven and generously fill the cavities with the stuffing. Cover the baking sheets with aluminum foil, shiny side down, and return the squashes to the oven for 30 minutes longer, or until tender when pierced with a fork.

To serve, cut each stuffed squash in half and sprinkle with the chopped parsley.

Notes: Good squash choices include sugar pumpkin, acorn, small butternut, delicata, or sweet dumpling.

• Extra stuffing can be put into a covered casserole dish and baked at 350 degrees for 30 minutes.

THROUGHOUT HISTORY chestnuts have evoked symbolic meanings and diverse practices in different cultures. In Japan, chestnuts symbolize both success and hard times. Always served as part of the New Year menu, chestnuts symbolize mastery and strength.

Per serving: Calories 332, Protein 6g, Fat 13g, Carbohydrate 49g, Vitamin E .6mg

Chestnut and Quinoa
Stuffed Portobellos

Yield: 4 to 8 servings

HERE'S AN APPEALING WAY to enjoy chestnuts from October through January, and sometimes even into February, when they are readily available in markets and specialty stores. The recipe will be much easier to assemble if you prepare the fresh chestnuts the day before or purchase already cooked chestnuts in a jar.

4 jumbo portobello mushrooms (about 5 inches in diameter), or 8 smaller portobello mushrooms

1 $\frac{1}{4}$ cups water

$\frac{1}{2}$ cup quinoa

1 $\frac{1}{4}$ teaspoons salt

1 $\frac{1}{2}$ cups cooked, peeled chestnuts (see page 27), coarsely broken

$\frac{1}{2}$ pound button or cremini mushrooms, chopped

3 celery stalks, finely chopped

1 small onion, finely chopped

5 garlic cloves, crushed

PREHEAT the oven to 375 degrees and have ready a large baking dish, about 10 x 15 inches.

Remove the stems from the portobello mushrooms, chop them, and set them aside to include with the stuffing ingredients. Reserve the mushroom caps separately.

To make the stuffing, combine 1 cup of the water, quinoa, and $\frac{1}{2}$ teaspoon of the salt in a 2-quart saucepan. Cover and bring to a boil over high heat. Turn the heat down to low and cook for 20 minutes, or until the quinoa is soft and all the water is absorbed. Cool slightly and transfer to a large bowl along with the chestnuts.

Combine the cremini mushrooms, celery, onion, $\frac{1}{4}$ cup water, garlic, olive oil, and portobello mushroom stems in a large skillet, and cook and stir for 5 to 6 minutes, or until the onion is soft and transparent. Add to the bowl with the chestnuts.

Lightly toast the bread. Cut it into small cubes, and add them to the chestnut mixture along with the maple syrup, cumin, remaining $\frac{3}{4}$ teaspoon salt, thyme, oregano, poultry seasoning, chili powder, and pepper.

Put the portobello mushroom caps into the baking dish, and generously fill the cavities with the stuffing mixture. Extra stuffing can be spooned into the bottom of the baking dish surrounding the mushroom caps.

1 tablespoon
extra-virgin olive oil

4 slices whole
grain bread

1¼ teaspoons
maple syrup

1 teaspoon
ground cumin

½ teaspoon dried thyme

½ teaspoon
dried oregano

½ teaspoon poultry
seasoning

½ teaspoon
chili powder

Freshly ground pepper

Parsley or thyme sprigs

Cherry tomato slices

Cover the baking dish with aluminum foil, shiny side down, and bake for 30 minutes. Garnish each serving with a sprig of parsley and a slice or two of cherry tomato and serve.

Note: For small appetites, cut each stuffed mushroom in half to make 8 servings.

Chestnut and Quinoa Stuffed Squash: During the winter, many delicious varieties of squashes (like sugar pumpkin, acorn, small butternut, delicata, and sweet dumpling) make appealing vessels for the stuffing. Preheat the oven to 375 degrees. Cut the squashes in half, brush the cut side with canola oil, and place them on a baking sheet, cut side down. Bake for 30 minutes. Remove them from the oven and fill the cavities with the stuffing. If you are stuffing just 2 or 3 squashes, transfer them to a baking dish. For several squashes, keep them on the baking sheet. Cover with aluminum foil, shiny side down, and bake for 30 minutes.

Per serving: Calories 281, Protein 7g, Fat 5g, Carbohydrate 53g, Vitamin E .4mg

Stuffed Artichokes

YOU COULDN'T ASK for a more visually appealing dish than these stuffed artichokes, which resemble king-size flowers in full bloom. For the perfect presentation, place a serving of cooked grains on the side of each dinner plate and sprinkle with finely minced dill weed, parsley, or green onion tops. The artichoke will fill the rest of the plate, starring as the main attraction.

3 large (not giant) fresh artichokes

1 onion, chopped

½ green bell pepper, chopped

½ red bell pepper, chopped

2 tablespoons extra-virgin olive oil

2 garlic cloves, finely minced

1 ¼ teaspoons salt

Freshly ground pepper

TO PREPARE the artichokes, remove a layer or two of the smaller leaves surrounding the base. Lay each artichoke on its side, and cut about 1 inch off the top with a sharp, heavy-duty knife and discard. Cut off the stem where it joins the bottom of the artichoke so the artichoke will stand upright. Reserve the stems. With a kitchen scissors, snip off the sharp tips of the remaining leaves of each artichoke, and use a small paring knife to trim off the outer skin from the stems.

To cook the artichokes, stand each one upside down, with the stem end up, in an 8- to 10-quart Dutch oven or stockpot. Put the stems into the pot as well. Add 1 inch of water, cover, and bring to a boil over high heat. Turn the heat down to medium and steam for 20 to 45 minutes, until just tender (the cooking time will depend on the size of the artichokes). Test for doneness by piercing the bottom or the heart with a fork. The artichokes should be firm, but the fork should enter without resistance. Remove them to a plate to cool.

To make the stuffing, preheat the oven to 325 degrees and have ready a 9 x 13-inch or 10 x 15-inch baking dish. While the artichokes are cooking, put the onion, bell peppers, olive oil, and garlic in a large nonstick skillet. Cook and stir for 7 to 8 minutes over high heat. Add the salt and pepper.

1 pound firm tofu, rinsed and drained

2 slices whole grain bread, diced

½ cup pine nuts

1 to 2 tablespoons nutritional yeast flakes

1 tablespoon freshly squeezed lemon juice

2 teaspoons soy sauce

Squeeze the tofu through your fingers into a large mixing bowl. Add the cooked onion and peppers, diced bread, pine nuts, nutritional yeast, lemon juice, and soy sauce, and mix until all the ingredients are well distributed.

To prepare each artichoke for stuffing, gently spread the leaves, taking care not to break them off. Reach into the center and remove the cone of lighter colored leaves by lifting them out. With a spoon, scoop out the hairy, inedible choke and discard it.

To stuff each artichoke, use a teaspoon to fill the center with the stuffing. Then stuff between the leaves, starting with the outer leaves and working inward.

Put the stuffed artichokes into the baking dish. Bake uncovered for 10 to 12 minutes, just to warm through. Serve whole for 3 large servings, or cut in half to make 6 generous portions.

Note: If you would like to serve some sauce on the side for dipping the artichoke heart, try Lemon Dill Silken Sauce (page 144).

Tofu Stuffed Enchiladas: Have ready 2¼ cups Savory Cashew Cream Sauce (page 141). Preheat the oven to 325 degrees and have ready a 7 x 9-inch baking dish. Prepare the stuffing for Stuffed Artichokes and spoon it into 6 corn tortillas or 4 whole wheat flour tortillas. Roll them up and lay them side by side in the baking dish. Thin the sauce slightly with 1 or 2 tablespoons of soymilk and spoon over the tortillas. Bake for 12 to 15 minutes to warm. To complete the meal, serve the enchiladas with a salad, rice, and beans.

Per serving: Calories 351, Protein 17g, Fat 22g, Carbohydrate 29g, Vitamin E .9mg

Stuffed Poblano Chiles

with Tomatillo Pistachio Salsa

Yield: 6 servings

IF YOU'RE NOT ACQUAINTED with fresh poblano chiles, called pasilla chiles in California, here are a few tidbits that may help. You never know if you've purchased the spicy or mild ones. The same bin may have some of each. A poblano chile could even be spicy at one end and mild at the other. However, these flavorful peppers are never as hot as jalapeño chiles. If poblano chiles are unavailable, you can use green bell peppers instead. To make the preparation easier, prepare the tomatillo pistachio salsa a day ahead. It keeps for several days in the refrigerator and retains its flavor quite well. Since poblano chiles can sometimes be a bit spicy, I prefer to keep the salsa unspiced. However, if you've got a bent for the spicy life, add one or more jalapeño chiles when processing the tomatillos and onion.

1 large broccoli crown (about ¾ to 1 pound), cut into quarters

1 pound extra-firm tofu, rinsed and drained

3 tablespoons freshly squeezed lemon juice

1 green onion, chopped

2 garlic cloves

1¼ teaspoons salt, plus more as needed

¼ teaspoon freshly ground pepper

6 large or 8 medium poblano chiles

TO MAKE the stuffing, put about ¼ inch of water into a 2-quart saucepan and add the broccoli. Cover and bring to a boil over high heat. Turn the heat down to low and steam for 5 to 6 minutes, until just tender. Quickly cool the broccoli by briefly rinsing it under cold water. Drain, chop it coarsely, and set it aside.

Crumble the tofu into the food processor. Add the lemon juice, green onion, 1 of the garlic cloves, salt, and pepper and process until creamy. Add the chopped broccoli and process until well incorporated. Adjust the seasonings, if needed.

Have ready a large bowl of cold water in the sink to cool the cooked chiles. Preheat the oven to 350 degrees and set aside a 7 x 9-inch baking dish.

Wash and dry the chiles and put them directly on the stove-top burners (gas or electric) over high heat. To save time, put a chile on each burner, and with tongs in hand, turn the chiles frequently, cooking them until they are blistered all over and almost blackened.

1 pound fresh tomatillos

1 large onion, coarsely chopped

Freshly squeezed lime juice

$1/2$ cup pistachios

2 tablespoons finely diced red bell pepper

Plunge the blackened chiles into the bowl of cold water to cool. Under running water, use your fingers to rub off the blackened skins. Using a serrated knife, cut around the top of the chiles to remove the stem and core. Rinse out any remaining seeds. Fill each chile with the tofu broccoli mixture and place them in the baking dish.

To make the tomatillo pistachio salsa, remove and discard the husks from the tomatillos and wash them under running water. Cut the tomatillos in half and put them into a 3- or 4-quart saucepan along with the onion. Add just enough water to cover. Cover, bring to a boil over high heat, and cook for 2 to 3 minutes.

Using a slotted spoon, transfer the tomatillos and onion to the food processor. Add the remaining garlic clove and process until combined but still chunky. Add the lime juice and salt to taste. Transfer to a bowl and stir in the pistachios.

Pour three-quarters of the salsa over the chiles in the pan; reserve the extra salsa to serve at the table. Sprinkle the red bell pepper over the top, and bake for 20 to 25 minutes to heat through.

Per serving: Calories 215, Protein 14g, Fat 10g, Carbohydrate 23g, Vitamin E 2.3mg

Thanksgiving Torte

Yield: 6 to 8 servings

Torte

2³⁄₄ cups plus
¹⁄₃ cup water

²⁄₃ cup wild rice

2¹⁄₈ teaspoons salt

³⁄₄ pound red rose or
white rose potatoes,
unpeeled, scrubbed, and
cut into 1-inch cubes

¹⁄₂ cup coarsely
chopped pecans

¹⁄₄ cup coarsely
chopped walnuts

1 (14-ounce) package
vegan ground sausage

4 large portobello
mushrooms, chopped

1 large onion, diced

2 tablespoons extra-
virgin olive oil

2 teaspoons
poultry seasoning

¹⁄₄ teaspoon freshly
ground pepper

¹⁄₂ teaspoon hickory
liquid smoke

2 ripe tomatoes, sliced

AN IDEAL VEGAN Thanksgiving dish, this elegant torte features the pleasing textures and savory flavors of wild rice, mushrooms, nuts, and sage. Served with a robust mushroom sauce on the side, it makes a lovely presentation, while adding a hearty main dish to the meal.

TO MAKE the torte, lightly oil a 9-inch springform pan, line the base with parchment paper (for easier cleanup), and set it aside. Combine 1³⁄₄ cups of the water, wild rice, and ³⁄₄ teaspoon of the salt in a 2-quart saucepan. Cover and bring to a boil over high heat. Turn the heat down to medium-low and steam for 45 to 50 minutes, or until the rice is tender. Drain any excess liquid and set the rice aside.

Combine the potato cubes, 1 cup of the water, and ¹⁄₈ teaspoon of the salt in a 2-quart saucepan. Cover and bring to a boil over high heat. Turn the heat down to medium and simmer for 5 to 7 minutes, or until the potatoes are fork-tender. Using a slotted spoon, transfer the potatoes to a medium bowl, mash them, and set them aside.

Preheat the oven to 375 degrees. Toast the pecans and walnuts in a 10-inch skillet over high heat, stirring constantly for 1 to 2 minutes. Immediately transfer them to a dish to cool.

Combine the vegan sausage, mushrooms, onion, remaining ¹⁄₃ cup water, olive oil, poultry seasoning, and pepper in a large, deep skillet. Cook over high heat for 5 to 7 minutes, or until the onion is transparent, stirring frequently with a wooden spoon or paddle to break up the sausage chunks. Drain and reserve any excess liquid. Add the remaining 1¹⁄₄ teaspoons salt and hickory liquid smoke to the sausage mixture and mix well.

Add the mashed potatoes to the skillet along with the toasted nuts and cooked wild rice. Mix well to combine the ingredients thoroughly. Adjust the seasonings, if needed.

Press the mixture firmly into the prepared springform pan, and attractively arrange the tomato slices over the top, covering most of the surface. Bake uncovered for 1 hour. Allow the torte to stand for 15 to 20 minutes before removing from the pan.

Mushroom Sauce

2 cups sliced button or cremini mushrooms

1³⁄₄ cups plus 3 tablespoons water

¹⁄₄ cup soy sauce

¹⁄₄ cup nonalcoholic dry red wine

2 tablespoons freshly squeezed lemon or lime juice

3 tablespoons cornstarch

PREPARE THE MUSHROOM SAUCE while the torte is baking. Combine the mushrooms, 1³⁄₄ cups of the water, soy sauce, red wine, and lemon juice in a 2-quart saucepan and bring to a boil. Turn the heat down slightly and simmer for 5 minutes.

Combine the cornstarch and remaining 3 tablespoons of water in a small bowl and stir with a spoon to make a runny paste. Add the paste to the bubbling sauce, a little at a time, stirring constantly for about 1 minute, until the sauce has thickened to the desired consistency.

To serve the torte, run a clean flatware knife around the edge of the springform pan, release the springform collar, and set the base with the torte on a platter. Serve the sauce in a gravy boat on the side.

Notes: To ease the feast-day preparations, make the torte the day before, store it in the refrigerator, and reheat it at 350 degrees for 15 to 20 minutes just before serving.

• The preparation comes together more quickly if you cook the wild rice before beginning the torte.

• Add a gourmet touch by serving the torte on a footed cake plate and garnish the edges with sprigs of fresh herbs and orange slices.

Per serving: Calories 401, Protein 17g, Fat 23g, Carbohydrate 36g, Vitamin E 2.4mg

Walnut Stuffed Eggplant

Yield: 4 servings

2 (1-pound) eggplants

1/2 pound ripe tomatoes, chopped

1/4 pound cremini or button mushrooms, sliced

1 cup chopped onions

4 large garlic cloves, minced

2 teaspoons extra-virgin olive oil

1 teaspoon salt

1/2 teaspoon ground cinnamon

Freshly ground pepper

2/3 cup walnuts

1 (6-ounce) can unsalted tomato paste

3 heaping tablespoons capers, well drained

2 to 3 small ripe tomatoes, sliced

Salt

A HEARTY Mediterranean dish with Greek ancestry, this entrée is pure heaven to walnut and eggplant lovers. Its exceptional flavor comes from the combination of cinnamon, tomato paste, and capers. Because the stuffed eggplant is so special, I keep the rest of the meal simple with stir-fried or steamed vegetables, bulgur wheat, and a tossed salad.

CUT the eggplants in half lengthwise, slicing through the stem end. Using a curved, serrated grapefruit knife, scoop out the flesh, leaving a 1/4-inch-thick shell, and coarsely chop the flesh. Put the chopped eggplant into a large, deep skillet or flat-bottom wok.

Rub the inside of the eggplant shells with a small amount of olive oil and place them on a baking sheet. Place the eggplant shells under the broiler, and broil them 3 inches from the heat source for 5 to 10 minutes, until fork-tender. Watch carefully to prevent burning. Remove the eggplant shells from the broiler and set them aside.

Preheat the oven to 375 degrees. Add the chopped tomatoes, mushrooms, onions, garlic, olive oil, salt, cinnamon, and pepper to the skillet with the chopped eggplant, and cook and stir for 7 to 10 minutes, until the vegetables are tender.

Coarsely grind the walnuts in a nut mill and add them to the skillet along with the tomato paste and capers. Mix well.

Fill the eggplant shells with the vegetable mixture and top with the tomato slices. Sprinkle with salt and pepper and bake, uncovered, for 25 to 35 minutes.

Per serving: Calories 282, Protein 9g, Fat 16g, Carbohydrate 35g, Vitamin E 3mg

Grains and Legumes

IF YOU'VE NEVER TASTED GRAINS LIKE BUCKWHEAT, BULGUR WHEAT, OR QUINOA,

you may be delighted with the first bite as you discover flavors and textures that expand your repertoire of food experiences. These are quick-cooking whole grains. Combined with nuts, these hearty complex carbohydrates provide long-lasting energy that keeps your blood sugar stable because they are slowly digested. A delectable dish like Sultan's Delight with Savory Pistachio Sauce (page 124) may be your introduction to the rich flavor and nutty qualities of bulgur wheat, a favored grain of Middle Eastern cooks.

Grains and legumes (beans, lentils, and peas) are the foundation of wholesome meals in many cultures today, as they were in ancient times. Nutritious and tasty, these staples offer satiety along with high fiber and low fat. Beans are the proud possessors of soluble fiber, a type of fiber that is completely digestible and provides a natural path to lower cholesterol. Another reason to boast about beans is their impressive content of antioxidants.

Neither grains nor legumes are difficult to cook. Some grains cook quickly, in 15 to 20 minutes, while others take longer and require a little advance planning. Grains such as barley, brown rice, and wild rice, which require 45 to 60 minutes to cook, offer such pleasing chewy texture you may enjoy serving them frequently.

Quick-cooking legumes, like lentils and green split peas, require no advance soaking and take 20 to 35 minutes, depending on the variety. For an extraordinary way to enjoy lentils, try Walnut Lentil Pie (page 44).

Preparing longer-cooking dried beans works best when the beans are soaked for about 8 hours, then cooked for 45 to 60 minutes for most varieties. Soaking shortens the cooking time and improves their digestibility.

In the United States most cooks soak their beans before cooking. However, in Latin America people usually cook their beans without soaking and instead plan on a lengthy simmering. They also plunge a few sprigs of the herb epazote into the cooking water to tame the gas-producing complex sugars called oligosaccharides.

Whether you decide to soak the beans or not, be sure to boil them vigorously for at least 5 to 10 minutes to destroy the indigestible lectins, compounds the beans produce to enhance their immune function while they are growing. It's important to cook beans thoroughly. Rushing the cooking process may result in uncooked or partially cooked starches, creating annoying flatulence. My personal preference is to soak the beans for at least 8 hours and discard the soaking water that contains the leached out oligosaccharides.

Canned beans are a welcome convenience and are just as nutritious as those cooked from scratch. While the perfectly organized home chef might be a plan-ahead kitchen whiz, I frequently operate on spontaneity and keep my pantry well stocked with canned beans. If their sodium content is a concern, simply drain and rinse the canned beans before using them. Rinsing won't eliminate all the sodium, but it will reduce it considerably.

Zesty Black Bean Patties

Yield: 9 to 10 (3-inch) patties

1/4 cup pine nuts

1/4 cup coarsely chopped walnuts

1 small onion, coarsely chopped

2 cups cooked black beans, rinsed and drained

1/2 cup oat bran or wheat germ

2 to 3 tablespoons water, as needed

1 teaspoon salt

3/4 teaspoon ground cumin

3/4 teaspoon ground coriander

3/4 teaspoon chili powder

1/4 teaspoon garlic powder

1/4 teaspoon freshly ground pepper

WHILE THESE PATTIES deliver a rich savory flavor, they look surprisingly like chocolate cookies dotted with chocolate chips. Enjoy these with fresh salsa on top, or tuck them into a whole wheat pita with lots of trimmings like chopped tomatoes, onions, cucumbers, and shredded lettuce. You can also enhance them with a dollop of Lemon Dill Silken Sauce (page 144) or Red Bell Pepper Cashew Sauce (page 142).

PREHEAT the oven to 400 degrees and lightly oil a large baking sheet. Combine the pine nuts and walnuts in the food processor and process until they are finely ground. Transfer to a large mixing bowl and set aside.

Put the onion into the food processor and pulse-chop until it is minced. Transfer to the bowl with the nut meal.

Measure 1/2 cup of the black beans and add them to the bowl with the nut meal. Put the remainder of the beans into the food processor. Add the oat bran, water, salt, cumin, coriander, chili powder, garlic powder, and pepper and process until well blended. Spoon the mixture into the nut meal and mix well.

Drop the mixture from a large spoon onto the prepared baking sheet to form nine or ten 3-inch patties. Flatten the patties slightly so they will bake evenly. Bake for 12 to 14 minutes. Turn the patties over with a metal spatula and bake 10 to 12 minutes longer.

Note: If you prefer to use canned beans rather than cooking beans from scratch, 1 1/2 (15-ounce) cans will give you the 2 cups of beans needed for this recipe. Rinse and drain the beans before using.

Per patty: Calories 111, Protein 5g, Fat 5g, Carbohydrate 14g, Vitamin E .1mg

Sultan's Delight
with Savory Pistachio Sauce

Yield: 6 servings

THIS PERSIAN-INSPIRED creation that features bulgur wheat is comprised of a colorful selection of vegetables with a flavorful nutty base that offers far more satiety than the traditional dish centered on white rice. If you're a purist and want to keep the sauce free of flecks, use ground white pepper instead of black.

Bulgur Wheat

3 cups water

1 1/2 cups bulgur wheat

1 1/4 teaspoons salt

Pistachio Sauce

1 cup pistachios

3 cups unsweetened soymilk

1 1/4 teaspoons salt

Freshly ground pepper

Garnish

1/3 cup currants or black raisins

2 to 3 tablespoons chopped pistachios

TO PREPARE the bulgur wheat, combine the water, bulgur wheat, and salt in a 2-quart saucepan. Cover and bring to a boil over high heat. Turn the heat down to low and cook for 15 minutes, or until the bulgur wheat is tender and all the liquid is absorbed.

TO MAKE the pistachio sauce, grind the pistachios to a fine meal in small batches in an electric mini-chopper/grinder or coffee grinder.

Combine the soymilk, salt, and pepper in a 2- or 3-quart saucepan and bring to a boil over medium-high heat. Watch closely so it doesn't boil over. Gradually add the ground pistachios to the bubbling liquid, stirring constantly with a wire whip for 1 to 2 minutes, until the sauce thickens. Remove from the heat and set aside. The sauce will thicken slightly as it cools.

TO PREPARE the garnish, put the currants into a small bowl, cover with hot water, and let stand 5 to 15 minutes, or until they are plump.

Vegetables

2 large carrots, peeled and coarsely grated

2 large zucchini, coarsely grated

1 small onion, chopped

2 garlic cloves, thinly sliced

2 tablespoons extra-virgin olive oil

2 tablespoons water

3/4 teaspoon salt

1/2 teaspoon dried oregano

1/2 teaspoon dried basil

1/2 teaspoon dried marjoram

Freshly ground pepper

1/4 cup whole pistachios

TO PREPARE the vegetables, combine the carrots, zucchini, onion, garlic, olive oil, water, salt, oregano, basil, marjoram, and pepper in a large, deep skillet and cook and stir over high heat for 5 to 7 minutes, or until the vegetables are tender. Stir in the whole pistachios.

To assemble the dish, mound the bulgur wheat on a large serving platter. Top with the vegetables, leaving a 1-inch border of bulgur wheat around the edges. Spoon a small amount of the pistachio sauce over the top. To garnish, drain the currants and sprinkle them over the top along with the chopped pistachios. Serve the remainder of the pistachio sauce at the table.

Persian Quinoa with Savory Pistachio Sauce: Replace the bulgur wheat with an equal amount of white or red quinoa.

Persian Buckwheat with Savory Pistachio Sauce: Replace the bulgur wheat with an equal amount of toasted or untoasted buckwheat. First bring the water to a boil; then add the buckwheat, cover, and cook for 15 minutes. Buckwheat is extremely porous and absorbs water quickly. Check about halfway through the cooking time to be sure there is sufficient water in the saucepan. Add more water, if necessary.

Per serving: Calories 475, Protein 18g, Fat 23g, Carbohydrate 56g, Vitamin E 1.8mg

Festive Wild Rice
with Dates and Pecans

Yield: 6 servings

WILD RICE and chopped pecans are excellent companions. The addition of nuts and dried fruits makes this recipe an especially good pairing with a savory entrée, a curried vegetable, or a legume dish.

4½ cups water

1½ cups wild rice

⅓ cup chopped dates

1½ tablespoons dried currants or raisins

1½ teaspoons salt

¾ teaspoon curry powder

¾ teaspoon onion powder

⅔ cup coarsely chopped pecans, toasted (see page 28)

1 Italian parsley sprig

COMBINE the water, wild rice, dates, currants, salt, curry powder, and onion powder in a 2-quart saucepan. Cover and bring to a boil over high heat. Turn the heat down to medium-low and cook for 45 minutes, or until the rice is tender and all the water is absorbed.

Stir in the toasted pecans, reserving a few for a garnish, and transfer the rice mixture to an attractive serving dish or bowl. Garnish with the reserved pecans and the sprig of Italian parsley.

Per serving: Calories 205, Protein 5g, Fat 9g, Carbohydrate 29g, Vitamin E .7mg

Company Rice

WHILE THE EVERYDAY grain dish might be simple, unadorned steamed rice, company rice begs for a fussier presentation. This dish is still a simple preparation, but the ingredients are a bit more lavish with the addition of cashews, pine nuts, and almonds.

3 cups water

¾ cup brown basmati rice

½ cup dried lentils

¼ cup barley flakes or pearl barley

¼ cup cashews

¼ cup pine nuts

¼ cup whole almonds

1 tablespoon organic canola oil

2 bay leaves

1½ teaspoons salt

1 garlic clove, minced

¼ teaspoon whole cumin seeds

¼ teaspoon ground cinnamon

Freshly ground pepper

COMBINE all the ingredients in a 3-quart saucepan. Cover and bring to a boil over high heat. Turn the heat down to low and cook for 35 to 45 minutes, or until the brown rice and barley are tender. Fluff the mixture with a fork and transfer it to an attractive serving bowl.

THE CASHEW TREE is a curious plant with multiple uses, yet we are only familiar with one of its fruits—the cashew nut. The cashew tree also produces an edible, pear-shaped fruit called the cashew apple. The fruit, extremely rich in vitamin C, is eaten raw, as well as made into jam, marmalade, candy, and juices.

Per serving: Calories 230, Protein 8g, Fat 12g, Carbohydrate 26g, Vitamin E 2.4mg

Nutty Grains Stuffing

Yield: 6 to 8 servings

A TASTY STUFFING recipe is an ideal addition to your culinary repertoire to serve as a side dish or to stuff vegetables like eggplant, peppers, or squashes.

2 pounds fresh chestnuts in the shell, cooked and peeled (see page 27), or 4 cups peeled cooked chestnuts

2¼ cups water, plus more as needed

3 teaspoons salt

1 cup buckwheat, toasted or untoasted

3 onions, coarsely chopped

4 slices whole grain bread, toasted and cubed

4 celery stalks, chopped

1¾ cups chopped green onions (about 1 bunch)

½ cup pine nuts

BREAK the chestnuts into coarse chunks, put them into a large bowl, and set them aside.

Combine 2 cups of the water and 1 teaspoon of the salt in a 2-quart saucepan. Cover and bring to a boil over high heat. Add the buckwheat, cover, and return to a boil. Turn the heat down to low and steam for 12 to 15 minutes. (Since buckwheat absorbs water quickly, check halfway through the cooking time to be sure there is sufficient water. Add more water, if necessary.)

Heat the remaining ¼ cup water in a large, deep skillet. Add the onions and cook and stir until they are nicely browned. Add more water as needed to prevent the onions from burning. Transfer them to the bowl with the chestnuts.

Add the cooked buckwheat to the chestnuts along with the bread cubes, celery, green onions, pine nuts, pecans, pumpkin seeds, olive oil, garlic, remaining 2 teaspoons salt, sage, oregano, marjoram, thyme, and pepper. Toss well. Adjust the seasonings, if needed.

Notes: If you are using fresh chestnuts in the shell, plan ahead and prepare them the day before to save time.

• For a side dish, transfer the stuffing to a 2-quart casserole dish, cover with aluminum foil, shiny side down, and bake at 350 degrees for 35 to 40 minutes.

1/3 cup coarsely chopped pecans

1/3 cup pumpkin seeds

2 tablespoons extra-virgin olive oil

3 garlic cloves, minced

2 teaspoons crushed dried sage

1/2 teaspoon dried oregano

1/2 teaspoon dried marjoram

1/2 teaspoon dried thyme

Freshly ground pepper

Nutty Bulgur Wheat Stuffing: Replace the buckwheat with an equal amount of bulgur wheat. To cook the bulgur wheat, combine 2 cups of the water, bulgur wheat, and 1 teaspoon of the salt in a 2-quart saucepan. Cover and bring to a boil over high heat. Turn the heat down to low and cook for 15 minutes. Proceed with the recipe as directed.

Nutty Barley Stuffing: Replace the buckwheat with an equal amount of pearl barley. To cook the barley, combine 3 cups water, 1 cup barley, and 1 teaspoon of the salt in a 2-quart saucepan. Cover and bring to a boil over high heat. Turn the heat down to low and cook for 50 to 60 minutes. Proceed with the recipe as directed.

Per serving: Calories 571, Protein 15g, Fat 21g, Carbohydrate 86g, Vitamin E 1.2mg

Noodles and Nuts

THIS SUMPTUOUS one-course meal starring almonds, vegetables, and pasta is ideal family fare. Dishes this flavorful make it easy to encourage the kids to eat more vegetables. To complete the meal, serve it with a salad, whole grain bread, and steamed vegetables.

1 (14- to 16-ounce) package Japanese soba noodles

2 tablespoons organic canola oil

3 garlic cloves, minced

1 (1-inch) piece fresh ginger, peeled and minced

1 large broccoli crown, coarsely chopped

3 ripe tomatoes, chopped

2 celery stalks, chopped

1 small onion, chopped

1 cup water

½ red bell pepper, diced

2 teaspoons sesame oil

1 teaspoon umeboshi vinegar or rice vinegar

Salt and freshly ground pepper

1 cup whole almonds

1 green onion, finely chopped

COOK the noodles in boiling water until tender, according to the package directions. While the noodles are cooking, heat the canola oil in a large, deep skillet. Add the garlic and ginger and cook over high heat for 1 minute. Add the broccoli, tomatoes, celery, onion, water, bell pepper, sesame oil, vinegar, salt, and pepper, and cook and stir for 2 to 4 minutes, until the vegetables are crisp-tender.

Grind the almonds into a fine meal in the food processor. Add to the simmering vegetables and stir for 1 to 2 minutes, or until thickened. Season with salt and pepper.

Drain the noodles and add them to the vegetable mixture, a little at a time, stirring with a wooden spoon to distribute them evenly. Adjust the seasonings, if needed. Heap the noodles and vegetables on a large platter, and garnish with the green onion.

Notes: Soba noodles are a type of Japanese pasta usually made from a combination of buckwheat and wheat.

• Processing whole almonds starts out at a nearly deafening clatter. You may want to hold your ears and warn anyone in the room.

Per serving: Calories 587, Protein 22g, Fat 25g, Carbohydrate 76g, Vitamin E 9mg

Red Lentil
Stuffed Tomatoes

Yield: 6 servings

ALTHOUGH LENTILS are tasty, nutritious legumes that can be simply prepared as a soup or casserole, I find them much more appealing when enhanced with pine nuts and spooned into hollowed out tomato halves. Serve them along with a whole grain such as quinoa, buckwheat, or wheat berries, and add a salad and a steamed vegetable to complete the meal.

3 large ripe tomatoes, cut in half horizontally

Salt and freshly ground pepper

2½ cups water

1 cup red lentils

½ teaspoon salt

1 red bell pepper, chopped

1 onion, chopped

½ yellow bell pepper, chopped

½ poblano chile or green bell pepper, diced

1 tablespoon extra-virgin olive oil

½ cup pine nuts

USING a curved, serrated grapefruit knife, remove the pulp and seeds from the tomato halves and put them into a 1-quart saucepan. Cook over high heat for about 5 minutes, or until the pulp is broken down. Sprinkle with salt and pepper and set aside.

Lightly sprinkle the tomato shells with salt and pepper, and set them aside.

Combine the water, lentils, and the ½ teaspoon salt in a 4-quart saucepan. Bring to a boil over high heat. Turn the heat down to medium and simmer uncovered for 15 to 20 minutes, stirring frequently, until the mixture breaks down into a purée.

Preheat the oven to 350 degrees and have ready a baking sheet or shallow baking pan. Combine the red bell pepper, onion, yellow bell pepper, poblano chile, and olive oil in a large, deep skillet, and cook and stir over high heat for 8 to 10 minutes, or until tender. Add the pine nuts and the cooked lentils and toss well. Adjust the seasonings, if needed.

Fill the tomato halves with the lentil mixture. Place them on the baking sheet or in the baking pan and warm them in the oven for 15 minutes. Spoon the warm tomato pulp over the stuffed tomatoes and serve.

Per serving: Calories 244, Protein 10g, Fat 11g, Carbohydrate 30g, Vitamin E .6mg

Pecan Praline Pumpkin Bread

Yield: 8 to 10 servings

MIX HOMEMADE, crunchy pecan pralines into a cinnamon-spiced pumpkin batter and out comes a tantalizing quick bread ideal for a potluck contribution or hostess gift. Of course, you can also enjoy it for breakfast with soy cream cheese or as an accompaniment to lunch, dinner, or festive occasions.

Pecan Pralines

¾ cup evaporated cane juice

⅓ cup water

2 tablespoons light corn syrup

Dash salt

1¼ cups pecans

1 teaspoon organic canola oil

TO MAKE the pecan pralines, combine the evaporated cane juice, water, corn syrup, and salt in a 2-quart saucepan. Stir with a wooden spoon over medium heat until the sugar is dissolved. Insert a candy thermometer and cook over medium-high heat until the syrup reaches 236 degrees. (See note next page.)

Remove the saucepan from the heat and stir in the pecans and canola oil. Stir vigorously for 1 to 2 minutes, or until the syrup becomes thick and clings to the pecans. Spoon into a dish to cool. When cool, break the pecans into small, coarse pieces and set them aside.

Pumpkin Bread

2⅔ cups all-purpose whole wheat flour

2 teaspoons baking powder

1½ teaspoons ground cinnamon

1½ teaspoons ground nutmeg

1 teaspoon baking soda

¾ teaspoon salt

¼ teaspoon ground ginger

½ cup water

¼ cup whole flaxseeds

1½ cups evaporated cane juice

1 cup cooked mashed pumpkin

½ cup organic canola oil

TO MAKE the pumpkin bread, preheat oven to 325 degrees and oil a 7 x 9-inch glass baking pan.

Sift the flour, baking powder, cinnamon, nutmeg, baking soda, salt, and ginger into a large mixing bowl and form a well.

Combine the water and flaxseeds in the blender and blend about 1 minute, until thick and viscous (it will be similar in consistency to thick oatmeal). Add to the flour mixture.

Stir in the evaporated cane juice, pumpkin, and canola oil and mix well, making sure all the flour is completely incorporated and there are no lumps in the batter. The batter will be very thick and somewhat dry.

Stir in the pecan pralines and mix well to distribute them evenly. Spoon the batter into the prepared baking pan and bake for 45 to 55 minutes. Cool completely in the pan before slicing.

Note: You can make the pecan pralines without a candy thermometer by boiling the evaporated cane juice, water, corn syrup, and salt until it reaches the soft-ball stage. To test, have a cup of cold water near the stove. After about 5 minutes of boiling, dip a spoon into the boiling syrup and drop about a half-teaspoon of it into the water. If it forms a soft ball when gathered up with the fingers, it has reached the desired temperature (between 234 and 238 degrees). Test again in a few minutes, if needed.

Per serving: Calories 514, Protein 8g, Fat 26g, Carbohydrate 67g, Vitamin E 3mg

Raisin Walnut Bread

CONVENIENTLY MADE in the food processor, this dense, nutty, and highly textured bread is an irresistible treat that lends itself to numerous variations. Slice it thickly and enjoy it as is or top it with nut butter, Date 'n' Raisin Tofu Spread (page 174), or Apricot Cashew Butter (page 169). This recipe does not require lengthy rising or kneading because it's yeast free.

5¼ cups water

2 cups whole wheat or spelt berries

⅔ cup black raisins

¼ cup golden raisins

1 cup coarsely chopped walnuts

¼ cup plus 2 tablespoons sunflower seeds

½ teaspoon ground allspice

½ teaspoon ground cardamom

½ teaspoon ground cinnamon

½ teaspoon salt

1 tablespoon psyllium husks

COMBINE 4 cups of the water and the whole wheat berries in a bowl and let soak for 8 to 12 hours at room temperature.

Preheat the oven to 300 degrees and line a baking sheet with parchment paper (to prevent the bread from sticking to it).

Combine the black and golden raisins in a small bowl, cover them with warm water, and set them aside until they are plump.

Place the walnuts, sunflower seeds, allspice, cardamom, cinnamon, and salt into a large mixing bowl. Toss well and set aside.

Drain the wheat berries and put them into the food processor. Add 1 cup of the remaining water and process for about 2 minutes, until the wheat berries are ground into a moist, coarse meal. Stop the machine occasionally to scrape down the sides of the work bowl. If your food processor has a small capacity, process the wheat berries and water in two batches.

Combine the remaining ¼ cup water and the psyllium husks in a small bowl or cup and stir to completely moisten. Within a few seconds the mixture will thicken. Add it to the food processor and process it into the wheat berries.

Transfer the wheat berry mixture to the bowl with the walnuts and spices. Drain the raisins, add them to the wheat berry mixture, and mix well to distribute the ingredients evenly.

Spoon the mixture onto the prepared baking sheet in two equal piles. Use your hands to form two 5 x 7-inch oval loaves.

Bake for 1 hour and 30 minutes. For a crusty surface, bake the breads uncovered. For a softer crust, cover the loaves with aluminum foil, shiny side down, and remove the foil the last 15 minutes of baking.

Cool the loaves completely before serving or storing. To store, wrap each loaf in a separate zipper-lock plastic bag and store it in the refrigerator. The loaves keep well for one week. For longer storage, wrap the loaves in heavy-duty zipper-lock plastic bags and freeze for up to three months.

Note: The wheat berries may be sprouted before making the bread, if desired. Sprouting has many benefits. Whole grains contain certain fibers, such as phytates, that interfere with the body's ability to absorb particular minerals like iron and zinc. Sprouting breaks down the phytate content of whole grains and makes the minerals available for absorption. Sprouting also increases the grains' vitamin C content considerably and generally makes the grains more digestible.

After soaking the wheat berries, place them in a wide-mouth jar, cover the top with cheesecloth, and secure it with a rubber band. Without removing the cheesecloth, fill the jar with water to moisten the grains, then drain off the water. Place the jar on its side on the countertop, cover it with a kitchen towel, and set it aside for 24 to 36 hours, rinsing and draining the grains three or four times during the day. The next day the berries will develop tiny white tails indicating they have sprouted and increased their digestibility. The berries will swell to a little over 4 cups. You can then proceed with making the bread.

recipe variations on next page

Per serving: Calories 262, Protein 8g, Fat 11g, Carbohydrate 37g, Vitamin E 2.4mg

Sweet Raisin Walnut Bread: Add 10 pitted dates to the food processor while processing the wheat berries.

Savory Walnut Bread: Omit the raisins, allspice, cardamom, and cinnamon. After grinding the wheat berries in the food processor, transfer them to a bowl and add ⅔ cup dehydrated onions, ½ cup capers, well drained, 6 garlic cloves, minced, and ½ teaspoon salt. Mix well. Proceed with the recipe as directed.

Savory Tomato Walnut Bread: Omit the raisins, allspice, cardamom, and cinnamon. Soak 2 ounces sun-dried tomatoes in warm water to cover until softened (about 5 minutes). Drain and chop the tomatoes and add them to the ground wheat berries along with ½ teaspoon garlic powder and ½ teaspoon fennel seeds, crushed. Proceed with the recipe as directed.

WHILE WALNUTS WERE APPRECIATED for the excellent nourishment they provided, their shells served a host of unique purposes we might never have considered. Pliny, a Roman natural scientist of the first century CE, suggests finely crushing the shells to use for filling dental cavities. Imagine shaving with the edge of heated walnut shells instead of a razor! King Louis XI's barber engaged in this practice because he thought it would prevent nicks. To keep bread from sticking, European bakers would spread powdered walnut shells on the base of their ovens.

Sauces

A COMPLEMENTARY SAUCE IS AS SIGNIFICANT AS YOUR OUTER LAYER OF CLOTHES

—you wouldn't dream of leaving the house in your undies! Upscale restaurants consider sauces so important, they staff their kitchens with a special chef, a saucier, whose sole task is to create exquisite sauces for the dishes on their menu.

Sometimes a little dollop of just the right topping gives a dish that gourmet flair. Can one serve pasta without sauce? Or baked potatoes without a topping? Become your own saucier and stir a little magic into your meals.

Polenta almost always needs an enhancer. Perhaps Red Bell Pepper Cashew Sauce (page 142) would be the perfect partner. Try Savory Cashew Cream Sauce (page 141) on steamed cauliflower, my family's favorite.

Mushroom aficionados just might fall in love with the very versatile Shiitake Mushroom Sauce (page 139) over pasta, cooked grains, or baked potatoes.

Because pasta ranks high as a comfort food, it deserves special treatment. While restaurants have added a host of vegetables to create variety in their pasta dishes, they seldom include nuts to thicken and enrich a tomato-based sauce. Cashew Tomato Eggplant Sauce (page 140) is a conversation-piece sauce that sends diners back for seconds.

While nuts are the focus of the recipes in this cookbook, you'll find one sauce, Lemon Dill Silken Sauce (page 144), contains no nuts at all. This little gem is an all-purpose topping that accompanies many of the dishes made with nuts.

Tomato Cashew Pasta Sauce

Yield: 6 servings

3½ pounds ripe Roma tomatoes

1 onion, cut into quarters

½ green bell pepper, diced

4 to 6 garlic cloves, crushed

1½ to 2 teaspoons chopped fresh basil, or ½ teaspoon dried

½ teaspoon dried oregano

½ teaspoon fennel seeds, crushed in a mortar and pestle

½ teaspoon dried rosemary, crushed in a mortar and pestle

¼ teaspoon dried marjoram

1 cup finely ground cashews

1¼ teaspoons salt

WHEN GUESTS COME OVER for a pasta dinner, serve this easy, versatile, and creamy tomato sauce. It's surprising how the addition of ground cashews can make an ordinary sauce exceptional. If you want to serve two sauces, pair this one with a pesto for color and flavor contrast.

COARSELY chop the tomatoes in the food processor. If you prefer a smoother, less chunky sauce, process them a little longer, until they reach the desired consistency. Transfer the tomatoes to a large, deep skillet.

Finely chop the onion in the food processor and add it to the skillet. Add the bell pepper, garlic, basil, oregano, fennel seeds, rosemary, and marjoram to the skillet, and cook and stir over medium-high heat for 12 to 15 minutes.

Add the ground cashews and salt to the simmering sauce, and cook a few minutes longer, until thickened. Adjust the seasonings, if needed, and serve.

Per serving: Calories 217, Protein 7g, Fat 13g, Carbohydrate 25g, Vitamin E .3mg

Shiitake Mushroom Sauce

NOTHING QUITE COMPARES to the woodsy flavor that dried shiitake mushrooms lend to sauces. Even fresh shiitakes lack the earthy quality of the dried mushrooms. To prepare this sauce, plan ahead for the hour it takes to soak the mushrooms. Then savor each spoonful you serve over cooked quinoa, pasta, polenta, or baked potatoes.

20 dried shiitake mushrooms

4 cups boiling water

¾ cup macadamia nuts

1 large onion, finely chopped

2 cups mushroom soak water

3 to 4 garlic cloves, thinly sliced

1 tablespoon extra-virgin olive oil

1 (14- to 16-ounce) package soft tofu

¼ cup plus 2 tablespoons soy sauce

PUT the mushrooms into a large bowl. Pour the boiling water over them to cover, and soak the mushrooms for 1 hour.

While the mushrooms are soaking, coarsely grind the macadamia nuts in the food processor and set them aside.

After the mushrooms have soaked, squeeze out the excess water, one handful at a time, and reserve the soak water. Using a kitchen scissors, cut off the tough stems and discard them.

Finely chop the mushroom caps in the food processor. Transfer them to a large, deep skillet along with the onions, 1 cup of the mushroom soak water, garlic, and olive oil. Cook and stir over high heat for about 7 minutes. Turn the heat down to medium.

Crumble the tofu into the food processor and process briefly until smooth. Add it to the mushrooms.

Add the remaining 1 cup mushroom soak water, soy sauce, and ground macadamias, and simmer another 2 to 3 minutes to blend the flavors. For a thinner sauce, add more mushroom soak water.

Note: Don't toss out the leftover mushroom soak water. Instead, use it as a broth or flavoring for soups and sauces. The soak water also makes an especially tasty base for gravy.

Per serving: Calories 236, Protein 8g, Fat 17g, Carbohydrate 17g, Vitamin E .4mg

Cashew Tomato Eggplant Sauce

Yield: 6 servings

2/3 cup cashews

2 1/2 pounds ripe Roma tomatoes

1 large eggplant (about 1 pound), unpeeled, cut into 1/2-inch cubes

1 onion, diced

3/4 cup water

1/2 green bell pepper, chopped

4 garlic cloves, pressed

2 teaspoons extra-virgin olive oil

1 1/2 teaspoons salt

1/2 teaspoon dried marjoram

1/2 teaspoon dried thyme

1/2 teaspoon dried rosemary, crushed in a mortar and pestle

1/2 teaspoon fennel seeds, crushed in a mortar and pestle

Freshly ground pepper

Dash cayenne

A PLEASANT CHANGE from the familiar tomato sauce that dresses pasta, this recipe offers a more complex blend of flavors. Cashews contribute sweetness and creaminess, while the eggplant and fennel add a Mediterranean influence.

GRIND the cashews into a fine meal in several batches in an electric mini-chopper/grinder or coffee grinder and set aside.

Coarsely purée the tomatoes in the food processor. Transfer the tomatoes to a large, deep skillet and add the eggplant, onion, half the water, bell pepper, garlic, olive oil, salt, marjoram, thyme, rosemary, fennel, pepper, and cayenne. Cook over high heat for 5 to 6 minutes, stirring frequently. Turn the heat down to medium-high and cook 20 to 25 minutes longer, stirring often, until the mixture is reduced and slightly thickened.

Stir in the remaining water and raise the heat to high. When the mixture begins to bubble, add the ground cashews and stir 1 to 2 minutes, until the sauce has thickened.

Per serving: Calories 179, Protein 6g, Fat 10g, Carbohydrate 22g, Vitamin E .6mg

Savory Cashew Cream Sauce

Yield: 2¼ cups

EASILY MASTERED, this highly versatile, cashew-thickened sauce is a treasure and only takes moments to whip up. It's perfect over starchy dishes, steamed vegetables, and broiled tomatoes. For an enjoyable dining experience, serve the sauce as a fondue for dipping baked tofu, tempeh, or seitan, along with raw and steamed vegetables.

⅔ cup coarsely chopped cashews

2 cups unsweetened soymilk

2 tablespoons nutritional yeast flakes

1 tablespoon freshly squeezed lemon juice

1 teaspoon salt

Dash cayenne

Freshly ground pepper

Dash nutmeg (optional)

GRIND the cashews to a fine meal in batches in an electric mini-chopper/grinder or coffee grinder.

Combine the soymilk, nutritional yeast, lemon juice, salt, cayenne, and pepper in a 2-quart saucepan and bring to a boil over medium-high heat. Watch closely so the mixture doesn't boil over. Turn the heat down slightly, keeping the mixture bubbling gently.

Add the ground cashews, stirring with a wire whip until the mixture thickens, about 1 minute. If the sauce seems too thick, thin it with 1 to 2 tablespoons of additional soymilk. Garnish with a sprinkling of nutmeg, if desired, and serve.

Note: This sauce is especially tasty over steamed cauliflower. For an attractive presentation, steam a whole head of cauliflower for 10 to 12 minutes, or until tender. Transfer the whole cauliflower to a serving platter and top it with Savory Cashew Cream Sauce. Surround the platter with a variety of other steamed vegetables, such as broccoli, carrots, and squash. Sprinkle the sauced cauliflower with a dash or two of paprika or freshly minced herbs, such as dill weed, marjoram, or thyme, and serve it proudly.

Per serving (½ cup): Calories 192, Protein 10g, Fat 12g, Carbohydrate 14g, Vitamin E .2mg

Red Bell Pepper Cashew Sauce

Yield: about 3 cups

THIS RICH, creamy, cashew-based sauce can be prepared quickly and makes a feather-light topping for grains, polenta, and baked potatoes. It's a perfect marriage with delicately seasoned foods.

¾ cup cashews

4 red bell peppers

1½ cups regular or unsweetened soymilk

1 teaspoon salt

GRIND the cashews into a fine meal in small batches in an electric mini-chopper/grinder or coffee grinder and set aside. Place a large bowl of cold water in the sink.

Line a baking sheet with aluminum foil, shiny side down, and arrange the peppers so they are lying down on the foil. Place the baking sheet 3 inches from the broiler heat source and broil the peppers, turning them one-quarter turn every 5 minutes, until they are completely blackened and soft.

Plunge the peppers into the bowl of cold water to quickly cool them. Using your fingers, rub off and discard the skins. Remove and discard the stem, seeds, and core.

Process the peppers in the food processor until completely smooth. Transfer to a 2-quart saucepan and add the soymilk, salt, and ground cashews. Bring to a simmer over medium heat, stirring frequently with a wire whip for 1 to 2 minutes, until the sauce has thickened. Serve the sauce well warmed. Stored in a covered container in the refrigerator, leftover Red Bell Pepper Cashew Sauce will keep for four to five days.

Per serving (½ cup): Calories 150, Protein 6g, Fat 10g, Carbohydrate 12g, Vitamin E 1mg

Cashew Tomatillo Sauce

Yield: 4 servings

WHEN TOMATILLOS are in season during spring and summer, enjoy them in this unique sauce that offers delightful tang in a thick, creamy cashew base. Serve it over pasta, baked potatoes, or grains. Dressed up with a sprinkling of fresh herbs, the sauce becomes a tasty hot dip.

⅔ cup coarsely chopped cashews

1½ pounds fresh tomatillos

1 poblano chile or green bell pepper, diced

1 small onion, diced

2 large garlic cloves, minced

1½ teaspoons salt

½ teaspoon ground cumin

Freshly ground pepper

1 cup unsweetened soymilk

GRIND the cashews into a fine meal in batches in an electric mini-chopper/grinder or coffee grinder. Remove and discard the outer husks from the tomatillos and wash them thoroughly. Chop the tomatillos and transfer them to a large, deep skillet.

Add the poblano chile, onion, garlic, salt, cumin, and pepper to the skillet and cook and stir over high heat for 6 to 7 minutes. Add the soymilk and stir well. When the mixture begins to bubble gently, add the ground cashews a little at a time, stirring with a wire whip for 1 to 2 minutes, until thickened and smooth.

Per serving: Calories 241, Protein 9g, Fat 14g, Carbohydrate 25g, Vitamin E 1mg

Lemon Dill Silken Sauce

Yield: about 1 cup

See photo facing page 97.

HERE'S A QUICK-FIX sauce you can rely on for complementing dishes such as Walnut Lentil Pie (page 44). Although the sauce contains no nuts, it serves as a topping to accompany a banquet of nutty dishes in this book. If you don't use it up all at once, it will wait patiently for several days in the refrigerator until you're ready to dress up another dish.

1 (12-ounce) box soft silken tofu

1 to 3 tablespoons freshly squeezed lemon juice

1 teaspoon salt

1 teaspoon minced fresh dill weed, or ¼ to ½ teaspoon dried

⅛ teaspoon freshly ground pepper

COMBINE all the ingredients in the blender or food processor, and process for about 1 minute, or until smooth. Stored in a covered container in the refrigerator, Lemon Dill Silken Sauce will keep for five days.

Per serving (2 tablespoons): Calories 24, Protein 2g, Fat 1g, Carbohydrate 1g, Vitamin E 0mg

Wasabi Pistachio Vegetable Aspic, page 80

Sandwiches

"Too few people understand a really good sandwich." But a good sandwich could have many interpretations. For some, it's the bread that really counts, while other sandwich aficionados say it's all in the dressing. And can we ignore the main focus of the sandwich—the stuff that rests between the bread and the dressing? When you come right down to it, it's all bundled together in one neat package where neither the bread, the dressing, nor the filling can stand apart, but rather form a blessed union.

Though the sandwich originated in England, Americans have adopted it as a major part of everyday life. The sandwich goes to work in a brown bag, is the mainstay of every fast food restaurant, satisfies at the dinner table, becomes the perfect meal on the run, and even starts the day at the breakfast table.

Intense hunger pangs call for something hearty. Count on the Great Garbanzo Burger (page 148) with its satisfying combination of nuts, beans, and grains. On the lighter side, choose the Nutty Carrot Sandwich (page 147) or the Sunchoke Pecan Sandwich (page 146).

Adventurous souls will enjoy the open-faced Pistachio Kalamata Cheese Melt (page 149) for its visual presentation, robust nature, and zesty flavors.

Almond, Mushroom and Spinach over Pasta
with Savory Cashew Cream Sauce, page 100

Sunchoke Pecan Sandwich

Yield: 3 to 4 sandwiches

1 ripe avocado

1½ tablespoons freshly squeezed lemon juice

¼ teaspoon salt

Dash cayenne

¼ to ½ cup organic canola oil

2 cups coarsely shredded sunchokes

½ cup raw or toasted pecans (see page 28), coarsely chopped or coarsely ground

¼ red bell pepper, finely diced

Salt and freshly ground pepper

6 to 8 slices whole grain bread

12 to 16 large basil leaves

3 ripe tomatoes, sliced

3 to 4 butter lettuce leaves

RAW SUNCHOKES, sometimes called Jerusalem artichokes, are spotlighted as the featured ingredient in this unique sandwich. Crunchy pecans and a smooth, creamy avocado sauce pair up in supporting roles. Serve the sandwich with a salad and fruit for a tasty light meal.

TO MAKE the avocado sauce, wash the avocado, cut it in half, scoop out the flesh, and place it in the blender. Add the lemon juice, salt, and cayenne and blend briefly. With the machine running, slowly add the canola oil, using just enough to create a thick, creamy sauce. Stop the machine occasionally to scrape down the sides of the blender jar and stir the mixture.

To make the sunchoke filling, combine the sunchokes, pecans, and red bell pepper in a medium bowl. Add enough of the avocado sauce to moisten and hold the mixture together. Season with salt and pepper, if needed.

Spread a thin coating of the avocado sauce over one side of each of the bread slices. Spread the sunchoke mixture over half the bread slices and top with the basil leaves, tomato slices, and lettuce. Place the remaining bread slices over the filling and cut the sandwiches in half.

Per serving: Calories 681, Protein 11g, Fat 46g, Carbohydrate 64g, Vitamin E 6mg

Nutty Carrot Sandwich

Yield: 4 sandwiches

UNITE PECANS and carrots and the result is a happy marriage of flavors that packs perfectly into a sandwich. Present the sandwiches with flair by cutting them into quarters and garnishing the plate with a fruit salsa.

3 large carrots, peeled and coarsely shredded

²/₃ cup pecans, finely ground

6 to 8 stuffed green olives, minced

1 small garlic clove, minced

¹/₄ to ¹/₂ cup vegan mayonnaise

8 slices whole grain bread

16 to 20 whole fresh basil or mint leaves

COMBINE the carrots, pecans, green olives, and garlic in a medium bowl. Add enough vegan mayonnaise to moisten them well and hold the ingredients together.

Spread one side of each slice of bread with a light coating of mayonnaise, and spoon the nutty carrot mixture on 4 of the slices. Arrange the basil leaves over the carrot mixture and top with the remaining bread.

IN ONE OF HIS HORTICULTURAL endeavors, Thomas Jefferson transplanted some pecan trees from the Mississippi Valley to his home in Monticello. At that time he presented some of the trees to George Washington, who planted them on March 25, 1775, at his Mount Vernon home. Washington referred to pecans as "Mississippi nuts." Three of those original trees still thrive on the property at Mount Vernon. The pecan was a favorite nut of both presidents, who regularly snacked on handfuls of them. In fact, George Washington was said to carry pecans in his pocket frequently.

Per serving: Calories 446, Protein 8g, Fat 26g, Carbohydrate 49g, Vitamin E 2.3mg

Great Garbanzo Burger

Yield: 10 giant or 16 medium burgers

A WARM whole wheat pita is the perfect pocket for this burger, especially when it is stuffed with lettuce, tomatoes, and onions. Other additions might include roasted vegetables like red, yellow, and green bell peppers, sliced eggplant, zucchini, or crookneck squash. For a unique treat, serve some oven-roasted sweet potatoes or yams with your burger. Instead of the standard mustard, ketchup, and mayo, try topping your burger with a zesty salsa, Lemon Dill Silken Sauce (page 144), or Tomato Cashew Dressing (page 86). Alternatively, serve the burgers as an entrée along with steamed vegetables and whole grains. Enjoy them topped with sauces like Cashew Tomatillo Sauce (page 143), Red Bell Pepper Cashew Sauce (page 142), Savory Cashew Cream Sauce (page 141), or Tomato Cashew Pasta Sauce (page 138).

½ cup coarsely chopped pecans

½ cup sunflower seeds

1 large onion, coarsely chopped

4 cups cooked garbanzo beans, or 3 (15-ounce) cans, rinsed and drained

1 cup oat bran, or ½ cup wheat germ and ½ cup oat bran

1 tablespoon nutritional yeast flakes

1 teaspoon salt

½ teaspoon garlic powder

½ teaspoon freshly ground pepper

2 tablespoons water

1 tablespoon psyllium husks

PREHEAT the oven to 400 degrees and lightly oil 2 large baking sheets or line them with parchment paper (for easier cleanup).

Grind the pecans and sunflower seeds in the food processor to the desired consistency. (Finely ground pecans will make a smooth burger; coarsely ground pecans will create a burger with a chunkier texture.) Transfer to a large mixing bowl and set aside.

Pulse-chop the onion in the food processor until minced. Add the garbanzo beans and process until well combined. Transfer the mixture to the bowl with the ground pecans.

Add the oat bran, nutritional yeast, salt, garlic powder, and pepper to the bowl. Combine the water and psyllium husks in a small bowl or cup and add to the bowl. Mix well until all the ingredients are thoroughly incorporated.

Using your hands, form the mixture into 10 to 16 burgers and place them on the prepared baking sheets. Bake for 15 minutes. Turn the burgers over with a spatula and bake for 10 to 12 minutes longer.

Per serving: Calories 170, Protein 8g, Fat 8g, Carbohydrate 22g, Vitamin E 2mg

Pistachio Kalamata Cheese Melt

Yield: 4 servings

THIS OPEN-FACED SANDWICH featuring pistachios and kalamata olives is ideal for breakfast or brunch when served with fruit or a tossed salad. The filling offers much diversity and makes a great-tasting topping for bread, toast, or crackers, a pungent topping for baked potatoes, a robust sandwich spread, or the perfect filling for a layered vegetable torte. With imagination, you may come up with a dozen other treatments for it.

1 pound extra-firm tofu

½ cup pistachios

18 pitted kalamata olives

¼ cup freshly squeezed lime juice

1 large garlic clove, coarsely chopped

4 slices whole grain bread

2 to 3 ripe tomatoes, sliced

4 to 8 slices vegan mozzarella cheese

TO MAKE the filling, break the tofu into chunks and put them into the food processor. Grind the pistachios into a fine meal in several batches in an electric mini-chopper/grinder or coffee grinder. Add to the tofu in the food processor along with the olives, lime juice, and garlic. Process until all the ingredients are well blended, stopping the machine occasionally to scrape down the sides of the work bowl.

To assemble the sandwiches, spread a generous layer of the filling over one side of each of the bread slices. Top with the tomato slices, covering the entire surface. Lay the vegan mozzarella cheese over the top, covering the whole surface.

Place the sandwiches on a baking sheet and broil them 3 inches from the heat source for about 2 minutes, or until the cheese has melted. Watch carefully to avoid burning the cheese. Serve with a knife and fork.

Note: If you cannot locate pitted kalamata olives, use a paring knife to cut the olive flesh from the pit. Regular black olives could be substituted, but they don't have the robust flavor of the kalamatas.

Per serving: Calories 381, Protein 22g, Fat 21g, Carbohydrate 33g, Vitamin E .5mg

FROM THE END OF THE MIDDLE AGES through the eighteenth century, almond and walnut milks made from blanched, pulverized, and soaked nuts were common in Europe. During medieval times, frumenty, a pudding made from whole wheat and almond milk, was traditionally served with meals of venison. Nut milks were often on hand to further enrich fatty desserts.

Vegetable Dishes

I SIMPLY CAN'T HIDE MY ENTHUSIASM FOR VEGETABLES,

those delightfully crisp, crunchy, and moist morsels that want so much to make us love them they give us more than we ask. We want flavor—they give us tantalizing taste plus vitamins and minerals. We want color—they give appealing brilliant hues plus phytochemicals. We rarely ask vegetables to bring us good health, yet they give us health benefits in so many ways.

With such diversity in the vegetable kingdom, one could never become bored with the choices available. Could a day be complete without vegetables? Hardly. Could anything compare to the divine sweetness and juiciness of a vine-ripened tomato in season? Make that an heirloom tomato and the flavor even intensifies.

Cooked or raw, vegetables offer us delightful flavors and textures and also provide us with appealing colors that create pleasant anticipation as we reach for a helping. Enjoy the offerings in this section, keeping in mind that substitutions are always an option. If you've run out of eggplant, leave it out or use zucchini instead. Or, if there is a vegetable on your not-so-favorite list, create the dish with one you do enjoy.

An important note to remember is that vegetables vary considerably in their flavor and moisture content. Because of this variability, a dish may require more or less liquid, or seasonings may need to be adjusted.

Treat your family to Gourmet Garden Loaf (page 156) that pairs walnuts and pine nuts and includes six different vegetables that look like someone sprinkled confetti in every serving. Hazelnuts, with their inherent sweetness and firm texture, become the focus of the tantalizing Hazelnut and Mushroom Curry (page 153) that cooks in only twenty minutes and keeps company with eggplant, zucchini, and tomatoes.

Explore new vegetables in the produce section of your supermarket. Shop in ethnic markets for exotic veggies that can be paired with nuts. Most of all, find joy in the wonderful world of vegetables and see how they come alive when nuts become an integral part of the vegetable preparation.

Carrot and Potato Hash Browns

Yield: 6 servings

VARIATION ON AN OLD THEME gives this familiar standard a splash of color, while the onions and carrots add a subtle hint of sweetness. The highlight of this dish is the delightful crunch provided by the toasted cashews.

5 red rose or white rose potatoes, unpeeled, coarsely shredded

4 carrots, peeled and coarsely shredded

1 onion, coarsely grated

1 green bell pepper, diced

1/2 cup water

2 tablespoons extra-virgin olive oil

2 garlic cloves, minced

1/2 cup coarsely chopped cashews, toasted (see page 28)

Salt and freshly ground pepper

COMBINE the potatoes, carrots, onion, bell pepper, water, olive oil, and garlic in a large, deep skillet and cook and stir over high heat for 15 to 20 minutes, until the vegetables are tender and golden brown. Add additional water, as needed, to keep the potatoes from sticking to the skillet. Add the cashews, season with salt and pepper, and serve as a side dish.

Per serving: Calories 238, Protein 5g, Fat 11g, Carbohydrate 33g, Vitamin E 1.1mg

Hazelnut and Mushroom Curry

Yield: 4 servings

3 Japanese eggplants,
sliced ½ inch thick, or
1 large eggplant,
cut into 1-inch chunks

2 zucchinis,
sliced ½ inch thick

2 ripe tomatoes,
chopped

½ pound cremini or
button mushrooms,
sliced

½ cup water

¼ cup nonalcoholic
dry red wine

1 tablespoon extra-virgin
olive oil

3 garlic cloves, minced

1 teaspoon curry powder

¼ teaspoon
ground cinnamon

¼ teaspoon turmeric

Salt and freshly ground
pepper

1 cup whole hazelnuts

WHILE SEASONING this family-style dish, I found the whole kitchen was enveloped in the lusty, inviting aromas of an Indian spice market. To complement the curry, serve it over brown or wild rice, and accompany the dish with some steamed vegetables and a tossed salad.

COMBINE the eggplant, zucchinis, tomatoes, mushrooms, water, wine, olive oil, garlic, curry powder, cinnamon, and turmeric in a large, deep skillet. Cook and stir over high heat for 10 to 12 minutes, or until the vegetables are soft and broken down. Season with salt and pepper.

While the vegetables are cooking, coarsely chop the hazelnuts in the food processor. Transfer the hazelnuts to a dry skillet, and toast them over high heat for about 2 minutes, stirring constantly. Watch carefully to prevent burning.

Add the hazelnuts to the vegetables, and stir for 1 to 2 minutes, or until the sauce thickens slightly. Adjust the seasonings, if needed, and serve.

Per serving: Calories 326, Protein 10g, Fat 27g, Carbohydrate 19g, Vitamin E 6.5mg

Paradise
Scalloped Potatoes
and Cashews

Yield: 4 to 5 servings

2/3 cup cashews

1/4 cup freshly squeezed
lemon juice

3 tablespoons
white miso

1 1/2 cups unsweetened
soymilk

2 tablespoons nutritional
yeast flakes

1 teaspoon salt

Dash cayenne

Freshly ground pepper

1 pound red rose or
white rose potatoes,
scrubbed and thinly
sliced

3 green onions, chopped

1 ripe tomato, diced

Paprika

2 tablespoons coarsely
ground walnuts

SCALLOPED POTATOES are an old-time creation that was probably popular in Grandma's kitchen. I've adapted this simple classic for the vegan table and enhanced it with cashews, miso, and nutritional yeast to create a dish that truly earns its name.

PREHEAT the oven to 375 degrees and have ready an 8 x 8-inch glass baking dish. Grind the cashews into a fine meal using an electric mini-chopper/grinder or coffee grinder. Transfer to a medium bowl and set aside.

To prepare the sauce for the potatoes, combine the lemon juice and miso in a small bowl. Blend with a spoon or small wire whip until smooth, and add to the ground cashews. Stir in the soymilk, nutritional yeast, salt, cayenne, and pepper, and mix until thoroughly combined.

Spoon a small amount of the sauce into the baking dish, using just enough to cover the bottom. Layer half of the potatoes, green onions, and tomatoes in the baking dish and cover with half of the sauce. Make another layer with the remaining potatoes, green onions, and tomatoes, and finish with the remaining sauce. Cover the baking dish with aluminum foil, shiny side down, and bake for 1 hour and 10 minutes.

Remove the dish from the oven, remove the foil, and sprinkle the top of the casserole with paprika and the ground walnuts before serving.

Per serving: Calories 308, Protein 13g, Fat 14g, Carbohydrate 36g, Vitamin E .3mg

Symphony in Squash

1 delicata squash (about ¾ pound)

1 small butternut squash (about 2 pounds)

1 small pie pumpkin (about 1½ pounds)

1 (15-ounce) can garbanzo beans, rinsed and drained

1 red bell pepper, cut into 1-inch chunks

1 onion, cut in half and sliced lengthwise

⅔ cup golden raisins

¼ cup whole hazelnuts

¼ cup chopped hazelnuts

¼ cup black currants

2 tablespoons extra-virgin olive oil

Salt and freshly ground pepper

2 tablespoons finely chopped green onions

THE FALL HARVEST is an inspiring season for restaurants and home chefs because of its bounty of colorful winter squashes that come to market. This recipe combines three types of squashes, adds an accent of hazelnuts, and pairs well with bean dishes, whole grains, and a hearty tossed salad.

PREHEAT the oven to 350 degrees and have ready a 9 x 13-inch glass baking dish.

Wash the squashes. Using a vegetable peeler or small, firm paring knife, peel off the skin. Cut the squashes in half using a large, firm chef's knife, and scoop out and discard the seeds. Cut the squashes into 1½-inch chunks and put them into an extra-large mixing bowl.

Add the garbanzos, bell pepper, onion, raisins, whole hazelnuts, chopped hazelnuts, and currants. Drizzle with the olive oil and sprinkle with salt and pepper. Stir well to distribute the oil and seasonings.

Transfer to the baking dish. Cover with aluminum foil, shiny side down, and bake for 45 to 60 minutes. Lift the foil and test the tenderness of the squashes with a fork. They should be soft enough for the fork to pierce through the flesh but still hold their shape.

Adjust the seasonings, if needed. Just before serving, sprinkle the green onions over the top.

Per serving: Calories 332, Protein 10g, Fat 10g, Carbohydrate 58g, Vitamin E 2.1mg

Gourmet Garden Loaf

THIS QUINOA-BASED loaf is a vegetable and nut lover's dream. Heaping with a confetti of broccoli, bell peppers, mushrooms, and onions, the dish becomes distinctive when embellished with the richness of walnuts and pine nuts. It's a perfect make-ahead entrée that can be quickly reheated. Serve it with Lemon Dill Silken Sauce (page 144) or Miso Mayo (page 171).

2½ cups water

1 cup quinoa

1 teaspoon salt

½ pound cremini or button mushrooms, sliced

1 broccoli crown, chopped

1 red bell pepper, chopped

1 small onion, chopped

½ green bell pepper, chopped

⅔ cup walnuts, coarsely ground

2 ripe Roma tomatoes, diced

⅓ cup pine nuts

¼ cup oat bran or wheat germ

2 garlic cloves, minced

1 teaspoon ground cumin

1 teaspoon ground coriander

1 teaspoon chili powder

½ teaspoon salt

1 tablespoon psyllium husks

PREHEAT the oven to 375 degrees and lightly oil a 9 x 13-inch glass baking dish.

Combine 2 cups of the water, quinoa, and salt in a 2-quart saucepan. Cover and bring to a boil over high heat. Turn the heat down to low and cook for 15 to 20 minutes, or until all the liquid is absorbed.

While the quinoa is cooking, combine the mushrooms, broccoli, red bell pepper, onion, green bell pepper, and ¼ cup of the remaining water in a large, deep skillet. Cook and stir for 2 to 3 minutes, just until tender. Transfer the vegetables to a large bowl, including any remaining liquid in the pan.

Measure 2 cups of the cooked quinoa and add it to the bowl. Refrigerate the remaining quinoa for a future recipe.

Add the walnuts, tomatoes, pine nuts, oat bran, garlic, cumin, coriander, chili powder, and salt to the bowl, and stir well to combine the ingredients.

Combine the psyllium husks and the remaining ¼ cup water in a cup or small bowl. Stir until completely moistened and add it to the bowl. Mix well until all the ingredients are thoroughly combined.

Spoon the mixture into the prepared baking dish, and pack it down to create a smooth surface. Bake uncovered for 35 to 45 minutes. Remove from the oven and let rest 10 minutes before serving. Cut the loaf into squares and serve.

Note: To reheat the loaf, warm it in the oven at 350 degrees for 15 to 20 minutes.

Per serving: Calories 254, Protein 9g, Fat 13g, Carbohydrate 30g, Vitamin E .3mg

Creamed Chestnuts

Yield: 6 to 8 servings

HERE'S A UNIQUE side dish you can serve in place of potatoes during fall and winter when fresh chestnuts are plentiful.

1¾ pounds fresh chestnuts in the shell, cooked and peeled (see page 27), or 5½ cups peeled cooked chestnuts

1 scant cup regular soymilk or rice milk

Salt and freshly ground pepper

Dash ground nutmeg

2 ripe Fuyu persimmon slices, quartered (optional)

PLACE the chestnuts into a 4-quart saucepan and add enough water to cover by 2 inches. Bring to a boil over high heat. Turn the heat down to medium-high and boil gently for 20 to 30 minutes, or until the chestnuts are soft enough to pierce with a fork.

Drain the water into a 2-cup measure, and add enough soymilk to equal 1½ cups. Pour into the food processor, add the chestnuts, and process until smooth. Season with salt and pepper. Transfer to an attractive serving bowl and sprinkle the top with a dash of nutmeg. Garnish with the optional persimmon slices, placing them around the outer edge, and serve.

Notes: The second cooking of the chestnuts will soften them further and result in a very delicate, creamy texture. For a thicker, firmer texture closer to mashed potatoes, eliminate the second cooking and place the chestnuts into the food processor. Add ¾ to 1 cup soymilk or rice milk and process until thick and smooth. Transfer to an ovenproof dish, and warm in the oven at 350 degrees for 15 to 20 minutes.

• To save preparation time, use 2 (15-ounce) jars cooked and peeled whole chestnuts. They are available at specialty shops, natural food stores, and some grocery stores. Each jar contains about 2½ cups chestnuts.

• Creamed Chestnuts may be prepared a day ahead and chilled in an ovenproof serving dish. Reheat it gently in the oven at 325 degrees for 15 to 20 minutes. Garnish just before serving.

Per serving: Calories 260, Protein 4g, Fat 3g, Carbohydrate 54g, Vitamin E 0mg

Stuffed Roasted Peppers with Brazil Nuts and Citrus Marinated Mushrooms

A HANDY MAKE-AHEAD vegetable dish with a nutty crunch is a welcome treat for any occasion. Marinate the mushrooms and Brazil nuts overnight, roast the peppers a day ahead, then simply assemble the ingredients and serve the dish heated, at room temperature, or chilled. For an appealing presentation, line a serving dish with lettuce leaves. Arrange the peppers on the dish, and top each pepper with a sprig of herbs or fresh edible flowers like nasturtiums, pansies, or dianthus.

2 pounds cremini mushrooms, sliced

½ cup Brazil nuts, coarsely chopped

⅓ cup organic canola oil

⅓ cup extra-virgin olive oil

⅓ cup orange or tangerine juice

2 tablespoons plus 1 teaspoon balsamic vinegar

½ teaspoon salt

½ teaspoon dry mustard

⅛ teaspoon freshly ground pepper

6 red bell peppers

PLACE the mushrooms and Brazil nuts into a deep bowl. Combine the canola oil, olive oil, orange juice, balsamic vinegar, salt, dry mustard, and pepper in a small bowl and pour over the mushrooms. Stir well, cover the bowl, and marinate 8 to 12 hours in the refrigerator.

To prepare the peppers, have ready a bowl of cold water in the sink. Wash the bell peppers and place them whole on a baking sheet. Put them under the broiler, 3 inches from the heat source, and broil for 2 to 3 minutes. Turn them one-quarter turn and broil about 2 minutes longer. Keep turning until the peppers are slightly blistered all over, but not completely blackened. Be careful not to overcook the peppers or they will not retain their shape.

When the peppers are blistered all over, plunge them into the bowl of cold water. Let cool for 1 to 2 minutes, then use your fingers to rub off the blistered skins. Carefully cut the peppers in half lengthwise and discard the core and seeds.

Remove the mushrooms and Brazil nuts from the refrigerator, stir, and lift them from the marinade using a slotted spoon. Fill each pepper half with the marinated mushrooms and Brazil nuts. Serve immediately or thoroughly chilled. To serve warm, preheat the oven to 350 degrees. Place the stuffed peppers on a baking sheet and warm them in the oven for 12 to 15 minutes.

Per serving: Calories 105, Protein 3g, Fat 9g, Carbohydrate 5g, Vitamin E 1.2mg

Relishes and Condiments

SOMETIMES IT'S THOSE LITTLE SIDE DISHES AND ENTRÉE ACCOMPANIMENTS
that add sparkle to a meal. Most relishes are uncomplicated, simple preparations that require only a few ingredients. You can, however, continue to add ingredients and create a more complex infusion of flavors.

Perhaps a vegetable salsa with a bit of heat is just what the entrée needs. At other times a sweet fruit-based relish with a splash of exotic spice and a crunch of nuts adds the finishing touch to a lunch or dinner.

What makes these dishes special is their diversity of ingredients that flow with the seasons. When cherries were in season, I created Cherry Relish (page 163). In summer, a nearby farm stand sells green tomatoes that are perfect for Green Tomato Comfit (page 165). Persimmons and cranberries are harvest season specialties that inspired Persimmon Cranberry Relish (page 161).

Use the recipes as a springboard to create your own relishes and accompaniments. For example, start with Cherry Relish as a basic recipe, but use peaches, mangoes, or plums in place of the cherries.

Experimenting with a variety of flavored vinegars is another way to alter the seasonings of salsas and relishes. Herbs and spices offer unlimited possibilities. A few leaves of chopped fresh herbs, a clove of garlic, or grated ginger breathe life into a simple relish.

Spices are wondrous treasures that can transform an ordinary relish into an exotic taste delight. A dash of nutmeg, cinnamon, allspice, cardamom, or star anise can create a dramatic change in a relish.

When seasonal fruits forget to be sweet, tease flavor into them with a squeeze of lemon or lime juice. For a savory approach, add a pinch of salt to heighten the flavor. And for texture and crunch, don't forget the nuts!

Apple Relish

THE TRADITIONAL NAME for this recipe is charoset, a Hebrew word that describes a mixture of fruits, nuts, and wine eaten at the Passover seder. This wine-free version features dried fruits and cinnamon typically used in Sephardic charoset recipes. The fruits almost always include apples that are shredded or finely diced. While European-style charoset is usually a simple combination of apples, sweet wine, and walnuts, the Sephardic Jews from Spain and the Middle East enhance their relish with a variety of dried fruits and add sweetening. This Sephardic-style combination is so tasty and nutritious it ought to be enjoyed throughout the year. Serve it as a sweet accompaniment to any savory meal.

1 large, crisp, sweet red apple, unpeeled

1 large green apple, unpeeled

⅔ cup sweet Concord grape juice

⅓ cup chopped dates

⅓ cup diced dried peaches or apricots

⅓ cup golden raisins

¼ cup sliced almonds

¼ cup finely chopped walnuts

1¼ teaspoons ground cinnamon

½ teaspoon almond extract

Evaporated cane juice

CORE and finely chop or coarsely shred the apples. Transfer to a large bowl, add the remaining ingredients, and mix well. Sweeten with evaporated cane juice to taste. Refrigerate the relish and allow it to marinate for 4 to 12 hours. Stored in a covered container in the refrigerator, Apple Relish will keep for three to five days.

Per serving (¼ cup): Calories 78, Protein 1g, Fat 3g, Carbohydrate 14g, Vitamin E .7mg

Persimmon Cranberry Relish

Yield: about 3 cups

THE ART OF BALANCING flavors is easy when you invite tart cranberries and sweet persimmons to the dinner table in the form of a relish to complement both savory and sweet dishes. Toasted nuts put the final touch on this simple condiment.

2 cups fresh cranberries

3 ripe Fuyu persimmons

¼ cup evaporated cane juice

¼ cup water

½ cup toasted cashews (see page 28), coarsely chopped

6 pitted dates, minced

⅓ cup black raisins

2 tablespoons pine nuts, toasted (see page 28)

2 dashes ground cinnamon

Dash ground cloves

1 cinnamon stick

PICK through the cranberries and discard any that are spoiled. Wash and dry the cranberries and place them in the food processor. Pulse-chop until they are minced but not puréed. Transfer to a large bowl.

Remove and discard the persimmon stems. Cut 1 slice of a persimmon, cut the slice in half, and set both halves aside for the garnish. Cut the remaining persimmons into eight wedges. Place them in the food processor and pulse-chop until minced. Transfer to a medium bowl.

Remove ½ cup each of the minced cranberries and minced persimmons and place in the food processor. Add the evaporated cane juice and water and process until completely smooth. Pour into the bowl with the minced cranberries.

Add the minced persimmons and the cashews, dates, raisins, pine nuts, cinnamon, and cloves, and mix well to distribute the ingredients evenly. Spoon into an attractive serving bowl and garnish with the reserved persimmon slice and cinnamon stick.

Per serving (¼ cup): Calories 122, Protein 2g, Fat 4g, Carbohydrate 22g, Vitamin E .6mg

Cinnamon Fruit and Cranberry Relish

Yield: 5 cups

THANKSGIVING WOULD SEEM incomplete without a cranberry delicacy on the table. A departure from the familiar relish, this easy prep features pecans and a touch of cinnamon, adding flair to the holiday table.

1 (12-ounce) package fresh cranberries

3 crisp, sweet apples, unpeeled, cored, and quartered

24 pitted dates, cut in half

1 cup black raisins

½ cup golden raisins

½ cup toasted pecans (see page 28), coarsely chopped

3 tablespoons maple syrup

½ teaspoon ground cinnamon

2 or 3 ripe Fuyu persimmons, sliced

COMBINE the cranberries, apples, dates, raisins, and pecans in the food processor and pulse-chop until fine. Transfer to a large mixing bowl and add the maple syrup and cinnamon, stirring well. (The relish will be very moist but will thicken after it chills.)

Line the sides of a clear glass serving bowl with the persimmon slices. Transfer the relish to the bowl, and chill for 8 to 12 hours before serving.

Per serving (¼ cup): Calories 127, Protein 1g, Fat 2g, Carbohydrate 29g, Vitamin E .4mg

Cherry Relish

Yield: 4 to 5 cups

DURING CHERRY SEASON, bring this zesty and nutty fruit relish to the table and serve it alongside a savory entrée. You'll discover it satisfies those sweet cravings people often feel at the end of a meal.

1 ripe mango, diced

1 sweet apple, diced

1 heaping cup pitted fresh cherries, cut in half

½ cup golden raisins

½ cup coarsely chopped pecans

1 tablespoon raspberry vinegar

COMBINE all the ingredients in an attractive serving bowl, and toss well to distribute them evenly.

OF THE MANY FAVORITE American dishes inspired by the pecan, none surpasses the beloved pecan pie with its rich, dark, custard-like filling and heavily encrusted, crunchy pecan topping. Exactly where the pie originated is a mystery, but some suggest the wife of a Karo Corn Syrup executive may have developed the pie more than seventy years ago in an effort to create recipes to help sell the product. Other historians presume the pecan pie originated in the backwoods of Georgia or Alabama where even the poorest of families had the pie's basic ingredients of corn syrup and pecans in their pantries.

Per serving (¼ cup): Calories 52, Protein 1g, Fat 2g, Carbohydrate 8g, Vitamin E .2mg

Nutty Dozen Seasoning Mix

Yield: ¾ cup

SEASONING A DISH with more than just a sprinkling of salt and a dash of pepper can often take as long as it does to create it. We tend to judge the flavor of a dish with the first bite, and quickly lose interest when that first impression is perceived as bland. Keep this seasoning mix on hand and count on a sprinkling or two to finish that special gourmet creation.

½ cup whole almonds

2 tablespoons hulled sesame seeds

½ teaspoon salt

½ teaspoon chili powder

½ teaspoon onion powder

½ teaspoon garlic powder

½ teaspoon dried oregano

½ teaspoon ground nutmeg

½ teaspoon paprika

¼ teaspoon freshly ground pepper

¼ teaspoon ground cumin

¼ teaspoon dried thyme

GRIND the almonds to a fine meal in two batches in an electric mini-chopper/grinder, coffee grinder, or food processor. Transfer to a small bowl and add the remaining ingredients. Stir well to thoroughly blend the herbs and spices with the ground almonds. Stored in a covered container in the refrigerator, Nutty Dozen Seasoning Mix will keep for up to six months.

ALMONDS HAVE BEEN CENTRAL to many cultural traditions around the world. In classical times, Romans presented gifts of sugared almonds to important dignitaries as well as personal friends. At weddings, they tossed almonds at the bride and groom as a symbol of fertility.

Per tablespoon: Calories 44, Protein 2g, Fat 4g, Carbohydrate 1g, Vitamin E 1.6mg

Green Tomato Comfit

FINDING GREEN TOMATOES in the supermarket is unlikely, but you may find them in abundance with a visit to the local farm stand or farmers' market during the summer or early fall. Green tomatoes greet the taste buds with a delightfully zesty tang and make an ideal relish to accompany a savory main dish.

1 large green tomato, diced

½ small onion, diced

½ to 1 jalapeño chile, minced

2 to 3 garlic cloves, minced

1 tablespoon extra-virgin olive oil

½ cup pine nuts

Salt and freshly ground pepper

1 tablespoon finely chopped green onions

COMBINE the tomato, onion, chile, garlic, and oil in a large, deep skillet. Cook and stir over high heat for 10 to 12 minutes, or until the tomato and onion are softened.

Add the pine nuts and season with salt and pepper. Stir to distribute the pine nuts evenly. Spoon the comfit into an attractive serving bowl and garnish it with the green onions.

Per serving: Calories 277, Protein 5g, Fat 25g, Carbohydrate 13g, Vitamin E 1mg

NOSTALGIC MEMORIES linger when chestnuts appear each fall. Some of our parents and grandparents still recall holiday seasons with street vendors selling roasted chestnuts on the sidewalks of New York and Philadelphia, as well as in many smaller cities. For just a few pennies people could buy bags of hot chestnuts, which they ate as a warming snack while they shopped or strolled along the streets.

Spreads and Dips

WHEN MY FRIEND, WHO ENTERTAINS FREQUENTLY, REFERRED TO SPREADS AND DIPS

as "eat-and-talk food," I began observing more closely how people gravitate to the little bowl next to the veggie platter. Often it doesn't matter what's in that bowl—people just naturally congregate and begin to chat. My hope is to offer dips and spreads so tasty that conversation stops mid-sentence and sparks comments like, "Wow! This is great!"

While dips are considered party food, spreads invite themselves to everyday meals and nibbles beginning with breakfast and ending with late-night snacks.

Savor the fruity tang or zesty flavor of a special spread on your breakfast toast, or use a spread to dress up sandwich bread. A little snack of crackers with a topping that tingles the taste buds might be just the perfect on-the-go tidbit to stave off hunger when dinner is delayed.

What can be more all-American than the ultra-creative sandwich? All too often, sandwich fillings and spreads are unimaginative. Mustard and mayo are long-standing favorites, but why not reach for a spread that's a little more flamboyant, one that has extraordinary character with distinctive flavor?

Instead of the old standards, offer your family and guests spreads that blossom with irresistible charm. Creations like savory Sun-Dried Tomato Tofu Spread (page 172) actually double as a great sandwich filling as well as a spread. On the sweeter side, include Date 'n' Raisin Tofu Spread (page 174) or Bean Butter (page 182) for breakfast or paired with nut butters in a sandwich.

Spanish Tapenade (page 180) and Cashew Mushroom Tapenade (page 181) make ideal party toppings on cocktail breads, pita bread, or crackers. Curry aficionados may gravitate toward Curried Tofu Spread (page 173), while those who favor the richness of cheese can enjoy Cheezy Tofu Spread with Pine Nuts (page 175). Both spreads serve as sandwich fillings.

Hazelnut and Fruit Spread

Yield: about 3½ cups

A HEALTHFUL ALTERNATIVE to sugary jams and jellies, this spread uses nothing processed and delivers flavor and satisfaction without sacrificing nutrition. Use it as a sandwich filling with fruit or tofu cream cheese.

½ cup sunflower seeds

½ cup hazelnuts

1 cup (6 ounces) dried apricots

1⅓ cups plus 1 tablespoon water

30 pitted dates

1 cup golden raisins

¼ cup evaporated cane juice

2 tablespoons freshly squeezed lemon juice

¾ teaspoon ground cinnamon

½ teaspoon almond extract

¼ teaspoon ground allspice

¼ teaspoon ground nutmeg

USING a hand-crank nut grinder or food processor, grind the sunflower seeds and hazelnuts into a coarse meal. Transfer to a medium bowl and set aside.

Combine the apricots and 1 cup of the water in a 2-quart saucepan, cover, and bring to a boil over high heat. Turn the heat down to low and steam for 5 minutes. Cool slightly and transfer the apricots and cooking liquid to the food processor.

Add the remaining water and other ingredients and process until completely smooth. Stop the machine occasionally to scrape down the sides of the work bowl.

Add the ground sunflower seeds and hazelnuts and pulse briefly until they are evenly incorporated. Spoon the spread into an attractive bowl and serve. Stored in a covered container in the refrigerator, Hazelnut and Fruit Spread will keep for up to three weeks.

Hazelnut and Fruit Pinwheels: To create finger food for a party, spread Hazelnut and Fruit Spread on a whole grain tortilla. Top with tofu cream cheese, roll up the tortilla, and slice it to make pinwheels.

Per serving (2 tablespoons): Calories 92, Protein 2g, Fat 3g, Carbohydrate 16g, Vitamin E 1.3mg

Apricot Cashew Butter

Yield: about 1 1/2 cups

DRIED FRUITS are a natural for creating delicious spreads for breakfast toast or to top pancakes and waffles. It takes only twelve minutes to whip up this delightful fruit butter. Treats like this one also make nice homemade gifts to bring to friends who invite you to dinner.

1 cup dried apricots

¾ cup water

¾ cup golden raisins

½ cup cashews

COMBINE the apricots and ½ cup of the water in a 1-quart saucepan. Cover and bring to a boil over high heat. Turn the heat down to low and steam for 10 minutes.

While the apricots are steaming, cover the raisins with warm water and let stand for about 5 minutes, or until they are plump. Drain the raisins and put them into the food processor. Grind the cashews into a fine meal in an electric mini-chopper/grinder or coffee grinder. Add the meal to the food processor.

Transfer the cooked apricots and their liquid to the food processor along with the remaining ¼ cup water. Process until completely smooth. Stored in a covered container in the refrigerator, Apricot Cashew Butter will keep for about two weeks.

Per serving (2 tablespoons): Calories 93, Protein 2g, Fat 3g, Carbohydrate 16g, Vitamin E 0mg

Super Soy Mayonnaise

Yield: 1½ cups

AN IDEAL MAYONNAISE substitute, soy makes a healthier spread that's much lower in fat. Enjoy it as a sandwich spread, a salad dressing, or a luscious dipping sauce for steamed artichokes.

1 (12.3-ounce) box firm silken tofu

½ cup finely ground cashews

1 tablespoon extra-virgin olive oil

1¼ teaspoons salt

1¼ teaspoons freshly squeezed lemon juice

1 garlic clove

COMBINE all the ingredients in the food processor or blender and process until smooth and creamy. Serve immediately or thoroughly chilled. Stored in a covered container in the refrigerator, Super Soy Mayonnaise will keep for one week.

IN ADDITION TO BEING an excellent food source, the cashew nut yields oil used for flavoring and cooking foods. The tree produces a sap or gum sometimes used in bookbinding and often incorporated into a varnish used to protect woodwork from insect damage.

Per serving (2 tablespoons): Calories 63, Protein 3g, Fat 5g, Carbohydrate 3g, Vitamin E .2mg

Miso Mayo

Yield: 2 cups

MAYONNAISE ALWAYS FEELS like such a splurge, with its high-fat and high-calorie content. But this homemade version, heightened with the subtle flavor of white miso, delivers great taste in a very low-fat base of silken tofu. It makes a unique a sandwich spread and adds pizzazz to potato salad.

½ cup coarsely chopped cashews

1 (12-ounce) box soft silken tofu

3 tablespoons freshly squeezed lemon juice

3 tablespoons white miso

1 garlic clove

¼ to ½ teaspoon salt

Freshly ground pepper

Dash cayenne

GRIND the cashews to a fine meal in two batches in an electric mini-chopper/grinder or coffee grinder. Transfer to the food processor.

Add the remaining ingredients and process until smooth and creamy. Serve immediately or thoroughly chilled. Stored in a covered container in the refrigerator, Miso Mayo will keep for one week.

Per serving (2 tablespoons): Calories 47, Protein 3g, Fat 3g, Carbohydrate 3g, Vitamin E 0mg

Sun-Dried Tomato Tofu Spread

Yield: 2 cups

THE DEFINITIVE FLAVOR of sun-dried tomatoes contributes a lively tang to this spread, while the walnuts lend toothy texture. Enjoy this savory spread as a topping for baked potatoes or polenta at dinner, or as a sandwich filling for lunch.

¾ cup sun-dried tomatoes (1.5 ounces)

1 pound firm or extra-firm tofu, rinsed and drained

½ cup coarsely ground walnuts

1 tablespoon white miso

1 teaspoon salt

1 large garlic clove

¼ teaspoon freshly ground pepper

PLACE the sun-dried tomatoes in a heatproof bowl and pour boiling water over them to cover. Let rest for about 5 minutes to soften. Using a slotted spoon, transfer the tomatoes to the food processor.

Add the remaining ingredients and process until almost smooth, leaving small bits of the sun-dried tomatoes for texture. Stop the machine occasionally to scrape down the sides of the work bowl. Spoon the spread into an attractive serving bowl. Serve immediately or thoroughly chilled. Stored in a covered container in the refrigerator, Sun-Dried Tomato Tofu Spread will keep for one week.

IN THE FRENCH countryside, it was tradition to hang a bag of walnuts from the ceiling beam in the kitchen to represent abundance. Walnuts also represented longevity.

Per serving (¼ cup): Calories 108, Protein 7g, Fat 8g, Carbohydrate 6g, Vitamin E 0mg

Curried Tofu Spread

Yield: about 3 cups

CURRY FANCIERS will appreciate this spread that can be quickly prepared in the food processor. It's especially satisfying on dense rye bread, breakfast toast, or party crackers. You can also employ it as a sandwich filling topped with sliced tomatoes, sweet onions, and sliced avocados, all piled on whole grain bread.

½ cup coarsely chopped Brazil nuts

1 pound extra-firm tofu, rinsed and drained

1 tablespoon plus ½ teaspoon rice vinegar

1 tablespoon freshly squeezed lemon juice

2 garlic cloves

1½ teaspoons salt

1½ teaspoons curry powder

¾ teaspoon ground coriander

½ teaspoon turmeric

½ teaspoon onion powder

¼ teaspoon plus ⅛ teaspoon freshly ground pepper

¼ teaspoon dry mustard

PUT the Brazil nuts into the food processor and process to a coarse, chunky meal. Add the remaining ingredients and process until well blended and creamy.

If the mixture seems too dry or crumbly, add 1 to 2 teaspoons of water to moisten. Transfer the spread to an attractive serving bowl. Serve immediately or thoroughly chilled. Stored in a covered container in the refrigerator, Curried Tofu Spread will keep for one week.

Per serving (¼ cup): Calories 71, Protein 4g, Fat 6g, Carbohydrate 2g, Vitamin E 0mg

Date 'n' Raisin Tofu Spread

Yield: 3 cups

IF SOMEONE ASKS how to make tofu taste good, offer some Date 'n' Raisin Tofu Spread. It's a no-fail recipe with exceptional flavor that surprises those new to tofu. Serve it on crackers, mini rice cakes, or whole grain bread.

1 pound extra-firm tofu, rinsed and drained

1 cup pitted dates, cut in half lengthwise

½ cup black raisins

½ cup coarsely ground walnuts

¼ cup water or regular soymilk

4 large dried Calimyrna figs, quartered

Dash salt

Dash ground nutmeg

3 raisins, for garnish

3 tiny mint leaves, for garnish

COMBINE the tofu, dates, ½ cup raisins, walnuts, water, figs, and salt in the food processor, and pulse-chop until the dried fruits are in very small pieces. Continue processing for 1 to 2 minutes, until the mixture turns medium-brown and the consistency is smooth. There should be no white specks of tofu visible.

Transfer to an attractive serving bowl. Sprinkle the top with a dash of nutmeg. Arrange the 3 raisins and the mint leaves in the center. Serve immediately or thoroughly chilled. Stored in a covered container in the refrigerator, Date 'n' Raisin Tofu Spread will keep for two weeks.

Note: Calimyrna figs are generally quite plump, about 1½ inches in diameter; however, if the figs are small, use 8 of them.

Date 'n' Raisin Tofu Pinwheels: To create an easy appetizer, generously spread Date 'n' Raisin Tofu Spread over whole wheat tortillas. Sprinkle finely diced apples over the top and roll up the tortillas tightly. Slice them to make pinwheels and arrange on a platter. Garnish with mint leaves and apple slices.

Per serving (¼ cup): Calories 139, Protein 5g, Fat 5g, Carbohydrate 22g, Vitamin E 0mg

Cheezy Tofu Spread with Pine Nuts

THIS CREAMY SPREAD is adaptive enough to serve at any meal. To prepare an open-faced sandwich for breakfast, spread a generous layer on whole grain bread, top with sliced tomatoes and vegan cheese, and melt it under the broiler. For a lunchtime sandwich, apply the spread generously to two slices of bread and add sliced tomato, onion, cucumber, avocado, lettuce, and sprouts. Include some pungent herbs like basil, arugula, or mint leaves for extra zest. For dinner, use it in place of ricotta for lasagne, stuffed pasta shells, and stuffed eggplant roll-ups.

1 pound extra-firm tofu

½ cup pine nuts

3 tablespoons unsweetened soymilk

2 tablespoons plus 1 teaspoon nutritional yeast flakes

2 teaspoons freshly squeezed lemon juice

1½ teaspoons red miso

1 teaspoon salt

¼ teaspoon freshly ground pepper

COMBINE all the ingredients in the food processor and process until smooth and creamy. Stop the machine occasionally to scrape down the sides of the work bowl. Serve immediately or thoroughly chilled. Stored in a covered container in the refrigerator, Cheezy Tofu Spread with Pine Nuts will keep for one week.

Per serving (¼ cup): Calories 122, Protein 8g, Fat 9g, Carbohydrate 4g, Vitamin E 0mg

Yin-Yang Nutty Bean Spread

Yield: about 4 cups

PREPARE TWO unique, savory spreads and take the Chinese yin-yang approach to an appealing presentation that represents an ideal balance of life's opposites. The macadamia-filled Chunky Cannellini Mac Spread sings a masculine hot, light, and active yang song while the Walnutty Black Bean Spread balances with a feminine cool, dark, and passive yin song. Place them side by side on a dish, forming the traditional yin-yang symbol. And, remember, since nothing is completely yin or yang, form a small spoonful of each spread into a small ball and place it on the opposite color.

Chunky Cannellini Mac Spread

1 (15-ounce) can cannellini beans (white kidney beans), drained

¾ cup macadamia nuts

2 teaspoons seasoned rice vinegar

1 teaspoon freshly squeezed lemon juice

½ teaspoon salt

½ teaspoon dried dill weed

COMBINE all the ingredients in the food processor and process until thick and slightly chunky. Stop the machine occasionally to scrape down the sides of the work bowl.

If you prefer a smoother spread, first process the macadamia nuts into a paste in the food processor. Then add the remaining ingredients and process until smooth.

Transfer to one side of a serving dish and set it aside. Wash and dry the processor work bowl and blade.

(Mac Spread only) Per serving (¼ cup): Calories 154, Protein 5g, Fat 10g, Carbohydrate 13g, Vitamin E .1mg

Walnutty Black Bean Spread

1 (15-ounce) can black beans, rinsed and drained

⅔ cup walnuts

1 tablespoon umeboshi plum vinegar

1 tablespoon water

1 teaspoon ground cumin

½ teaspoon chili powder

⅛ to ¼ teaspoon salt

2 tablespoons dried onion flakes

COMBINE the beans, walnuts, vinegar, water, cumin, chili powder, and salt in the food processor and process until smooth. Stop the machine occasionally to scrape down the sides of the work bowl.

Add the onion flakes and pulse until they are incorporated. Transfer to the serving dish beside the Chunky Cannellini Mac Spread and form the two spreads into the yin-yang symbol. Covered with plastic wrap and stored in the refrigerator, leftover Yin-Yang Nutty Bean Spread will keep for about one week.

Note: If there is a fair amount of leftover spread, you may want to reshape the yin-yang symbol on the dish prior to storing it.

IN PAST CENTURIES people discovered that all parts of the walnut could be processed to create colors and dyes. Furniture makers and finishers used the husks to create a rich walnut stain. Women developed a beauty secret to enhance their appearance: a hair dye made from the walnut hulls. Scribes made their brown ink from walnut hulls. Since prehistoric times, weavers extracted a rich dark brown dye from walnut juice, while they used the green husks to make a yellow dye. They also boiled the bark to extract a deep brown dye used for coloring wool.

(Black Bean Spread only) Per serving: Calories 110, Protein 5g, Fat 6g, Carbohydrate 11g, Vitamin E 0mg

Savory Fava Bean Spread

Yield: about 6 to 8 servings

NOT ONLY IS THIS RECIPE a flavorful spread, it also makes a delightful dip. For a hearty sandwich filling, layer it with tomatoes, onions, avocados, and sprouts.

1 (1-pound) can fava beans, drained (reserve the liquid)

½ cup coarsely ground pistachios

2 tablespoons extra-virgin olive oil

1 to 2 tablespoons freshly squeezed lemon or lime juice

1 large clove garlic

½ teaspoon salt

¼ teaspoon ground cumin

⅓ cup finely chopped onions

COMBINE the beans, 1 tablespoon of the bean liquid, pistachios, olive oil, lemon juice, garlic, salt, and cumin in the food processor and process until smooth.

Transfer to an attractive serving bowl, stir in the onions, and serve. Stored in a covered container in the refrigerator, Savory Fava Bean Spread will keep for about one week.

Note: If you plan to serve the spread at the table as part of a build-it-yourself meal, dampen a paper napkin slightly and wipe the edges of the bowl to create a fresh appearance. Then sprinkle the top with 1 tablespoon coarsely chopped pistachios and a dash of paprika.

Per serving: Calories 144, Protein 6g, Fat 9g, Carbohydrate 12g, Vitamin E .8mg

Hazelnut and Garbanzo Spread

Yield: about 2 cups

HAVING A REPERTOIRE of easy spreads pays off when you need a quick appetizer or canapé base. Spreads this wholesome also make great sandwich fillings.

½ ripe avocado, diced

2 green onions (white part only), minced

1 (1-pound) can garbanzo beans, drained (reserve the liquid)

½ cup hazelnut meal

5 tablespoons garbanzo liquid

1 tablespoon Dijon mustard

1 tablespoon freshly squeezed lime juice

¾ teaspoon salt

¼ teaspoon cayenne

PLACE the diced avocado and green onions into a medium bowl and set them aside.

Combine the remaining ingredients in the food processor and process until thick and smooth. Using a spatula, transfer the spread to the bowl with the avocado, and gently mix until the avocado and green onions are evenly distributed. Spoon into an attractive serving dish and enjoy.

Eggplant Cornucopias: These make an extraordinary starter to offer guests. Preheat the oven to 375 degrees. Slice 2 eggplants into rounds, place them on a baking sheet, and brush them with oil. Roast the eggplant slices for 25 to 30 minutes. Place 1 tablespoon of Hazelnut and Garbanzo Spread in the center of each slice, pinch the bottom together, and secure it with a toothpick.

Per serving (¼ cup): Calories 165, Protein 5g, Fat 10g, Carbohydrate 16g, Vitamin E 2mg

Spanish Tapenade

Yield: about 3 cups

IDEAL PARTY FARE, this easy-to-make chunky relish draws its assertive nature from pimiento-stuffed green olives. Adding flavor balance, pine nuts and Roma tomatoes tame the relish and give it perky colors. Serve the relish with little rounds of toasted rye bread, or spoon it over polenta or baked potatoes.

1 pound ripe Roma tomatoes

¾ cup pimiento-stuffed green olives, well drained

¾ cup pitted black olives, well drained

3 green onions, chopped

½ cup pine nuts

2 tablespoons extra-virgin olive oil

¼ teaspoon plus ⅛ teaspoon salt

⅛ teaspoon freshly ground pepper

CUT the tomatoes in half and seed them. Coarsely chop the tomatoes and put them into the food processor.

Add the remaining ingredients and pulse-chop to a coarse, chunky purée. Transfer to an attractive serving bowl. Serve immediately or thoroughly chilled. Stored in a covered container in the refrigerator, Spanish Tapenade will keep for one week.

Per serving (¼ cup): Calories 93, Protein 1g, Fat 9g, Carbohydrate 4g, Vitamin E 0mg

Cashew Mushroom Tapenade

Yield: about 2 cups

FOR THOSE WHO SHUN lengthy kitchen preps, this recipe is ideal. Just marinate, process, and serve the spread in eight different ways. Present the tapenade as an appetizer wrapped in a lettuce or napa cabbage leaf. Prepare it as a canapé by spreading it on whole grain crackers and topping with sliced green olives. Serve the tapenade over steamed brown rice. Enjoy the spread as a sandwich filling with sliced tomatoes and romaine lettuce. Serve it as a pâté on toasted pita bread or crackers. Use it as a filling for stuffed tomatoes. Spread the tapenade over polenta squares, top with thinly sliced tomatoes, and heat under the broiler. Spoon it over baked potatoes.

1 pound portobello mushrooms, coarsely chopped (about 4 giant mushrooms)

¼ cup soy sauce

¼ cup apple cider vinegar

¼ to ⅓ cup water

½ pound coarsely chopped cashews

PUT the mushrooms into a large, deep bowl. Add the soy sauce, vinegar, and enough water to create a marinade. Cover and marinate at room temperature for 2 hours, stirring occasionally.

While the mushrooms are marinating, grind the cashews into a fine meal in the food processor. Leave them in the processor.

Using a slotted spoon, remove the mushrooms from the marinade and add them to the cashews in the food processor. Pulse-chop until the mushrooms are well minced and the mixture is creamy.

Note: Button or cremini mushrooms can be substituted if portobello mushrooms are unavailable. However, portobello mushrooms lend a more pungent flavor and deeper color.

Per serving (¼ cup): Calories 39, Protein 3g, Fat 2g, Carbohydrate 4g, Vitamin E 0mg

Bean Butter

COMBINING UNLIKELY INGREDIENTS often turns up pleasing results. Blending beans, dates, and pecans provides the base for a delectable spread that goes especially well with earthy breads like rye, whole wheat, or multigrain. For an ideal snack to serve the kids, spread Bean Butter on two slices of bread, then slip sliced bananas or thinly sliced apples in between to make a tasty, quick-fix sandwich.

1 (15-ounce) can pinto beans, rinsed and drained

15 pitted dates

1/2 cup coarsely chopped pecans

1/4 cup plus 2 tablespoons water, as needed

COMBINE all the ingredients in the food processor and process until thick and smooth. Stop the machine occasionally to scrape down the sides of the work bowl and redistribute the ingredients. Add more water, 1 tablespoon at a time, for a creamier, softer consistency. For a sweeter spread, add more dates.

MANY OF THE NATION'S beloved pecan dishes—including pralines, sticky buns, candied pecans, fruitcake, pecan tarts, sweet potatoes or grits with pecans, and pecan stuffing for meat dishes—originated in the southern regions of the United States. Not to be overlooked is butter pecan ice cream, a favorite treat that Texas is proud to claim as its own.

Per serving (1/4 cup): Calories 92, Protein 2g, Fat 4g, Carbohydrate 14g, Vitamin E .4mg

Smoothies and Beverages

With one sip, they pave the way to solving most of life's troubles. They fill a void in life—actually, more than one void. Think of a hot summer day, sometime between lunch and late dinner. A heavy meal is unimaginable, but a little something cooling would feel perfectly refreshing. Got to have a smoothie! Problem solved. Many more troubles could disappear just as quickly with a blender and a great smoothie recipe.

Another compliment goes to smoothies for their great portability. Because you don't have to be chained to a dish with a knife and fork, you can enjoy your smoothie at the computer while reading your e-mail. Sip your fluffy refresher while soaking in the tub or chatting on the phone.

Smoothies are quick and simple. If you need an excellent justification to make a smoothie, think good health. Because smoothies are made with fresh fruits, and a base of soy, nuts, or juices, they provide plenty of energy, fiber, and loads of phytochemicals.

For a dreamy summer treat, freshen up with Maui Sunset Cooler (page 187), made with fresh ripe mango and flavored with pineapple and lime juice.

Turn to Almond Milk (page 189) for a pleasantly light beverage to serve with hot or cold cereal. Though soymilk is more familiar, the rich, creamy flavor and silky mouthfeel of Almond Milk is a welcome change.

Sometimes magical moments come in the form of relaxing hot beverages like warming Hot Peanut Butter Chocolate (page 188). Cool evenings make one seek the comfort of a steamy beverage.

Banana Date Smoothie

Yield: about 3 cups
(2 to 3 servings)

WITH NUTRITIOUS INGREDIENTS like cashews, bananas, and soy, a smoothie can quickly restore vigor and even take the place of a light meal. In summer, when a cool, refreshing beverage is so welcome, make the smoothie a few hours ahead and allow it to chill.

1 (12.3-ounce) box extra-firm lite silken tofu

1¼ cups regular soymilk

1 ripe banana, cut into chunks

10 pitted dates

⅔ cup coarsely chopped cashews

2 tablespoons maple syrup

¼ teaspoon vanilla extract

COMBINE all the ingredients in the blender and blend on high speed for 1 to 2 minutes, until smooth and creamy. Pour into tall glasses and serve with straws.

THE CASHEW NUTSHELL contains an oil used for waterproofing and as an adhesive. Natives in South America applied cashew nutshell oil in the treatment of skin ailments. The oil is found to have potent antibacterial properties. Not many plants can claim to provide so many benefits.

Per serving: Calories 544, Protein 23g, Fat 24g, Carbohydrate 68g, Vitamin E .4mg

Mango Macadamia Smoothie

Yield: 2 servings

HERE'S A PERFECT energy booster for a midday treat or a friendly late-night snack that's so thick and creamy you can devour it with a spoon. The spoons of choice are iced tea spoons, the ones with the extra-long handles, so you can reach the bottom of a tall glass to get every drop.

1 large ripe mango

½ cup regular soymilk

¼ (12.3-ounce) box extra-firm silken tofu (one 1-inch-thick slice)

½ cup macadamia nuts

3 tablespoons maple syrup

¼ teaspoon vanilla extract

⅛ teaspoon coconut extract

Dash ground cinnamon

COMBINE the mango, soymilk, tofu, macadamia nuts, maple syrup, vanilla extract, and coconut extract in the blender. Process on low speed for a few seconds. Gradually increase to high speed and blend for 1 to 2 minutes, until smooth and creamy. Pour into tall glasses and sprinkle with a dash of cinnamon.

IN SUMMER, when mangoes are in season at reasonable prices, buy several at a time. Keep them at room temperature until the flesh gives slightly when gently squeezed, and then refrigerate them.

Per serving: Calories 524, Protein 20g, Fat 30g, Carbohydrate 50g, Vitamin E .2mg

Banana Walnut Breakfast Smoothie

Yield: 2 (10-ounce) servings

A DELIGHTFUL DEPARTURE from the typical bowl of cereal for breakfast, this smoothie offers fruity flavors in a creamy base of silken tofu. To complete your breakfast, serve it with whole grain toast and a delectable fruit butter, such as Date 'n' Raisin Tofu Spread (page 174), or your favorite nut butter.

3 ripe bananas, cut into large chunks

⅓ cup walnuts

¼ teaspoon vanilla extract

1 (12-ounce) box soft silken tofu

2 tablespoons hulled sesame seeds

COMBINE the bananas, walnuts, and vanilla extract in the blender. Blend on low speed for 1 to 2 minutes, until smooth. Stop the machine occasionally to scrape down the sides of the blender jar and redistribute the ingredients.

Add the tofu and sesame seeds and blend for 1 to 2 minutes longer, until smooth and creamy. Serve immediately or thoroughly chilled.

THE ROMANS associated the walnut with Juno, the Roman goddess of women and marriage, and the wife of Jupiter. This association led to the unique wedding practice of throwing walnuts at the bride and groom as a symbol of fertility. Women often carried walnuts to promote fertility.

Per serving: Calories 374, Protein 13g, Fat 18g, Carbohydrate 46g, Vitamin E .3mg

Maui Sunset Cooler

IT'S COOL to go tropical. Toss some cashews, pineapple juice, bananas, and mango into the blender, add a splash of lime juice, and enjoy a tangy taste of Hawaiian paradise. When planning a dinner party, serve this refreshing beverage as a predinner starter along with an appetizer.

½ cup cashews

2 cups unsweetened pineapple juice

2 large ripe bananas

1¾ cups ice cubes

1 ripe mango

3 tablespoons maple syrup

2 tablespoons freshly squeezed lime juice

1 teaspoon vanilla extract

GRIND the cashews into a fine meal in an electric mini-chopper/grinder or coffee grinder.

Combine the remaining ingredients in the blender and blend on high speed for a few seconds. Add the cashews and blend until smooth and creamy.

Per serving: Calories 581, Protein 10g, Fat 17g, Carbohydrate 106g, Vitamin E .5mg

Hot Peanut Butter Chocolate

Yield: 2 servings

WHEN THE WINTER shivers send you on a quest for something soothing, turn to a cup of hot chocolate to bring warmth and comfort. This version, with the addition of creamy peanut butter, gives the traditional beverage a unique, tantalizing twist.

2 cups regular soymilk

3 tablespoons evaporated cane juice

2 rounded teaspoons unsweetened cocoa powder

½ teaspoon vanilla extract

3 heaping tablespoons unsalted creamy peanut butter

COMBINE the soymilk, evaporated cane juice, cocoa powder, and vanilla extract in a 2-quart saucepan. Warm over medium-high heat, stirring vigorously with a wire whip to incorporate the cocoa powder.

Add the peanut butter and stir with the wire whip to thoroughly incorporate it. Heat to the desired temperature, pour into mugs, and enjoy.

WOULD YOU BE SURPRISED to learn the peanut is actually a bean, and an odd one at that? While most of the beans in the legume family grow in pods on sprawling, climbing vines, the peanut plant is a singular bush that matures its pods underground.

Per serving: Calories 285, Protein 15g, Fat 11g, Carbohydrate 31g, Vitamin E 0mg

Almond Milk

Yield: 2½ cups

WHILE SOYMILK and rice milk are familiar beverages that have become vegetarian household staples, nut milk beverages offer nutritious alternatives. You'll be delighted to discover how easy they are to make.

½ cup whole almonds, unsoaked, soaked, or blanched

2½ cups water

2 pitted dates

Dash salt

IF USING unsoaked almonds, grind them into a fine meal in an electric mini-chopper/grinder or coffee grinder. Transfer to the blender and add the water, dates, and salt. If the almonds are soaked or blanched, they do not need to be ground and can be put directly into the blender with the water, dates, and salt.

Start the blender on low speed for a few seconds; then switch to high speed and process until creamy.

Strain through a fine mesh strainer to remove the almond pulp, and set the pulp aside (see notes). Stored in a covered container in the refrigerator, Almond Milk will keep for two to three days.

Notes: Almond Milk makes a thick, creamy milk that is ideal for Blancmange (page 228). For other purposes, thin the Almond Milk with water to achieve the desired consistency. To make sweeter Almond Milk, simply add more dates or a little light brown sugar, agave nectar, or maple syrup to taste.

• To use the pulp, combine it with 1 teaspoon evaporated cane juice and ¼ teaspoon almond extract. Mix well and use it as a topping over puddings, cereals, fruit salads, or desserts. Stored in a tightly covered container in the refrigerator, almond pulp will keep for up to four days.

Thick Almond Cream: Reduce the water to 1 cup and proceed as directed.

Per serving (1 cup): Calories 194, Protein 7g, Fat 15g, Carbohydrate 11g, Vitamin E 7.5mg

Making Nut Milks

To make nut milk, you do not have to soak the nuts beforehand, but many cooks prefer soaking because it enhances the digestibility of the nuts. To soak the nuts overnight, put them into a bowl or jar with water to cover by one inch, and discard the water in the morning or use it to water your houseplants.

For making almond milk, you may choose to blanch the nuts or use them whole. Blanching the nuts will result in a pure white nut milk, while nut milk made from whole almonds contains tiny flecks of brown skin.

The basic recipe for Almond Milk (page 189) is essentially the same as for making cashew, pistachio, walnut, hazelnut, Brazil nut, pine nut, macadamia nut, and pecan milk with some exceptions. The almonds do not break down completely and leave a fair amount of pulp that must be strained off. The other variable is that each kind of nut may produce a tasty nut milk with differing quantities of water. Experiment by starting with the basic recipe for Almond Milk, and increase or reduce the water to suit your taste or needs.

Using Nut Milks

Creamy and highly nutritious, nut milk adds a wonderfully rich dimension to your breakfast when poured over hot or cold cereal. Each nut variety offers its own unique flavor, adding much diversity.

Use nut milk for creating delicious sauces as well. A baked potato, for instance, is instantly enhanced with a cashew or pistachio milk sauce. Turn simple steamed vegetables into an exquisite dish with a creamy nut milk sauce heightened with herbs and spices.

Nut milks also work well to provide the base for a fruit smoothie or for thinning a shake that seems too thick to go through a straw. On cold winter nights, serve a warming mug of nut milk sweetened with evaporated cane juice and laced with cinnamon and vanilla.

Flavor your nut milks with all kinds of extracts from coconut to maple, and add sweet spices like cinnamon, allspice, ginger, nutmeg, cardamom, or star anise to create your own unique beverage.

Sweetened nut milk also complements baked apples, rice pudding, and frozen desserts. Thickened by simply reducing the amount of water added, creamy nut milk sauces pair perfectly with most fruity desserts. Have fun inventing new ways to enjoy this nutty beverage.

Desserts and Confections

FOR THOSE SPECIAL HOLIDAYS OR CELEBRATIONS,
bring on the sweets and have a nut-cracking good time. Mark the occasion with a captivating nutty dessert that will send the honored guests begging for seconds of tantalizers like Apple Date-Nut Pie (page 194) or Peanut Butter Carob Pie (page 192). A little extra time spent preparing these treats pays off in compliments and expressions of appreciation.

While you may not plan to include a dessert with every meal or even every day, you can give yourself permission to go nutty and choose a sweet finish when the occasional craving beckons. This section offers many quick and easy-to-make fruit parfaits that can be adapted to almost any season by varying the fruits available during that time of year.

These recipes are uniquely original—you won't find them in other cookbooks or on bakery shelves. None of the desserts contain dairy products, yet they employ ingredients that achieve the same creamy, rich, delectable results that leave a trail of happy dessert fanciers.

Peanut Butter Carob Pie

Yield: 6 to 8 servings

1 Nutty Wheat Pie Crust (page 200), baked, or 1 Nutty No-Bake Pie Crust (page 201)

1 large ripe banana, sliced

¼ cup carob chips or dairy-free semisweet chocolate chips

1 (12.3-ounce) box extra-firm silken tofu

¾ cup unsalted creamy peanut butter

⅓ cup evaporated cane juice

2 tablespoons maple syrup

2 teaspoons vanilla extract

1 (1-ounce) square dairy-free semisweet chocolate, or 2 heaping tablespoons chocolate chips

1 teaspoon water

½ teaspoon organic canola oil

PEANUT BUTTER SATISFIES in so many ways. Even a tablespoon or two infuses sauces, dressings, soups, and beverages with exceptional flavor. But a sensational, sweet, and chocolaty peanut butter dessert stirs the passions. Here's a no-bake treat that can be prepared a day in advance and even keeps well for a day or two after serving.

ARRANGE the banana slices in one layer along the bottom of the prepared crust, and sprinkle the carob chips over the bananas.

Combine the silken tofu, peanut butter, evaporated cane juice, maple syrup, and vanilla extract in the food processor and process until smooth and creamy. Pour over the carob chips and smooth the top with the back of a spoon.

Place the chocolate, water, and canola oil in a 1-quart saucepan. Warm over the lowest heat, stirring continuously, until the chocolate melts and the sauce is well blended.

Decorate the top of the pie with long zigzag lines by pouring the melted chocolate from the tip of a pointed teaspoon. Chill the pie in the refrigerator for 8 to 12 hours before serving.

PEANUTS ARE SO NUTRITIOUS that performer/producer Billy Rose survived on one five-cent bag of peanuts a day for three days when all he had to live on was fifteen cents.

Per serving (with No-Bake Crust): Calories 599, Protein 20g, Fat 33g, Carbohydrate 65g, Vitamin E 8.5mg

Peanut Butter Carob Pie

Cranberry Walnut Pie

TOSS SHOWY RED CRANBERRIES, walnuts, and raisins into a pie crust and the result is a stunning dessert that features a zippy sweet-and-tart flavor. This tantalizing treat is an ideal, easy-to-prepare, make-ahead holiday dessert. When cranberries come to market in late October or early November, buy several packages and enjoy combining them with sweet or dried fruits to temper their tartness.

1 cup walnuts, coarsely ground

1 (12-ounce) package fresh cranberries

½ cup golden raisins

½ cup evaporated cane juice

½ cup light brown sugar

½ teaspoon almond extract

3 tablespoons cornstarch

2 tablespoons freshly squeezed lemon juice

2 tablespoons water

1 Nutty Wheat Pie Crust (page 200), unbaked

PREHEAT the oven to 425 degrees. Put the walnuts into a large mixing bowl and set aside.

Sort the cranberries and discard any spoiled ones. Wash the cranberries in a strainer and drain them well.

Place 1 cup of the cranberries into the food processor and pulse-chop them coarsely. Transfer them to the bowl with the walnuts and add the remaining whole cranberries. Add the raisins, evaporated cane juice, brown sugar, and almond extract and toss well.

Combine the cornstarch, lemon juice, and water in a small bowl or cup, and stir to make a runny paste. Add it to the cranberry mixture and stir thoroughly.

Spoon the filling into the prepared pie crust and bake for 20 minutes. Turn the heat down to 350 degrees and bake for 30 minutes longer. Cool about 30 minutes. Serve warm, or cool completely and refrigerate until ready to serve.

Per serving: Calories 585, Protein 13g, Fat 30g, Carbohydrate 73g, Vitamin E 3.7mg

Pistachio Peanut Bonbons (left), page 206

Sticky Gooey Caramel Nuts (right), page 203

Apple Date-Nut Pie

THIS UNIQUE and unforgettably delicious no-bake apple pie is a compliment catcher that highlights almonds, walnuts, and pecans. Begin with a layer of cinnamon-spiced apples and add a decadent fluff of light, creamy, and nutty topping. Finish with a garnish of pecans, and dessert becomes an irresistible pièce de résistance.

Creamy Topping

½ cup (4.5 ounces) extra-firm silken tofu

⅓ cup plus 1 tablespoon freshly squeezed orange juice

¼ cup maple syrup

¼ teaspoon plus ⅛ teaspoon ground cinnamon

1 cup plus 2 tablespoons coarsely chopped walnuts

TO MAKE the topping, blend the tofu, orange juice, maple syrup, and cinnamon in the food processor. Add the walnuts and process until thick and creamy. Set aside.

TO MAKE the filling, combine the apples, prunes, ¼ cup of the water, 4 tablespoons of the maple syrup, and cinnamon in a 4-quart saucepan. Cover and bring to a boil over high heat. Turn the heat down to low and steam for 10 to 12 minutes, or until the apples are fork-tender and there is still a little liquid left in the saucepan. Add 1 to 2 tablespoons of the maple syrup or water, if needed, to provide about 2 tablespoons of liquid as a base for a sauce.

Combine the cornstarch with 3 tablespoons of the water to form a runny paste. When the apples are soft, return them to a boil and add the cornstarch mixture, a little at a time, stirring constantly for 1 to 2 minutes, until the sauce has thickened and clings to the apples.

Filling

4 or 5 large, crisp, sweet apples (such as Fuji), cored, peeled, and thinly sliced

13 pitted prunes, chopped

¼ to ½ cup water, as needed

4 to 6 tablespoons maple syrup

½ teaspoon ground cinnamon, plus more for garnish

3 tablespoons cornstarch

6 to 8 pecan halves

Crust

1 Nutty No-Bake Pie Crust (page 201)

Spoon the apples into the prepared crust and spread them to the edges. Then spoon the topping over the apple mixture, leaving a 1-inch border of apples exposed.

Decorate the top with the pecan halves, sprinkle lightly with cinnamon, and refrigerate for 8 to 12 hours before serving.

Note: For convenience, prepare the pie a day ahead, cover it lightly, and refrigerate.

TOWARD THE END of the seventeenth century, walnuts, along with chestnuts, became important staples in France. During the famine of 1663, the poor consumed their walnuts and then resorted to grinding up the shells along with acorns to create coarse, unpalatable bread.

Per serving: Calories 603, Protein 13g, Fat 30g, Carbohydrate 82g, Vitamin E 8.5mg

Totally Nutty Nougat Pie

1 Nutty Wheat Pie Crust
(page 200), unbaked

1 1/4 cups coarsely
broken mixed nuts

1 1/2 cups dark
corn syrup

1/2 cup dark brown
sugar, packed

1/2 cup tapioca flour
(see note next page)

2 tablespoons (1 ounce)
dairy-free margarine

1 teaspoon
vanilla extract

1 teaspoon imitation
black walnut extract

1/2 cup water

1/4 cup whole flaxseeds

1 1/2 cups mixed raw or
dry-roasted nuts (whole,
halves, or coarsely
broken pieces)

SIX KINDS OF NUTS jumped into my lap one day and begged to be baked into a pie. The result was a unique, firm, nougat-like filling embedded with toasted almonds, cashews, hazelnuts, pecans, pine nuts, and walnuts. One secret to binding the filling and giving the pie a beautiful glaze is stirring tapioca flour into the sweeteners and caramelizing the mixture before baking. The other is a thickened blend of flaxseeds and water. Refrigerating the cooled pie tempers it into its finished form. Because this dessert is super rich, cut it into small servings.

PREHEAT the oven to 425 degrees. Toast the 1 1/4 cups coarsely broken nuts in a nonstick skillet over high heat for 1 to 2 minutes, stirring continuously. Pour into a dish to cool. Spread the cooled pieces over the bottom of the pie crust.

To make the filling, combine the corn syrup, brown sugar, tapioca flour, margarine, vanilla extract, and imitation black walnut extract in a 4-quart saucepan and stir until the tapioca flour is completely incorporated. Set aside for 5 minutes to allow the tapioca flour to absorb some of the liquid. Bring to a boil over high heat, turn the heat down slightly to medium-high, and boil for 5 minutes to caramelize the sugars and thicken the mixture slightly.

While the filling is boiling, place the water and flaxseeds into the blender and process on low speed for a few seconds. Stop the machine to scrape down the sides of the blender jar, then continue blending for 1 to 2 minutes, until thick and viscous (the consistency will be similar to thick oatmeal).

Add the flaxseed mixture to the boiled filling and stir with a wire whip to combine thoroughly. Pour over the broken nuts in the crust, and arrange the 1½ cups raw or dry-roasted nuts over the top, covering the surface completely.

Place the pie on a baking sheet to catch any drips, and bake for 10 minutes. Turn the heat down to 325 degrees and bake for 30 minutes longer. Carefully remove the pie from the oven and allow it to cool completely. The filling will seem somewhat loose at first, but it will solidify as it cools. Once cool, place the pie in the refrigerator. The filling will firm completely once it is thoroughly chilled.

Note: Tapioca flour can be found in most natural food markets.

Per serving: Calories 785, Protein 14g, Fat 37g, Carbohydrate 109g, Vitamin E 3mg

Down-Home Pecan Pie

Yield: 1 (9-inch) pie

BECAUSE PECANS are native to the American South, they frequently turn up as pecan pie on Southern dessert menus. This version has all the eye-appealing and flavorful attributes of its traditional counterpart with the added benefit of being egg free. Taking the place of the eggs is a combination of tapioca flour and flaxseeds that gives the pie its unique, creamy texture. Tapioca flour performs the double duty of thickening the filling as well as providing an inviting glaze. Create a love-at-first-glance dessert by taking the time to sort out beautiful pecan halves for the topping and then arranging them side by side in concentric rings.

1 Nutty Wheat Pie Crust (page 200), unbaked

1¼ cups coarsely broken pecans

2 tablespoons (1 ounce) dairy-free margarine

1½ cups dark corn syrup

½ cup dark brown sugar

2 teaspoons vanilla extract

½ cup regular soymilk

½ cup tapioca flour, packed

PREHEAT the oven to 350 degrees and have ready a large baking sheet. Bake the Nutty Wheat Pie Crust for 5 minutes and set it aside on the baking sheet to cool.

Place the coarsely broken pecans in a nonstick skillet and toast them over high heat, stirring constantly, for 1 to 2 minutes, until fragrant. Watch carefully to avoid over-toasting or burning them. Pour the toasted pecans immediately into a dish to cool. When cool, spoon them into the bottom of the pie shell.

Melt the margarine over medium heat in a 2-quart saucepan. Add the corn syrup, brown sugar, and vanilla extract and bring to a full boil over medium heat, stirring frequently. Boil 5 minutes, then set aside to cool for about 30 minutes.

Place the soymilk in a bowl and stir in the tapioca flour. Set it aside for 5 minutes to allow the tapioca flour to absorb some of the liquid.

5 tablespoons whole flaxseeds

1¼ cups pecan halves

Meanwhile, place the flaxseeds in a small electric coffee grinder or mini-chopper/grinder and grind them to a fine meal. Add the flaxseeds and the soymilk mixture to the cooled corn syrup mixture. Stir to combine, and pour the mixture into the blender. Blend for 1 minute, until smooth. Pour over the toasted pecans.

Top the pie with the pecan halves, arranging them in concentric circles. Bake for 40 minutes. Cool thoroughly, then chill in the refrigerator. The pie will firm after it is thoroughly chilled.

Working with Flaxseeds

Flaxseeds processed in the blender with water can serve as a thickener and binder in baked goods. Because of their viscous nature, flaxseeds ground with water tend to cling to the blender, if allowed to dry. To ease the cleanup, fill the blender with water as soon as you remove the flaxseed mixture and allow it to soak for a few minutes before washing it.

Per serving: Calories 811, Protein 14g, Fat 41g, Carbohydrate 108g, Vitamin E 4mg

Nutty Wheat Pie Crust

Yield: 1 (9-inch) crust

CLASSIC RECIPES for pie crust can be a bit persnickety and have discouraged many from making pies. This easy, no-fail recipe is one you can always count on because it's very forgiving. If it breaks, simply patch it. When forming the edges, take your time sculpting it any way you like. You'll find the extra handling won't affect its pleasing, light texture one bit.

1½ cups whole wheat pastry flour

½ cup almond meal

2 tablespoons evaporated cane juice

½ teaspoon salt

½ cup organic canola oil

2 tablespoons cold water

COMBINE the pastry flour, almond meal, evaporated cane juice, and salt in a medium mixing bowl and mix well.

Add the canola oil and mix with a spoon until all the flour is incorporated. Add the water and stir thoroughly until the mixture forms a soft dough and all the water is absorbed.

Form the dough into a ball and roll it out between two sheets of waxed paper. Remove the top sheet of waxed paper, place the pie pan over the dough, and invert the dough and pan together. The remaining sheet of waxed paper will now be on top of the crust. Remove it carefully and trim the edges of the crust with a knife.

Set the crust aside while preparing the pie filling for a baked pie. For a no-bake pie, bake the crust in a preheated 350 degree oven for 10 minutes. Cool before filling.

Note: To use this recipe for a savory pie, such as a quiche or vegetable pie, omit the evaporated cane juice.

Per serving: Calories 305, Protein 10g, Fat 19g, Carbohydrate 26g, Vitamin E 3mg

Nutty No-Bake Pie Crust

Yield: 1 (9-inch) crust

FOR PIES that require no baking, rely on this recipe for a pie crust that magically comes together with only three ingredients. This crust plays a dual role. In addition to creating a base for a pie filling, it actually contributes nutty texture, flavor, and sweetness to the pie.

1 ½ cups whole almonds

1 ½ cups pitted dates, chopped

1 to 4 tablespoons water

GRIND the almonds into a fine but not powdery meal in the food processor. Add the dates and enough water to form a dough that holds together when pressed. Stop the machine occasionally to scrape down the sides of the work bowl and redistribute the ingredients. Press the mixture into the bottom and sides of a 9-inch pie pan.

AN EARLY EUROPEAN tradition of wrapping sugarcoated almonds in sheer netting and presenting them to wedding guests symbolized fertility, happiness, romance, good health, and fortune. Today we still carry on this tradition with white sugarcoated almonds sheathed in netting as a familiar wedding favor.

Per serving: Calories 292, Protein 8g, Fat 17g, Carbohydrate 34g, Vitamin E 8.4mg

Sugarplum Spiced Walnuts

Yield: 3½ cups

½ cup powdered sugar

2 teaspoons ground allspice

2 teaspoons ground cardamom

2 teaspoons ground cinnamon

2 teaspoons ground cloves

2 teaspoons ground ginger

2 teaspoons ground nutmeg

¼ teaspoon cayenne

¼ teaspoon salt

1 tablespoon organic canola oil

⅓ cup evaporated cane juice

¾ cup apple juice

3 cups coarsely chopped walnuts

AN IDEAL GIFT for special friends at holiday time, or simply an extra-special treat to serve on a dessert table, these nutty delights can be made well in advance of the holiday rush. They're good keepers if you store them in airtight containers. The success of this recipe depends on measuring all ingredients in advance. It actually comes together quickly once you have everything ready.

PLACE the powdered sugar in a medium bowl and set it aside.

To make the spice mixture, combine the allspice, cardamom, cinnamon, cloves, ginger, nutmeg, cayenne, and salt in a small bowl or cup. Stir the mixture well and set it aside near the stove.

To make the coating, pour the canola oil into a large nonstick skillet. Place the evaporated cane juice, apple juice, and walnuts in separate cups or bowls and set them aside near the skillet. Now you're ready to begin.

Heat the canola oil over high heat for about 1 minute. Add the evaporated cane juice and stir another minute until hot and bubbly. Pour in the apple juice and stir constantly for about 1 minute, until the sugar is completely dissolved.

Quickly stir in the walnuts and continue stirring over high heat until all the liquid evaporates and the mixture becomes sticky and shiny. Cook for 1 to 2 minutes longer, or until all the liquid is absorbed.

Sprinkle in 2 tablespoons of the spice mixture and toss to coat the walnuts, stirring for 1 minute. Turn off the heat and add the remaining spice mixture, tossing continuously.

Pour the spiced walnuts into the bowl with the powdered sugar and toss to give them a white dusting. Spread the walnuts in a single layer on a large dish or baking sheet to cool completely. Stored in an airtight container at room temperature, Sugarplum Spiced Walnuts will keep for up to one month.

Per serving (¼ cup): Calories 208, Protein 4g, Fat 17g, Carbohydrate 13g, Vitamin E .2mg

Sticky Gooey Caramel Nuts

Yield: about 1½ cups

See photo facing page 193.

LET THE FAMILY enjoy these nutty, easy-to-make confections that are really too sticky to serve to guests. Like potato chips, they're so addictive it's hard to stop at just one. Storage is rarely a problem—the recipe makes a small quantity that will disappear quickly.

⅓ cup whole almonds

⅓ cup pecan halves

⅓ cup coarsely chopped walnuts

¼ cup evaporated cane juice

3 tablespoons light brown sugar

¼ teaspoon salt

2 tablespoons light corn syrup

COMBINE the almonds, pecans, and walnuts in a small bowl or cup and set them aside close to the stove. Place the evaporated cane juice, brown sugar, and salt in a 10-inch nonstick skillet and mix well until evenly combined. Add the corn syrup and turn the heat to medium-high.

When the mixture begins to bubble, about 1 minute, stir well for 1 to 2 minutes to combine the corn syrup and completely dissolve the sugars.

Add the reserved nuts and stir constantly for 1 to 2 minutes, until all the liquid is absorbed and the nuts are well coated. Transfer to a clean dish. When the nuts are cool enough to handle, separate the clumps, and allow them to dry for several hours. They will still retain their sticky surface, and you'll have to pry them off the dish. But that's half the fun.

Per serving (¼ cup): Calories 199, Protein 3g, Fat 12g, Carbohydrate 22g, Vitamin E 2.3mg

Chili Nuts

Yield: about 1½ cups

THESE ARE FOR spice enthusiasts who can't get enough of the lively heat that chiles dish out. The recipe's medium heat level makes the nuts quite tolerable even for the chile shy.

1 cup mixed nuts (such as walnuts, pecans, and almonds)

¼ cup evaporated cane juice

2 tablespoons light corn syrup

1 teaspoon cayenne

½ teaspoon ground ginger

½ teaspoon freshly ground pepper

¼ teaspoon salt

¼ teaspoon chili powder

COMBINE the nuts in a small bowl and set them aside near the stove.

Combine the remaining ingredients in a 10-inch nonstick skillet. Turn the heat to medium-high and cook, stirring constantly, until the spices are well incorporated.

Add the nuts and cook, stirring constantly, for 1 to 2 minutes, until they are well coated and the mixture sticks to them.

Transfer to a clean dish to cool. Separate the nuts when they are cool enough to handle. You can enjoy them while still quite warm, but the flavor will improve when they have cooled completely.

Per serving (¼ cup): Calories 181, Protein 3g, Fat 12g, Carbohydrate 17g, Vitamin E 0mg

Maple Cinnamon Nuts

THESE LITTLE CHARMERS combine the delightful tingle and warmth of cinnamon with the old-fashioned flavor of maple syrup.

1 cup mixed nuts (such as walnuts, pecans, and almonds)

¼ cup maple syrup

1 tablespoon ground cinnamon

COMBINE the nuts in a small bowl and set them aside near the stove.

Combine the maple syrup and cinnamon in a 10-inch nonstick skillet and turn the heat to medium-high. Heat and stir the mixture briefly, for about 30 seconds. Add the nuts and stir continuously for about 1 minute to coat and toast them.

Transfer to a clean dish to cool. Break the nuts apart when they are cool enough to handle. The cinnamon flavor will become more intense when the nuts have cooled completely.

ONE CUSTOM in Poitou, France, was to have the bride and groom dance around the city's gigantic walnut tree. The villagers believed that by participating in this dance the bride would produce an abundance of milk for her baby.

Per serving (¼ cup): Calories 172, Protein 3g, Fat 12g, Carbohydrate 14g, Vitamin E 0mg

Pistachio Peanut Bonbons

Yield: about 20 bonbons

See photo facing page 193.

SWEET INDULGENCES like these nut-crusted, fruity confections awaken our pleasure centers with every delectable bite. Since these nutty delights will keep well for two to three weeks in the fridge, they make great nibbles to serve to guests who drop by, or to bring to a friend as a hostess gift.

1¼ cups almond meal

1 cup chopped prunes

½ cup unsalted chunky peanut butter

¼ cup plus 2 tablespoons maple syrup

¼ cup carob chips or dairy-free semisweet chocolate chips

¼ cup coarsely chopped pistachios or chopped salted roasted peanuts

COMBINE the almond meal, prunes, peanut butter, maple syrup, and carob chips in a large bowl and mix well with a large, firm spoon. The mixture will be thick and stiff, but it's important to distribute the ingredients evenly.

Put the chopped pistachios into a separate bowl. To make the bonbons, work with 1 teaspoon of the prune mixture at a time, and roll it into a small ball between the palms of your hands. Dip one side into the chopped pistachios and place it on an attractive serving dish with the pistachio side up. Continue rolling the remainder of the mixture in the same fashion until all the mixture is used. Serve immediately or cover with plastic wrap and chill. Stored in the refrigerator, Pistachio Peanut Bonbons will keep for two to three weeks.

THE COMMON PEANUT has become so universally enjoyed throughout the world that most people never connect it with South America, its place of origin. The ancient Incas of Peru first cultivated wild peanuts and offered them to the sun god as part of their religious ceremonials. Their name for the peanut was ynchic.

Pistachio Peanut Log: Spread a 25-inch-long piece of waxed paper horizontally on the countertop. Spread the chopped pistachios or peanuts horizontally along the center portion of the waxed paper.

Pile the prune mixture over the pistachios and form it into a long roll, about 18 inches long and 1 to 1½ inches in diameter. Cover the surface with the pistachios.

Fold the waxed paper over to cover the log and twist the ends to seal it completely. Cover the roll with plastic wrap to hold in the moisture and chill for 8 to 12 hours.

To serve, cut the log into ¼-inch-thick slices. Wrapped well and stored in the refrigerator, Pistachio Peanut Log will keep for two to three weeks. Yield: 15 to 20 servings

Per bonbon: Calories 153, Protein 8g, Fat 7g, Carbohydrate 17g, Vitamin E .1mg

Apricot and Hazelnut Morsels

Yield: about 50 morsels

WELL ENDOWED with the tangy flavor of dried apricots, these delicacies practically melt in the mouth. You can make them well in advance of serving, and store them in the refrigerator.

2 cups pitted dates

1 1/4 cups dried apricots

1/2 cup hazelnuts, coarsely ground

1/4 cup plus 2 tablespoons water

1/2 cup hazelnuts, finely ground

COMBINE the dates, apricots, coarsely ground hazelnuts, and water in the food processor and process until finely ground. Stop the machine occasionally to scrape down the sides of the work bowl and redistribute the ingredients.

Put the finely ground hazelnuts into a small, deep bowl. Roll the apricot mixture by hand into 1-inch balls. Roll the balls in the finely ground hazelnuts until completely coated.

Arrange on an attractive serving platter, cover with plastic wrap, and refrigerate until ready to serve. Stored in the refrigerator, Apricot and Hazelnut Morsels will keep well for about one week. (They can be stored a little longer, but they will begin to lose their freshness.)

Note: For an appealing presentation and ease of serving, place a waxed doily on the serving platter before arranging the morsels.

Per serving (2 morsels): Calories 93, Protein 1g, Fat 4g, Carbohydrate 15g, Vitamin E .9mg

Cherry Almond Mousse

Yield: 4 servings

A **DESSERT** that celebrates the cherry season and titillates the taste buds, this sweet, two-layered mousse is a taste sensation, accented by a blissful marriage of almonds and fresh cherries. Serve the mousse in long-stemmed glasses or small, clear glasses, to highlight its two-tone effect.

Mousse

⅓ cup blanched almonds

1 heaping cup pitted sweet cherries

1 (12.3-ounce) box extra-firm silken tofu

¼ cup plus 3 table-spoons evaporated cane juice

1 teaspoon almond extract

Topping

1 cup pitted sweet cherries

2 tablespoons evaporated cane juice

¼ teaspoon almond extract

4 whole cherries, for garnish

HAVE READY 4 long-stemmed glasses or clear juice glasses. To make the mousse, grind the almonds into a fine meal in a food processor, electric mini-chopper/grinder, or coffee grinder (see note below). Set aside.

Combine the cherries, silken tofu, evaporated cane juice, and almond extract in the blender. Blend on low speed, stopping occasionally to scrape down the sides of the blender jar and redistribute the ingredients. Turn to high speed, add the ground almonds, and blend until creamy. Pour the mousse into the glasses. Set aside, and rinse and dry the blender.

TO MAKE the topping, combine the cherries, evaporated cane juice, and almond extract in the blender and process into a thin sauce. Pour over the mousse and top with a whole cherry. Chill for several hours before serving.

To serve, place the wine glasses on individual plates and bring them to the table. Serve with spoons and enjoy.

Note: If you prefer a smoother, creamier mousse, grind the almonds in a mini-chopper/grinder. If you grind the almonds in the food processor, they will be more granulated, which will give slightly more texture to the finished mousse.

Strawberry Almond Mousse: Replace the cherries with an equal amount of fresh strawberries.

Per serving: Calories 246, Protein 11g, Fat 8g, Carbohydrate 36g, Vitamin E 3mg

Fruity Pecan Balls

DRIED FRUITS and nuts blossom in these scrumptious confections that are easy to assemble. At the end of a dinner party, guests often feel too full for a big dessert. But they rarely refuse these little treats when they're passed around the table. Take them on a picnic, pack them for a hike, present them as a gift, or simply indulge in a tasty little morsel.

3 cups coarsely chopped pecans

1 cup broken pecan halves

½ cup hulled sesame seeds

½ cup sunflower seeds

2¾ cups pitted dates

1¼ cups (7.5 ounces) moist dried peaches

6 tablespoons water

3 teaspoons vanilla extract

1 small bunch grapes (optional)

PUT the chopped pecans into a bowl and set them aside.

Combine the broken pecan halves, sesame seeds, and sunflower seeds in the food processor and grind into a coarse meal. Transfer to a large bowl.

Process the dates, dried peaches, water, vanilla extract, and ground nuts and seeds in three batches in the food processor. Process until the mixture almost forms a paste. Stop the machine occasionally to scrape down the sides of the work bowl and redistribute the ingredients. Transfer to a bowl, cover with plastic wrap, and chill for 3 to 12 hours in the refrigerator to firm for easier handling.

To make the balls, lightly oil your hands and roll about 1 teaspoon of the fruit mixture at a time between your palms. Roll the balls in the chopped pecans, pressing the pecans into the surface. Arrange the balls on an attractive serving dish and garnish with a small bunch of grapes, if desired. Stored in an airtight container in the refrigerator, Fruity Pecan Balls will keep for two weeks.

Fruity Pecan Logs: Divide the mixture into thirds, and place each third on an 18-inch-long piece of waxed paper. Form the mixture into 3 logs and chill them in the refrigerator to firm. Spread the coarsely chopped pecans in a large baking pan, and roll the fruit logs in the nuts. Cut the logs into ½-inch-thick slices and arrange them on a serving platter. Yield: 3 logs (25 slices per log)

Golden Raisin and Walnut Balls: Replace the peaches with an equal amount of golden raisins, and replace the pecans with an equal amount of walnuts. This variation brings out the delightful flavor of the sesame seeds.

THE PECAN, because of its pure American heritage, is honored by having the month of April declared as National Pecan Month. Because of its popularity in Texas, the pecan became the state's official tree in 1919 by an act of the Texas legislature.

Per serving (2 balls): Calories 232, Protein 4g, Fat 16g, Carbohydrate 23g, Vitamin E 1.8mg

Chestnut Mousse
with Chocolate Truffle

Yield: 7 to 8 servings

OTHER THAN ROASTING or boiling chestnuts for a Thanksgiving or Christmas stuffing, home chefs tend to ignore them. This enchanting dessert, nestled between two layers of chocolate, demonstrates the versatility of chestnuts by serving them as a sweet indulgence. Cooking and peeling fresh chestnuts can be labor intensive, but you can sidestep this task by purchasing the ones that come in a can or jar already cooked and peeled. You'll still have to cook them a little longer to soften them for the mousse, but you'll appreciate the convenience.

Chestnut Mousse

2 cups regular soymilk or rice milk

1 pound fresh chestnuts in the shell, cooked and peeled (see page 27), or 1¾ cups peeled cooked chestnuts

½ cup evaporated cane juice

1 tablespoon organic canola oil

½ teaspoon vanilla extract

HAVE READY seven or eight 4-ounce dessert cups or long-stemmed glasses. To make the mousse, combine the soymilk, chestnuts, evaporated cane juice, canola oil, and vanilla extract in a 3-quart saucepan. Simmer uncovered over medium heat for 20 to 40 minutes, or until the chestnuts are very soft when pierced with a fork.

WHILE the chestnuts are cooking, prepare the truffle. Combine the soymilk and evaporated cane juice in a 1-quart saucepan. Turn the heat to medium-high and cook, stirring frequently, until the sugar is dissolved.

Turn the heat down slightly and add the chocolate. Stir continuously until the chocolate is completely melted. Add the vanilla extract and stir with a wire whip until the sauce is smooth and creamy. Set it aside.

When the chestnuts are soft, drain and reserve the liquid. Transfer the chestnuts to the food processor and process until smooth and creamy, adding all the cooking liquid a little at a time.

Spoon a dollop of the truffle into the bottom of each dessert cup. Fill the cups with the mousse and finish with another dollop of truffle. Garnish with the coarsely ground pecans and chill for several hours before serving.

Chocolate Truffle

½ cup regular soymilk (see note)

3 tablespoons evaporated cane juice

2 (1-ounce) squares dairy-free unsweetened chocolate

¼ teaspoon vanilla extract

¼ cup coarsely ground pecans or walnuts

Note: If the chestnuts are not very sweet, or if the soymilk has a low sugar content, add 2 tablespoons or more of evaporated cane juice to improve the flavor of the mousse.

Chestnut Mousse Pie: Prepare one Nutty Wheat Pie Crust (page 200). Bake it for 10 minutes in a preheated 350-degree oven. Cool and fill it with the Chestnut Mousse and top it with the Chocolate Truffle. Sprinkle the ground pecans over the top and chill well before serving.

IN FRANCE, marron glacé, a candied chestnut prepared in a typically French cooking style that involves sixteen different processes, is always served at Christmas and New Years time. The French claim they originated this treat in the time of Louis XIV, but apparently a candied chestnut confection was served 150 years earlier in Piedmont, a northwestern area of Italy close to the border of Switzerland and France.

Per serving: Calories 307, Protein 6g, Fat 11g, Carbohydrate 48g, Vitamin E .5mg

Apricot Almond Freeze

Yield: 8 servings

½ cup plus 8 whole almonds

1½ pounds ripe apricots, pitted

2 cups water

½ cup plus 3 tablespoons evaporated cane juice

½ teaspoon vanilla extract

½ teaspoon almond extract

8 fresh mint leaves

HAVE READY 2 metal 9 x 5-inch loaf pans.

Grind ½ cup of the almonds into a fine meal in the food processor.

Place half the apricots into the blender along with the water, evaporated cane juice, and vanilla and almond extracts. Start blending on low speed. Increase to high speed and gradually add the remaining apricots, blending until the apricots are completely smooth.

Pour into a large bowl and stir in the almond meal. Divide the mixture equally between the loaf pans and put them into the freezer for 30 minutes.

Remove the pans from the freezer and stir the mixture. Return to the freezer for another 30 minutes and stir again. Return to the freezer for a final 30 minutes and stir once more. Spoon into 8 small dessert bowls. Garnish by standing 1 of the remaining whole almonds in the center of each serving and placing a mint leaf next to it.

Note: Although this frozen apricot treat is an easy prep that can be made about two hours before serving, you may prefer to prepare it a day ahead by freezing it completely. Then, about an hour before serving, allow it to thaw slightly at room temperature, just until slushy.

Summer Fruit Freeze: Replace the apricots with an equal amount of fresh strawberries, peaches, plums, nectarines, or red flame grapes.

Per serving: Calories 160, Protein 4g, Fat 6g, Carbohydrate 24g, Vitamin E 3mg

Red Berry Sauce

THIS SAUCE can be drizzled over frozen desserts, cakes, soy yogurt, fresh fruit, pancakes, waffles, parfaits, or mousse. By varying the sauce as seasonal fruits come to market, you can make this a year-round treat.

1 (1.25-pound) package fresh or frozen strawberries or raspberries

5 tablespoons evaporated cane juice

1 tablespoon freshly squeezed lemon or lime juice

COMBINE all the ingredients in the blender and blend on low speed until the sauce becomes thick and smooth. Chill it in the refrigerator until ready to use.

SWEDES EMPLOY the almond as a symbol of good fortune at Christmas time, serving rice pudding with an almond hidden in one of the servings. The one who finds it is promised an especially fortuitous year.

Per serving (1/4 cup): Calories 32, Protein 0g, Fat 0g, Carbohydrate 8g, Vitamin E .1mg

Fruited Coeur à la Crème with Macadamias and Strawberry Sauce

Yield: 6 servings

FRENCH FOR "heart of cream," Coeur à la Crème is a classic dessert that lends itself perfectly to a dressed-up vegan rendition. Win the heart of that someone special on Valentine's Day by preparing this heart-shaped, ambrosial dessert with a macadamia filling. Then slather it with delicious Red Berry Sauce just before serving.

2 sweet apples (Pink Lady, Gala, or Fuji)

½ cup water

5 tablespoons evaporated cane juice

3 tablespoons maple syrup

1 cup macadamia nuts

2 teaspoons vanilla extract

LINE a 4-cup heart-shaped mold with a large piece of plastic wrap, leaving plenty of excess to drape over the sides. Set it aside.

Peel and core the apples. Cut them into 8 wedges and put them into a 2-quart saucepan with the water and 2 tablespoons of the evaporated cane juice. Cover and bring to a boil over high heat. Turn the heat down to low and steam for 10 minutes. Remove from the heat and let rest for 10 minutes, covered.

Create a macadamia paste by combining the remaining 3 tablespoons evaporated cane juice and the maple syrup in a 1-quart saucepan. Stir continuously for 1 to 2 minutes over medium-high heat, until the sugar dissolves. Transfer to the food processor. Add the macadamia nuts and 1 teaspoon of the vanilla extract and process until smooth and creamy. Transfer the paste to a small bowl. Wash and dry the food processor work bowl and blade.

20 pitted dates

1 (12.3-ounce) box
extra-firm silken tofu

2 fresh strawberries

2 to 3 cups Red Berry
Sauce (page 215),
as needed

Drain the cooked apples and transfer them to the food processor. Add the dates, silken tofu, and remaining 1 teaspoon vanilla extract and process until smooth and creamy.

Spoon half of the tofu mixture into the prepared mold and spread it to the edges. Crumble the macadamia paste over the top and press it down lightly. Spoon the remaining tofu mixture over the top, spreading it to the edges to cover the macadamia paste. Cover the mold by folding the excess plastic wrap over the top, and refrigerate for 8 to 12 hours.

Shortly before serving, open the plastic wrapping and invert the coeur onto an attractive platter. Cut the strawberries in half lengthwise and garnish the center of the coeur with them. Spoon 1/3 to 1/2 cup of the Red Berry Sauce over the top, allowing it to cascade down the sides. Pour the remainder of the sauce into a bowl or pitcher and pass it at the table for guests to add as much as they like.

Per serving: Calories 420, Protein 8g, Fat 19g, Carbohydrate 63g, Vitamin E .4mg

Chocolate Peanut Butter Mousse

SOME CLAIM they simply cannot live without chocolate. Others are utterly entranced with peanut butter. Combining the two in a divinely sweet dessert results in a mousse so captivating you may want to eat dessert first.

Yield: 6 servings

2 ripe bananas

1 (12-ounce) box soft silken tofu

1/2 cup coconut milk

3 heaping tablespoons unsalted creamy peanut butter

1 teaspoon vanilla extract

3/4 teaspoon ground cinnamon

1/4 teaspoon ground nutmeg

1 (12-ounce) package dairy-free semisweet chocolate chips

1/2 cup evaporated cane juice

6 small mint sprigs

6 fresh strawberries or raspberries

COMBINE the bananas, tofu, coconut milk, peanut butter, vanilla extract, cinnamon, and nutmeg in the food processor and process until creamy.

Place the chocolate chips and evaporated cane juice in a 1-quart saucepan and place over low heat. Warm, stirring frequently, until the chips are melted and the mixture has no lumps.

Add the melted chocolate to the tofu mixture in the food processor and process until smooth. Spoon into 6 custard cups or dessert dishes and chill for 4 to 8 hours, until firm.

Just before serving, garnish each dish with a sprig of mint and a berry.

Note: For an extravagantly rich mousse, use a coconut milk with at least 8 grams of fat. If you are aiming for a lower-fat mousse, look for "lite" coconut milk, which contains 2 to 4 grams of fat.

Per serving: Calories 499, Protein 9g, Fat 26g, Carbohydrate 60g, Vitamin E .1mg

Spiced Treasure Island

NOT A CAKE, pie, or torte, this pudding-like dessert stands alone as a proud little island, rich with pleasing aroma, spiciness, moistness, sweetness, visual appeal, and delectable fruity flavor. Prepare it ahead along with the special Treasure Sauce (page 220), and serve it during the holiday season when sugar and spice are such an integral part of festive gatherings.

4 cups regular soymilk

1 cup evaporated cane juice

1 tablespoon organic canola oil

¾ teaspoon ground cardamom

¼ plus ⅛ teaspoon ground cloves

¼ teaspoon salt

1 cup barley flakes

1 large carrot, peeled and coarsely shredded

¾ cup black raisins

¾ cup golden raisins

¼ cup pine nuts

½ cup whole almonds, toasted (see page 28)

1¼ cups Treasure Sauce (page 220), as needed (optional)

LINE a deep 5-cup mold with clear plastic wrap, leaving plenty of excess to drape over the sides. Set aside.

Combine the soymilk, evaporated cane juice, canola oil, cardamom, cloves, and salt in a 4-quart saucepan. Bring to a boil, uncovered, over high heat. Watch closely so the mixture doesn't boil over.

Immediately add the barley flakes, carrot, raisins, and pine nuts. Return the mixture to a boil, then turn the heat to low. Cover and steam for 40 minutes, or until all the liquid is absorbed and the mixture becomes thick and pudding-like. Remove from the heat and let stand, covered, for 10 minutes.

Spoon into the prepared mold, packing it firmly. Allow to cool, uncovered. Then drape the plastic wrap over the pudding and refrigerate it for 8 to 12 hours, until thoroughly chilled.

To serve, unmold onto an attractive serving platter and poke the toasted almonds partway into the pudding so they stand up like porcupine quills. Serve with Treasure Sauce on the side, if desired.

Per serving (no sauce): Calories 535, Protein 15g, Fat 16g, Carbohydrate 89g, Vitamin E 3.9mg

Treasure Sauce

THOUGH THIS SAUCE is optional to serve with Spiced Treasure Island (page 219), it adds a touch of elegance and eye appeal. Treasure Sauce gives a chocolate cake the lavish treatment. It enriches warm apple pie or other fruit pies, bread puddings, warm, soft puddings, baked apples, and even pancakes and waffles.

2 cups regular soymilk
(see note)

¼ cup evaporated
cane juice

1 teaspoon
vanilla extract

Dash salt

2 tablespoons
cornstarch

2 tablespoons water

COMBINE the soymilk, evaporated cane juice, vanilla extract, and salt in a 2-quart saucepan and bring to a boil over medium-high heat. Watch carefully so the mixture doesn't boil over.

Combine the cornstarch and water in a small cup or bowl and stir to make a thin paste. Add to the bubbling soymilk, stirring continuously with a wire whip for about 1 minute, until thickened.

Note: Rich soymilk is recommended for this recipe. It contains about 3.5 to 4 grams of fat, and will make the sauce creamy and luxurious.

Per serving (¼ cup): Calories 94, Protein 4g, Fat 2g, Carbohydrate 15g, Vitamin E 0mg

Almond Paradise Baked Apples

Yield: 4 servings

DELICIOUSLY HOMESPUN, this enhanced version of baked apples is no trouble to prepare and creates its own fruity sauce. Almonds take the spotlight in this dessert, which provides a satisfying conclusion to a meal. I've included rose water in this recipe for its delightful infusion of flavor. However, if you don't have any on hand, it can easily be omitted without harming the outcome of the recipe.

4 large crisp apples (Braeburn, Rome Beauty, Fuji, Gala, or Pink Lady)

⅔ cup whole almonds

3 tablespoons water

½ to ¾ cup evaporated cane juice

1 teaspoon rose water (optional)

½ teaspoon almond extract

¼ cup black raisins

¼ cup golden raisins

1½ cups unsweetened pineapple juice

PREHEAT the oven to 350 degrees. Wash and core the apples, arrange them in an 8-inch square baking dish, and set them aside.

To make the filling, grind the almonds to a fine meal in batches in an electric mini-chopper/grinder or coffee grinder. Transfer to the food processor.

Add the water, 2 tablespoons plus 2 teaspoons of the evaporated cane juice, the optional rose water, and almond extract and process into a creamy paste. Spoon into a small bowl and stir in the raisins.

Using a pointed spoon, fill the apple cavities with the almond filling, packing it firmly all the way down into the bottom of the cavity. Mound the remaining filling over the top of the apples.

To make the sauce, combine the pineapple juice and the remaining evaporated cane juice in a small bowl, adding more or less evaporated cane juice to achieve the desired sweetness. Pour it into the bottom of the baking dish around the apples. Cover the dish with aluminum foil, shiny side down.

Bake for 50 to 90 minutes. Test the apples with a fork after 50 minutes. If they are not tender, continue baking until a fork slides into the apples easily. To serve, place the apples into dessert bowls and spoon some of the sauce into each bowl. Serve with spoons, though some people may prefer a knife and fork as well.

Note: The baking time for this recipe has a wide range. Some apple varieties, like Rome Beauty, are softer and bake in 50 to 60 minutes, while very firm apples, like Fuji, take longer.

Per serving: Calories 438, Protein 7g, Fat 13g, Carbohydrate 81g, Vitamin E 6mg

Double Devastation Brownies

Yield: 9 servings

1 cup coarsely chopped walnuts

½ cup dairy-free semisweet chocolate chips

¾ cup dark brown sugar

⅓ cup unsweetened cocoa powder

1 cup all-purpose whole wheat flour

1 tablespoon plus 1½ teaspoons instant decaffeinated coffee crystals

2 teaspoons baking powder

½ teaspoon salt

¾ cup evaporated cane juice

½ cup regular soymilk

2 tablespoons organic canola oil

1 teaspoon vanilla extract

1¾ cups boiling water

IT'S WELL KNOWN that chocolate fanciers can never get enough of the stuff. You can't miss with a dessert that whips cocoa and chocolate chips into a unique brownie loaded with walnuts and brown sugar. Adding to the irresistible double chocolate is a hint of coffee. This remarkable brownie even makes its own fudge sauce. Serve it in dessert bowls, and if you like, top the brownie with vegan whipped cream. Though the brownies are delicious served cold, they are even better served warm.

PREHEAT the oven to 350 degrees and oil an 8-inch square glass baking pan. Measure the walnuts and chocolate chips into a small bowl. Combine the brown sugar and ¼ cup of the cocoa in another small bowl.

Sift together the flour, remaining cocoa, instant coffee crystals, baking powder, and salt in a large bowl. Then form a well in the center. Add the evaporated cane juice, soymilk, canola oil, and vanilla and stir well. The mixture will be very thick and somewhat dry. Stir in the walnuts and chocolate chips and mix well.

Spoon the batter into the prepared baking pan, spreading it evenly. Sprinkle the brown sugar and cocoa mixture over the top. Pour the boiling water over the top of the batter and bake for 40 to 45 minutes. Remove and cool.

Per serving: Calories 347, Protein 6g, Fat 15g, Carbohydrate 51g, Vitamin E .6mg

Almond Macaroon Sandwich Bars

Yield: about 24 cookies

SPECIAL GUESTS deserve special cookies. When your favorite aunt or uncle comes to visit, prepare a batch of these indulgent macaroon sandwich bars made with rich whole grains. They store well in the refrigerator or freezer, and are the ideal make-ahead treat.

2 cups whole almonds

½ cup plus 1 tablespoon evaporated cane juice

½ cup water

1½ teaspoons almond extract

1 teaspoon vanilla extract

1¼ cups whole wheat pastry flour

1¼ cups old-fashioned rolled oats

1 cup dark brown sugar

¾ cup (6 ounces) dairy-free margarine

PREHEAT the oven to 325 degrees and have ready an 8-inch square glass baking pan.

Grind the almonds medium-fine in the food processor. Add the evaporated cane juice, water, and almond and vanilla extracts and process until the mixture is thoroughly combined and forms a soft paste. Set it aside and allow the mixture to thicken slightly.

Combine the flour, rolled oats, brown sugar, and margarine. Blend into fine crumbs using a pastry blender or a fork.

Spoon half the flour mixture into the baking dish, and press firmly with the back of a spoon to form a compact layer.

Using a rubber spatula, spread the almond mixture over the flour layer, covering it completely. Top with the remaining flour mixture, spreading it to the edges, and press gently.

Bake for 40 to 45 minutes, or until the top is a delicate golden brown. Cool completely before cutting into squares. Covered tightly, Almond Macaroon Sandwich Bars will keep for two weeks in the refrigerator or up to three months in the freezer.

Per serving: Calories 183, Protein 4g, Fat 10g, Carbohydrate 22g, Vitamin E 3.4mg

Nutty Granola Bars

SOMETIMES you just get the munchies and nothing will quell that urge but a fruity, nutty, and highly textured "cookie" that offers chewy, crunchy sweetness with every bite. When those cravings clutch your vulnerable palate, haul out the fixings and prepare a batch of these treats. The recipe makes quite a large quantity, so you can share some, freeze some, and munch some.

4½ cups granola

3 cups chopped dates

1½ cups muesli

1 cup black raisins

1 cup golden raisins

1 cup chopped sweetened dried pineapple

¾ cup unsweetened shredded dried coconut

¾ cup coarsely chopped walnuts

½ cup sunflower seeds

½ cup hulled sesame seeds

PREHEAT the oven to 200 degrees and lightly oil 2 jelly-roll pans. Combine the granola, dates, muesli, raisins, pineapple, coconut, walnuts, sunflower seeds, sesame seeds, cashews, flaxseeds, and pumpkin seeds in a giant mixing bowl. Toss all the ingredients together with a wooden spoon and break up the very large clumps of granola.

Add the peanut butter, brown rice syrup, and maple syrup, and mix well to distribute the moist ingredients evenly throughout. (Using your hands will work best.) The mixture will be very lumpy.

Divide the mixture equally between the 2 prepared pans and press it firmly into each pan with your hands. Make sure the edges are firmly pressed together and are fairly even. Use a knife to score the mixture into 2-inch squares.

Baking Tip

Cleanup is a cinch when baking cookies on parchment-lined baking sheets. Even better, the parchment paper can be reused for baking the second batch and then discarded.

½ cup coarsely
chopped cashews

⅓ cup whole flaxseeds

⅓ cup pumpkin seeds

1½ cups salted chunky
peanut butter

1½ cups brown
rice syrup

½ cup maple syrup

Bake for 2 hours for bars with a chewy texture, or for 2½ to 3 hours for crisp bars. Remove the pans from the oven and cut the bars all the way through. Cool completely. Stored in heavy-duty zipper-lock plastic bags, Nutty Granola Bars will keep for two weeks at room temperature, one month in the refrigerator, or up to three months in the freezer.

Notes: As an alternative to baking the granola bars, you can dehydrate them. Press the mixture onto three Teflex sheets, score, and dehydrate the bars at 105 degrees for 2 to 3 hours on the first side. Invert onto another dehydrator tray and dehydrate on the second side for 2 to 3 hours longer.

• If you prefer a bar that is less lumpy, you can pulse-chop the granola in the food processor until the lumps become a coarse meal. Proceed with the recipe as directed.

• Vary the flavors by substituting different dried fruits and nuts; or adding spices such as cinnamon, allspice, cardamom, or ginger; or extracts such as vanilla, maple, coconut, or fruity flavorings.

Per bar: Calories 266, Protein 7g, Fat 12g, Carbohydrate 34g, Vitamin E 1.1mg

Cranberry Peanut Butter Dainties

RICHER THAN traditional peanut butter cookies, these treats make ideal surprises for the brown bagger and can also be packed in kids' lunches.

2 cups dark brown sugar, packed

¾ cup unsalted chunky peanut butter

¼ cup (2 ounces) dairy-free margarine

½ cup plus 2 tablespoons water

2 tablespoons whole flaxseeds

2 cups whole wheat pastry flour

1 cup old-fashioned rolled oats

2 teaspoons baking soda

1½ teaspoons ground cinnamon

1⅓ cups sweetened dried cranberries

PREHEAT the oven to 350 degrees. Line 2 baking sheets with parchment paper and set them aside.

Combine the brown sugar, peanut butter, and margarine in a large bowl and mix well with a wooden spoon.

Place ¼ cup of the water and the flaxseeds into the blender and process on low speed for a few seconds. Stop the machine to scrape down the sides of the blender jar, then continue blending for 1 to 2 minutes until thick and viscous (the consistency will be similar to thick oatmeal). Add to the peanut butter mixture and stir it in well.

Combine the flour, rolled oats, baking soda, and cinnamon in a medium bowl. Add to the peanut butter mixture, stirring well until evenly incorporated.

Add the cranberries and the remaining ¼ cup plus 2 tablespoons water and mix well to form a stiff dough. Using your hands, roll the dough into small balls, about 1 inch in diameter, and place them 3 inches apart on the prepared baking sheets. Use the bottom of a glass or a spatula to flatten the cookies slightly.

Bake for 12 to 14 minutes for soft, chewy cookies, or 15 to 17 minutes for crisp cookies. Cool 2 to 3 minutes on the baking sheets before transferring the cookies to a dish. Stored in an airtight container or heavy-duty zipper-lock plastic bags, Cranberry Peanut Butter Dainties will keep for one week at room temperature, two to three weeks in the refrigerator, or up to three months in the freezer.

Per cookie: Calories 72, Protein 2g, Fat 2g, Carbohydrate 12g, Vitamin E .1mg

Peanut Butter Hammers

Yield: about 30 cookies

YOU KNOW YOU HAVE a winner when cookie lovers reach for second and third helpings. These little treats could be called "convenience cookies" because they can be made in stages. Make the dough and chill it for up to two days. Bake the cookies and store them until you have the time to double-dip them first into chocolate, then into chopped peanuts.

½ cup (4 ounces) dairy-free margarine

½ cup unsalted chunky peanut butter

½ cup evaporated cane juice

½ cup dark brown sugar, packed

2 tablespoons water

1 tablespoon whole flaxseeds

1 ½ cups whole wheat pastry flour

¾ teaspoon baking soda

½ teaspoon baking powder

1 cup crushed salted peanuts

5 (1-ounce) squares dairy-free semisweet or bittersweet chocolate

PREHEAT the oven to 375 degrees and line 2 baking sheets with parchment paper.

Combine the margarine, peanut butter, evaporated cane juice, and brown sugar in a large mixing bowl and mix thoroughly. Put the water and flaxseeds into the blender and blend on low speed for about 1 minute, until thick and viscous (the consistency will be similar to thick oatmeal). Add the flaxseed mixture to the peanut butter mixture and incorporate thoroughly.

Measure the flour, baking soda, and baking powder into a medium mixing bowl, stir well, and add it to the peanut butter mixture. Combine thoroughly to create a thick dough. Cover the bowl and chill the dough for at least 1 hour or up to 12 hours.

Spoon out 1 tablespoon of dough at a time and use your fingers to create logs that are 2 to 3 inches long and ½ inch in diameter. Place the logs 3 inches apart on the prepared baking sheets.

Bake for 10 to 13 minutes, or until delicately browned. The cookies will be too soft to handle. Cool them completely on the baking sheets and they will firm up.

To create the hammers, measure the peanuts into a small bowl. Melt the chocolate in a small saucepan over the lowest heat. Dip one end of each log into the chocolate, then immediately dip it into the peanuts to create a peanut coating. Cool. Stored in an airtight container, Peanut Butter Hammers will keep for two weeks at room temperature or three months in the freezer.

Per cookie: Calories 137, Protein 4g, Fat 9g, Carbohydrate 14g, Vitamin E .1mg

Blancmange

Yield: 6 servings

HERE IS A VEGAN version of a classic French dessert with a long history dating back to the fourteenth century, though its true origin is derived from a medieval Arab dish. Blancmange is a snowy-white molded dessert with the definitive flavor of sweetened almonds, reminiscent of marzipan. Blancmange, also written as blanc mange and blanc manger, literally means white eating or white food, which describes the white appearance blanched almonds give the original recipe. I prefer the nutritional benefits and higher fiber of whole almonds with the skins.

Cashew Cream

2/3 cup cashews

1 cup water

1 pitted date

Dash salt

Almond Liquid

2 cups Almond Milk
(page 189), or packaged
almond milk

1/2 cup evaporated
cane juice

3 tablespoons
agar flakes

1/2 teaspoon
almond extract

1/4 teaspoon
vanilla extract

Mint sprig

1 pound grapes

LIGHTLY OIL a 3-cup mold and set it aside.

TO MAKE the Cashew Cream, grind the cashews to a fine meal in an electric mini-chopper/grinder or coffee grinder. Transfer to the blender and add the water, date, and salt. Start the blender on low speed for a few seconds, then switch to high speed and process for 1 to 2 minutes, until the liquid is smooth and creamy. Measure 1 cup of the Cashew Cream and put it into a 3-quart saucepan. Stored in a sealed container in the refrigerator, Cashew Cream will keep for one week. Leftover Cashew Cream can be used as a topping for fruit salad, pies, puddings, or other desserts.

ADD the almond milk, evaporated cane juice, agar flakes, and almond and vanilla extracts. Bring to a boil over medium-high heat. Watch closely so the mixture doesn't boil over. Turn the heat down to medium and simmer gently for 10 minutes, stirring frequently with a wire whip to thoroughly dissolve the agar. Pour into the prepared mold and refrigerate for 8 to 12 hours, until thoroughly chilled.

To serve, gently loosen the edges with a flatware knife and unmold onto an attractive serving platter. Garnish with the mint and serve with the grapes.

Note: If you make Blancmange with homemade almond milk, sweeten the strained almond pulp with 3/4 teaspoon evaporated cane juice and add 1/4 teaspoon almond extract. Stir the mixture well and serve it on the side.

Per serving: Calories 233, Protein 6g, Fat 14g, Carbohydrate 24g, Vitamin E 3.4mg

Crème Anglaise

Yield: about 2½ cups

ELEGANT AND RICH, this custard-like sauce is traditionally made with whole milk and egg yolks. Still clinging to its French roots, the vegan version is equally rich and delicious with soymilk as the base.

2 cups unsweetened soymilk

¼ cup evaporated cane juice

¾ teaspoon vanilla extract

Dash salt

3 tablespoons cornstarch

3 tablespoons water

COMBINE the soymilk, evaporated cane juice, vanilla extract, and salt in a 2-quart saucepan and gently bring to a simmer.

Combine the cornstarch and water in a cup or small bowl and stir to form a runny paste. Add the paste to the bubbling soymilk mixture, a little at a time, stirring constantly for about 1 minute, until it has thickened to the desired consistency. Transfer to an attractive serving bowl and serve with a ladle. Chill the leftovers. Stored in a covered container in the refrigerator, Crème Anglaise will keep for about five days.

Per serving (½ cup): Calories 100, Protein 4g, Fat 2g, Carbohydrate 17g, Vitamin E 0mg

Hazelnut Cranberry Bread Pudding

Yield: 6 servings

THE HIGHLIGHT of this make-ahead fruity dessert is its homespun, spicy, and sweet-tart flavor with nutty accents. Add the easy-fix Crème Anglaise to top it off and you'll take this folksy dessert to new heights.

½ cup hazelnuts

4 slices whole grain bread

1 (12-ounce) package fresh cranberries

2 large ripe Bosc or Anjou pears, quartered and sliced

1 cup dark brown sugar

1 cup water

2 cinnamon sticks

PREHEAT the oven to 350 degrees and lightly oil a 3-quart glass baking dish.

Place the hazelnuts on a baking sheet and roast them for 10 minutes. Remove the nuts from the oven and wrap them in a clean dish towel. Rub them vigorously to remove the loosened skins. Don't worry if some of the skins cling to the nuts—these will add appeal to the finished dessert. Cool the hazelnuts completely. When cool, put them into a zipper-lock plastic bag. Pound them gently with a hammer to break them into coarse pieces and set them aside.

Toast the bread until crisp. Cool, break it into 1-inch pieces, and put them into a large mixing bowl.

Pick over the cranberries and discard any spoiled ones. Wash them and put them into the bowl with the bread pieces. Add the sliced pears.

Combine the brown sugar, water, and cinnamon sticks in a 2-quart saucepan. Bring to a boil over high heat, turn the heat down to medium-high, and simmer gently for 10 minutes. Cool and add to the bowl with the cranberries.

½ cup golden raisins

¼ cup regular soymilk

2 tablespoons freshly squeezed lemon juice

½ teaspoon ground cinnamon

¼ teaspoon ground nutmeg

2½ cups Crème Anglaise (page 229)

Stir in the raisins, soymilk, lemon juice, cinnamon, and nutmeg and mix well. Spoon the mixture into the prepared baking dish and cover with aluminum foil, shiny side down. Bake for 45 minutes.

Remove the foil and stir the mixture gently to break up the cranberries. Sprinkle the top with the reserved hazelnuts, cover with the aluminum foil, and return to the oven to bake for 15 minutes longer. Serve warm with Crème Anglaise on the side.

Note: Leftover Hazelnut Cranberry Bread Pudding is delicious. To reheat it, place the bread pudding into a cold oven and warm it at 350 degrees for 15 to 20 minutes.

Per serving (no cream): Calories 384, Protein 5g, Fat 9g, Carbohydrate 77g, Vitamin E 2.6mg

Nutty Chocolate Frozen Bananas

Yield: 6 servings

HOW DO YOU SEND chocoholics into ecstasy? Give 'em chocolate, of course. And a frozen banana is the perfect vehicle for the chocolate. For an after-dinner course that's eating fun for everyone, make this a do-it-yourself dipping-and-rolling dessert. A few simple preparations the day before make the dessert virtually trouble free.

3 ripe bananas

1 cup walnuts

6 (1-ounce) squares dairy-free unsweetened chocolate

1¼ cups evaporated cane juice

½ cup boiling water

PEEL the bananas and cut them in half crosswise. Insert a sturdy wooden skewer deeply into the center of the cut end of the banana halves and place them on a metal baking pan. Freeze for 3 to 12 hours.

Coarsely grind the walnuts in a hand-crank nut mill, put them into a wide-mouth bowl, and set them aside.

To prepare the chocolate sauce, melt the chocolate squares in a 1-quart saucepan over very low heat, stirring frequently. Put the evaporated cane juice into a small bowl and add the boiling water. Stir well to dissolve the sugar completely. When the chocolate is thoroughly melted, turn off the heat and add the sweetened water, stirring until shiny and smooth.

Pour the chocolate sauce into a wide-mouth bowl. Remove the skewered bananas from the freezer and place them on a platter. Place the bowls of chocolate sauce and walnuts on the table. Instruct each person to firmly hold the skewer, roll the banana in the chocolate sauce to coat it, then roll it in the ground nuts.

Notes: Choose bananas that are ripe but not overripe.

• For variety, replace the walnuts with an equal amount of pecans, peanuts, pistachios, almonds, or hazelnuts. For harder nuts like almonds or hazelnuts, put them into a zipper-lock plastic bag, place the bag on a firm surface, and crush the nuts with a hammer. Combining two or more kinds of nuts also makes an ideal topping. Toast the nuts to bring out a more intense flavor.

Per serving: Calories 414, Protein 8g, Fat 27g, Carbohydrate 56g, Vitamin E .2mg

Very Berry Parfait
with Macadamia Nuts

Yield: 4 servings

WHENEVER BLUEBERRIES meet up with other berries, those unabashed little blueberries take over. But thoughtfully placed in this light dessert with a macadamia surprise at the bottom, they allow the parfait to display its colors with individuality. Because berries lose flavor so quickly, plan to make and serve the parfait the same day.

⅓ cup macadamia nuts

1 (12.3-ounce) box extra-firm silken tofu

¾ cup chopped fresh strawberries

¾ cup pitted sweet cherries

¼ cup evaporated cane juice

¼ teaspoon vanilla extract

¼ teaspoon strawberry extract

¼ teaspoon freshly squeezed lemon juice

¼ cup fresh or frozen blueberries

4 mint sprigs

COARSELY chop the macadamia nuts in a hand-crank nut mill and set them aside.

To make the parfait, place the silken tofu, strawberries, cherries, evaporated cane juice, vanilla and strawberry extracts, and lemon juice into the blender. Process on low speed for a few seconds, redistributing the ingredients as necessary. Switch to high speed and process until completely smooth.

Reserve 1 tablespoon of the macadamia nuts. Divide the remaining nuts equally among 4 short, wide-mouth glasses. Spoon a small amount of the parfait over the nuts, using 1 to 2 tablespoons per glass, and stir the mixture.

Pour the remaining parfait over the nut layer. Top with the blueberries and a sprinkling of the reserved nuts. Garnish with the mint sprigs, placing one sprig at the edge of each parfait.

Per serving: Calories 198, Protein 9g, Fat 10g, Carbohydrate 20g, Vitamin E .2mg

Glossary

Agar

Sometimes called agar-agar or kanten, this product is a tasteless, translucent sea vegetable that is the vegetarian alternative to gelatin. Agar comes in flakes, powder, or bars, and must be boiled in liquid for up to 10 minutes until it is completely dissolved. Unlike gelatin, agar will set up at room temperature within an hour, though it will become firmer with refrigeration.

Agar flakes can be found in the macrobiotic section of many natural food markets; however, macrobiotic products can be a bit pricey. You can buy bars of agar very reasonably at Japanese markets and some Chinese markets. The bars are available in plain, translucent form or with red coloring. I purchase the plain bars, break them into small pieces, and put them into the blender. Within a minute or two of blending, I have flakes that are perfect for gelling and binding desserts. Store the flakes in an airtight container at room temperature. If a recipe calls for a whole bar, soak it in water for 5 to 10 minutes to soften before boiling.

Agave Nectar

This thick liquid sweetener is similar in consistency to honey and has a flavor that could be considered a cross between honey and maple syrup. Agave nectar is extracted from the juice of the agave cactus native to Mexico. For baking, use ¾ cup agave nectar to replace 1 cup sugar, and lower the oven temperature by 25 degrees. Because it is 90 percent fructose, this sweetener is low on the glycemic index. It makes an excellent sweetener for smoothies, nut milks, and desserts. Look for agave nectar at natural food markets.

Barley Flakes or Pressed Barley

Barley flakes are made from pearl barley that has been lightly toasted and then pressed with heavy rollers. The process shortens the cooking time from 50 to 60 minutes to 30 to 35 minutes. Barley flakes offer the same pleasing texture as pearl barley, and can be cooked for breakfast or served as a dinner grain. The uncooked flakes can also be added to breads or homemade muesli, and are valued for their nutty texture and high fiber. Barley flakes can be found in natural food markets.

Carob Chips

Carob is made from long brown pods that grow on the carob tree, which originated in the Middle East, worked its way westward into the Mediterranean, and more recently (historically) was introduced into California, Australia, South Africa, India, and Mexico. The pods are ground into a fine, dark brown powder that looks similar to cocoa powder. It is often used to give beverages and mousses a chocolate-like flavor. Carob powder is the base for making carob chips, a popular alternative to chocolate chips; however, carob chips do not melt as smoothly or completely as chocolate chips. Both carob powder and carob chips are available in natural food markets.

Chiles (Fresh)

Chiles are rated on a scale of 1 to 10, with 10 registering the hottest.

Anaheim chiles were developed around 1900 for canning in Anaheim, California, and are sometimes called California chiles or chiles verde. They are usually green (though some are red), long (about six inches in length), and thin, with a mild heat level of 2. Because of their gentle heat, they are ideal to perk up a dish when just a little spice is needed.

Jalapeño chiles originated in Mexico and are the most popular variety used in America. Deep green in color, these two-inch-long chiles taper to a point and are used raw as well as cooked. Though their heat level of 5 is considered medium, they are rather fiery. Use them cautiously. Jalapeños are ideal for salsa, stir-fries, salads, and any dish that would benefit from a little heat. Purchase them in almost any large chain grocery or Latino market.

Poblano chiles (called pasilla chiles in California) are very dark green with shiny skin. Their four-inch length and plump, conical shape make them ideal for stuffing with seasoned tofu, rice, or vegetables. Poblano chiles, with their mild heat level of 3 or 4, are typically used for making chiles rellenos. Look for these chiles in supermarkets with a large Latino clientele or in Latino markets.

Serrano chiles are thin, bullet shaped, and two and a half to three inches long. They can be red or green with a heat level of 6 to 7. Use these with timidity for salsa, salads, and stir-fries. While serrano chiles are always available in Latino markets, many supermarkets also sell them.

Evaporated Cane Juice

Evaporated cane juice is granulated crystals of dehydrated sugarcane juice that can be used exactly like white sugar. Conventional table sugar has been processed to refine the sugar crystals and remove the natural molasses, a practice that gives sugar its characteristic snowy-white color. Because evaporated cane juice has not been processed in this fashion, it retains some of the natural molasses flavor and hue, resulting in a warm ivory color. Evaporated cane juice is available in natural food markets and some supermarkets.

Guar Gum

Guar gum is a fine white powder made from the seeds of a legume called cluster bean or guar plant that grows in India and Pakistan. The powder is an excellent thickening agent and stabilizer that requires no cooking and can be dissolved in hot or cold water. I find it invaluable for thickening oil-free salad dressings. Look for guar gum in natural food markets. Many natural food markets will special order it for you if it is not one of their regularly stocked products.

Miso

Miso is a thick, salty condiment paste typically made from soybeans, although sometimes other legumes are used instead. Some varieties may be combined with barley or rice. Miso is used to flavor soups, sauces, dressings, and just about anything that needs a flavor boost. The soybean-grain combination is cooked, salted, and inoculated with a mold called koji, which begins a fermentation process taking from six months to three years. Chinese and Japanese families consider soybean miso an important source of protein because it contains all eight essential amino acids. Because miso is a living, cultured food and contains lactobacillus bacteria (a "friendly" strain of bacteria), it is considered a valuable aid to the digestive system. Natural food markets are the best source of miso because the varieties they carry are generally organic, unpasteurized, and contain live beneficial bacteria. (Miso with live cultures must be kept under refrigeration.) Imported miso, sold at Asian markets, has to be pasteurized, which destroys the live cultures and stops the fermentation.

White miso, sometimes referred to as mild miso, is lighter in color, has a shorter fermentation period, and produces a more delicate flavor. Red miso, sometimes called dark or strong miso, has been fermented longer and therefore has a bolder flavor.

Miso should be added at the end of the cooking process to avoid excess heat, which destroys the live cultures. Miso should be stored in the refrigerator; it will keep for several months.

Nut Meal

Nut meal is simply nuts that are finely ground. Make your own nut meal by grinding whole nuts in small batches in an electric mini-chopper/grinder or coffee grinder. For a coarser meal, whirl whole nuts in the food processor until you achieve the desired consistency. Be prepared for the startlingly loud noise when you begin the grinding process with whole almonds.

Nutritional Yeast Flakes

Far different from the yeast used in baking bread, this is a specially grown yeast product made for nutritional enhancement and for adding a cheesy flavor to foods. One teaspoon to two tablespoons added to savory recipes can create a flavor that hints of cheese. Rich in B vitamins, the variety called "vegetarian support formula" also contains vitamin B_{12}. Look for nutritional yeast flakes in natural food markets.

Pomegranate Syrup

Sometimes called pomegranate molasses, pomegranate syrup is a thick liquid with a pleasingly potent sweet-tart flavor used to season everything from appetizers to salads to main dishes. Usually available in bottles, pomegranate syrup is sold in Greek, Middle Eastern, and sometimes Italian markets.

Psyllium Husks

Psyllium, a natural dietary fiber, is well known for its colon cleansing abilities. However, in several of my recipes I use psyllium husks because they have the ability to bind ingredients and can take the place of eggs or egg whites in baked goods. I find the husks invaluable for binding nut loaves, casseroles, kugels, and even potato pancakes. Combine 1 tablespoon psyllium husks with ¼ cup water and set aside for just a few seconds. Stir the mixture into the recipe before baking or cooking. You can find psyllium husks in natural food markets as well as many drug stores.

Quinoa

This tiny, nutritious, ivory-colored whole "grain" is the fruit of an herbal plant that looks almost like millet before cooking. Originally grown in the high altitudes of Peru and Bolivia, quinoa was an important staple of the ancient Incas who considered it their "mother grain." Primarily a diet staple, quinoa was also used by the Incas in their religious ceremonies. It is delicious and distinctly different from other grains in appearance. The germ is on the outside of the grain, and when cooked, it encircles the grain, giving it the appearance of little flat circlets in the saucepan. Delicate, light, and pleasing in flavor, quinoa can take the place of rice in salads, casseroles, and side dishes. It can also be used as a breakfast cereal. Because quinoa is gluten free, it's ideal for those with gluten intolerance. Be sure to rinse quinoa in a strainer under running water for a full minute before cooking, to remove the natural saponin coating that can impart a bitter flavor. Quinoa cooks in 15 to 20 minutes. It can be found in natural food markets.

Rose Water

Frequently used in Middle Eastern cooking, rose water is made by distilling water with the petals of roses to produce a delightful flavoring liquid. A tincture of roses, rose water added in small amounts is a unique and refreshing flavor enhancement in dessert recipes. Rose water may be used to enhance other foods as well. Look for rose water in bottles in Middle Eastern and Greek markets.

Tomatillos

Originally from Central and South America and cultivated by the Aztecs, these small green tomatoes, about the size of plump cherry tomatoes or slightly larger, are covered with a thin, paper-like cellulose husk. Eaten raw or cooked, these unique little tomatoes impart a delicately tart, lemony flavor to salads, salsas, and sauces. Store tomatillos in their husks and remove them just before using. Wash the tomatillos thoroughly. Notice the characteristic slightly sticky surface that remains even after washing. Stored in the refrigerator, they will keep well for about three weeks. Look for tomatillos in Latino markets or supermarkets with a Latino clientele.

Umeboshi Vinegar

This unique vinegar is made from the brine used to salt and pickle ume plums, a savory Japanese delicacy. This vinegar is a familiar ingredient in macrobiotic cooking. Because of its tangy, salty, sour flavor, the vinegar makes a great seasoning for everything from stir-fries to salads. Its flavor is assertive, so it is best used sparingly. Store it at room temperature. Look for umeboshi vinegar in natural food markets in the macrobiotic section.

Vegan Parmesan

This dairy-free imitation Parmesan cheese may be made from ground nuts or ground textured soy protein and seasonings. Look for it in the dairy cooler at natural food markets. Store it in the refrigerator.

Wasabi Paste or Powder

Wasabi is Japanese horseradish ground into a powder or paste. The paste comes in a tube that should be stored in the refrigerator once it is opened. Read labels to find a brand that is lactose free. The powder comes in a tiny can and can be stored at room temperature. It needs to be blended with water just prior to serving. The wasabi paste has a more distinct flavor that holds up better when added to foods. Typically, wasabi is served at sushi bars and is mixed with soy sauce for dipping. Its unique flavor and spicy bite lend an appetizing touch to many foods like salad dressings and sauces. Look for wasabi paste and powder in Asian markets and natural food markets.

Xanthan Gum

This powdered natural carbohydrate is used as a thickener, emulsifier, and stabilizer in hot or cold foods. Xanthan gum is produced by a culture fermentation and is free of wheat, corn, gluten, fat, and dairy products. It adds good structure and texture to gluten-free baked goods when used in conjunction with gluten-free flours (for cakes, use 1/4 teaspoon per cup of flour; for breads, use 1 teaspoon per cup of flour). Because it is soluble in water, it is also ideal for thickening oil-free salad dressing (use 1/4 teaspoon to thicken 1 1/2 cups of dressing). Look for xanthan gum in natural food markets.

Resources

Retail Nut Suppliers

Allen Creek Farm

Fresh chestnuts, dried chestnuts, chestnut flour, chestnut knives, nutritional information, and many recipes for cooking with chestnuts and chestnut flour.

29112 NW 41st Avenue
Ridgefield, WA 98642
Phone: 360-887-3669
www.ChestnutsOnLine.com

Bono Macs of Hawaii

Sun-roasted macadamias in the shell, macadamias on a lei, macadamia nut oil, macadamia cookbook, and a special macadamia nutcracker that also cracks black walnuts and Brazil nuts.

27205 Waterford Drive
Santa Clarita, CA 91354-2422
Phone: 661-644-3057
wwwibonomacs.com

Diamond Organics

Organically grown nuts, nut butters, tahini, and seeds, in addition to a full line of organically grown fruits and vegetables.

1272 Highway 1
Moss Landing, CA 95039
Phone: 888-674-2642
www.diamondorganics.com

Girolami Farms

Fresh, organic, California-grown whole chestnuts in the shell, peeled and cooked chestnuts, and English walnuts in the shell and shelled. Offers a chestnut roaster, chestnut cookbook, gift baskets, and a special knife for opening chestnuts.

11502 East Eight Mile Road
Stockton, CA 95212
Phone: 209-931-0158
www.chestnutsforsale.com

Jaffe Bros.

Organically grown and untreated natural foods such as shelled and unshelled nuts, unsalted nut butters, seeds and sprouting materials, peas and beans, grains and flour, whole grain pastas, olives, and dried fruits.

28560 Lilac Road
Valley Center, CA 92082
Phone: 760-749-1133
www.organicfruitsandnuts.com

Living Tree Community Foods

Organically grown nuts, nut butters, tahini, and seeds.

PO Box 10082
Berkeley, CA 94709
Phone: 800-260-5534; 510-526-7106
www.livingtreecommunity.com

NutsOnline

Nuts, dried fruit, and seeds, including hard-to-find piñon nuts.
1201 E. Linden Avenue
Linden, NJ 07036
Phone: 800-558-6887
www.NutsOnline.com

SunOrganic Farm

Organically grown nuts, nut butters, tahini, and seeds.
411 S. Las Posas Road
San Marcos, CA 92078
Phone: 888-269-9888
www.sunorganic.com

Western Mixers, Inc.

Bulk and small orders of shelled and in-shell nuts and seeds, gift packs, and trail mixes of almonds, pistachios, cashews, Brazil nuts, and mixed nuts. Available raw, roasted, salted, blanched, sliced, and slivered.
Treasured Harvest Division
2910 San Fernando Road
Los Angeles, CA 90065
Phone: 323-344-5270
www.nutsite.com

Nutritional and Educational Information

Almond Board of California

Excellent source of nutritional information and research results on the latest studies.
1150 Ninth Street, Suite 1500
Modesto, CA 95354
Phone: 209-549-8262
www.almondsarein.com

California Macadamia Society

Macadamia nut health information and sources for purchasing nuts, nutcrackers, and macadamia trees.
PO Box 1298
Fallbrook, CA 92088
http://users.aol.com/CalMacSociety

California Pistachio Commission

Nutrition and health information, history, recipes, and instructions for how to grow your own pistachios.
1318 E. Shaw Avenue, Suite 420
Fresno, CA 93710-7912
Phone: 559-221-8294
www.pistachios.org

Diamond of California

Comprehensive Web site features research and health information. Suggestions for purchasing, storing, and toasting tree nuts. Recipes, gift items, cookbooks, and a catalog of products.

1050 South Diamond Street
Stockton, CA 95205
Phone: 209-467-6000
www.diamondwalnut.com

International Tree Nut Council, Inc.

Supports research, promotes worldwide nut consumption, and creates international standards within the nut industry. Publishes Cracker magazine, an international publication dedicated to the tree nut industry. Provides complete nutritional profiles on all tree nuts and articles pertaining to nuts.

Calle Boule 2, 3
43201 REUS
Spain
Phone: +34-977-331-416
www.treenuts.org

Planters Division/Kraft Foods Global, Inc.

Online newsletter gives nutritional information including vitamin and mineral content of individual nuts, as well as facts, articles, and history of nuts.

1 Kraft Court
Glenview, IL 60025
Phone: 800-543-5335
www.nutnutrition.com

The Peanut Institute

Supports extensive nutrition research and education programs to promote and encourage healthful lifestyles by including peanuts in the diet.

PO Box 70157
Albany, GA 31708-0157
Phone: 888-8PEANUT; 229-888-0216
www.peanut-institute.org

Appendix: Nutrition Tables for Nuts

Arginine, Phytosterols, and Antioxidants

Nuts are a rich source of arginine, the amino acid researchers believe helps to relax blood vessels and permit better blood flow. Arginine, the precursor to nitric oxide, is employed by the body to help open blood vessels and deliver more oxygen to the heart.

Phytosterols are natural plant fats found in fruits, vegetables, grains, nuts, and seeds that support recommended cholesterol levels and play a role in lowering excess blood lipids and reducing risk for heart disease. Phytosterols are nature's way of interfering with the absorption of cholesterol during digestion and aiding the body in the removal of surplus cholesterol. Phytosterols may offer some protection from colon cancer.

Antioxidants—a combination of vitamins, minerals, and enzymes found in plant foods—protect our tissues from oxidation that contributes to many degenerative diseases like cancer, heart disease, Alzheimer's disease, and Parkinson's disease. During the normal digestion process, unstable molecules called free radicals are formed. These molecules can cause damage to our DNA, cell membranes, and immune system. Antioxidants interfere with the oxidation of these free radicals and help prevent cell damage.

The figures in table 12.1 indicate the arginine content in grams for 3.5 ounces, or 100 grams, of nuts. The phytosterols are given in milligrams for 3.5 ounces. The last column shows the total antioxidant capacity (TAC) for 1 ounce of nuts.

Table 12.1 Arginine, phytosterols, and antioxidants in various nuts

Nut	Arginine (grams per 3.5 ounces nuts)	Phytosterols (milligrams per 3.5 ounces nuts)	Antioxidants (TAC per 1 ounce nuts)
Almonds, raw	2.73	120	1265
Brazil nuts, raw	1.36	NA	403
Cashews, raw	1.51	158	567
Chestnuts, raw	0.55	0	NA
Hazelnuts/Filberts, raw	1.68	116	2739
Macadamia nuts, raw	1.10	114	481
Peanuts, dry-roasted	2.89	220	899
Pecans, raw	0.93	102	5095
Pine nuts, raw	2.19	141	204
Pistachios, raw	1.84	214	2267
Walnuts, raw	1.83	72	3846

Table 12.2 Fatty acid composition of raw nuts, demonstrating the high levels of beneficial fats

Nut	% of Total Fat	% of Saturated Fat	% of Mono-unsaturated Fat	% of Poly-unsaturated LA (omega 6)†	% of Poly-unsaturated ALA (omega 3)‡
Almonds	80	8	52	23	0
Brazil nuts	91	22	30	33	0
Butternuts	84	2	18	59	15
Cashews	72	14	42	17	0
Chestnuts	8	2	3	3	0
Hazelnuts/Filberts	87	7	70	9	0
Macadamia nuts	95	16	74	7	0
Peanuts	76	11	38	25	0
Peanut oil	100	19	48	33	0
Pecans	91	8	59	26	1
Pine nuts	89	14	33	37	0
Pistachios	75	9	53	11	0
Walnuts	87	8	20	58	14
Walnut oil	100	11	24	54	11

†LA is linoleic acid, omega-6 essential fatty acid.
‡ALA is alpha linolenic acid, omega-3 essential fatty acid.

Table 12.3 Protein, carbohydrates, fiber, and fats in various nuts

Nut, 100gm (3.5 ounces)	Protein (gm)	Carbs (gm)	Fiber (gm)	Total Fat (gm)	% of Fat Calories	Saturated Fat (gm)	Monoun- saturated Fat (gm)	Polyun- saturated Fat (gm)	ALA (gm)
Almonds, whole, raw	21.3	19.7	11.8	50.6	78.9	3.9	32.2	12.2	0
Almond butter	15.1	21.2	3.7	59.1	84.0	5.6	38.3	11.9	0.42
Almonds, dry-roasted	22.1	19.3	11.8	52.8	79.6	4.0	33.7	12.7	0
Brazil nuts, whole, raw	14.3	12.8	5.4	66.2	90.9	16.2	23.0	23.8	0.06
Butternuts, whole, raw	24.9	12.0	4.7	57.0	83.8	1.3	10.4	33.7	8.72
Cashew butter	17.6	27.6	2.0	49.4	75.8	9.8	29.1	8.2	0.17
Cashews, dry-roasted	15.3	32.7	3.0	46.4	72.7	9.2	27.3	7.7	0.16
Chestnuts, cooked	2.0	27.8	NA	1.4	1.1	0.3	0.5	0.5	0.06
Hazelnuts, whole, raw	15.0	16.7	9.7	60.8	87.1	4.5	45.7	7.8	0.01
Macadamia nuts, whole, raw	7.9	13.8	8.6	10.6	95.0	12.1	58.9	1.3	0.21
Peanut butter	24.1	21.6	6.6	8.5	76.3	9.6	23.6	14.1	0.08
Peanuts, dry-roasted	23.7	21.5	8.0	8.5	76.4	6.9	24.6	15.7	0
Pecans, raw	9.2	13.9	9.6	72.0	93.7	6.2	40.8	20.6	1.0
Pecans, dry-roasted	9.5	13.5	9.5	74.3	94.1	6.3	43.9	19.6	1.0
Pine nuts, raw	24.0	14.2	4.5	50.7	80.6	7.8	19.1	20.7	0.12
Pistachios, dry-roasted	21.2	27.1	10.3	45.7	72.6	5.5	24.1	13.6	0.26
Pistachios, raw	20.5	29.2	10.0	43.2	70.5	5.3	22.7	12.8	0.25
Walnuts, black, whole, raw	24.4	12.1	5.0	56.6	83.9	3.6	12.7	33.5	3.31
Walnuts, English, whole, raw	15.2	13.7	6.7	65.2	89.7	6.1	8.9	38.1	9.08

Table 12.4 Mineral content of various nuts

Nut, 100gm (3.5 ounces)	Calcium (mg)	Copper (mg)	Iron (mg)	Magnesium (mg)	Manganese (mg)	Potassium (mg)	Selenium (mcg)	Zinc (mg)
Almonds, whole, raw	248.0	1.1	4.29	275.0	2.5	728.0	7.9	3.3
Almond butter	270.0	0.9	3.7	303.0	2.4	758.0	NA	3.0
Almonds, dry-roasted	266.0	1.2	4.5	286.0	2.6	746.0	7.9	3.5
Brazil nuts, whole, raw	176.0	1.8	3.4	225.0	0.8	600.0	2960.0	4.6
Butternuts, whole, raw	53.0	0.5	4.0	237.0	38.7	421.0	17.2	3.1
Cashew butter	43.0	2.2	5.0	258.0	0.8	546.0	11.5	5.2
Cashews, dry-roasted	45.0	2.2	6.0	260.0	0.8	565.0	11.7	5.6
Chestnuts, cooked	46.0	0.4	1.7	54.0	0.9	715.0	0	0.3
Hazelnuts, whole, raw	114.0	17.3	4.7	163.0	6.2	680.0	4.0	2.5
Macadamia nuts, whole, raw	85.0	0.8	3.7	130.0	4.0	368.0	3.6	0.2
Peanut butter	41.0	0.5	1.9	159.0	1.87	747.0	1.3	2.8
Peanuts, dry-roasted	54.0	0.7	2.3	176.0	2.1	658.0	1.3	3.1
Pecans, raw	70.0	1.2	2.5	121.0	4.5	410.0	6.0	4.5
Pecans, dry-roasted	72.0	1.7	2.8	132.0	4.9	424.0	4.0	5.1
Pistachios, dry-roasted	108.0	1.3	4.2	120.0	1.3	1033.0	8.0	2.3
Pistachios, raw	107.0	1.3	4.3	121.0	1.2	977.0	7.0	2.2
Walnuts, black, whole, raw	58.0	1.0	3.1	202.0	4.3	524.0	17.0	3.4
Walnuts, English, whole, raw	104.0	1.6	2.9	158.0	3.4	441.0	4.6	3.1

Table 12.5 Vitamin content of various nuts

Nut, 100gm (3.5 ounces)	Thiamine B_1 (mg)	Riboflavin B_2 (mg)	Niacin B_3 (mg)	Pyridoxine B_6 (mg)	Folate (mcg)	Vitamin E (IU)
Almonds, whole, raw	0.24	0.8	3.9	0.13	29.0	26.18
Almond butter	0.13	0.6	2.9	0.08	65.2	20.3
Almonds, dry-roasted	0.07	0.86	3.9	0.13	33.0	26.3
Brazil nuts, whole, raw	1.0	0.12	1.6	0.25	4.0	7.6
Butternuts, whole, raw	0.38	0.14	1.0	0.56	66.2	3.5
Cashew butter	0.3	0.18	0.27	0.25	68.3	1.56
Cashews, dry-roasted	0.2	0.2	0.24	0.25	69.2	0.57
Chestnuts, cooked	0.15	0.1	0.73	0.23	38.4	0
Hazelnuts, whole, raw	0.64	0.11	1.8	0.56	113.0	15.18
Macadamia nuts, whole, raw	1.2	0.16	2.47	0.28	11.0	0.54
Peanut butter	0.13	0.11	13.69	0.45	92.0	10.0
Peanuts, dry-roasted	0.44	0.09	13.52	0.26	145.3	7.8
Pecans, raw	0.66	0.13	1.68	0.21	22.0	3.66
Pecans, dry-roasted	0.45	0.1	1.68	0.09	16.0	3.75
Pine nuts, raw	0.81	0.19	3.57	0.11	57.3	3.5
Pistachios, dry-roasted	0.84	0.16	1.43	1.7	50.0	4.26
Pistachios, raw	0.87	0.16	1.3	1.7	51.0	4.6
Walnuts, black, whole, raw	0.22	0.11	0.69	0.55	65.5	2.62
Walnuts, English, whole, raw	0.34	0.15	1.91	0.54	98.0	2.94

References

Adams, Ruth, and Frank Murray. 1973. *The good seeds, the rich grains, the hardy nuts for a healthier, happier life*. New York: Larchmont.

Adams, Ruth, and Frank Murray. 1975. *All you should know about health foods*. New York: Larchmont.

Anderson, Jean, and Barbara Deskins. 1995. *Nutrition bible*. New York: Morrow.

Apicius. 1958. *The Roman cookery book: A critical translation of the art of cooking*. Trans. Barbara Flower and Elisabeth Rosenbaum. London: Nevill.

Apicius. 1977. *Cookery and dining in imperial Rome*. Ed. and trans. Joseph Dommers Vehling. New York: Dover.

Awad, A. B., K. Chan, A. Downie, and C. S. Fink. 2000. Peanuts as a source of B-sitosterol, a sterol with anti-cancer properties. *Nutr and Cancer* 36:238–41.

Barnett, Robert A., ed. 1991. *The American health food book*. New York: Dutton.

Booth, Sally Smith. 1971. *Hung, strung and potted*. New York: Potter.

Clark, Morton Gill. 1967. *A world of nut recipes*. New York: Funk.

Clarkson, P. 1996. Oral L-arginine improves endothelium-dependent dilation in hypercholeterolimic young adults. *J Clin Invest* 97:1989–94.

Colquhoun, D. M., J. A. Humphries, D. Moores, and S. M. Somerset. 1996. Effects of a macadamia nut enriched diet on serum lipids and lipoproteins compared to a low fat diet. *Food Aust* 48:216–22.

Davidson, Alan. 1999. *The Oxford companion to food*. Oxford: Oxford Univ. Press.

Davis, Brenda, and Vesanto Melina. 2000. *Becoming vegan*. Summertown, TN: Book Publishing Company.

East West Journal. 1987. *Shopper's guide to natural foods*. Garden City Park, NY: Avery.

Erasmus, Udo. 1993. *Fats that heal, fats that kill*. Burnaby, BC: Alive Books.

Fraser, G. E., J. Sabate, W. L. Beeson, and T. M. Strahan. 1992. A possible protective effect of nut consumption on risk of coronary heart disease. The Adventist health study. *Arch Intern Med* 152:1416–24.

Hu, F. B., M. J. Stampfer, J. E. Manson, E. B. Rimm, G. A. Colditz, B. A. Rosmer, F. E. Speizer, C. H. Hennekers, and W. C. Willett. 1998. Frequent nut consumption and risk of coronary heart disease in women: Prospective cohort study. *BMJ* 317:1341–45.

Jenkins, D. J., C. W. Kendall, A. Marchie, D. A. Faulkner, J. M. Wong, R. de Souza, A. Emam, T. L. Parker, E. Vidgen, K. G. Lapsley, E. A. Trautwein, R. G. Josse, L. A. Leiter, and P. W. Connelly. 2003. Effects of a dietary portfolio of cholesterol-lowering foods vs lovastatin on serum lipids and C-reactive protein. *JAMA* 290:502–10.

Jiang, R., J. E. Manson, M. J. Stampfer, S. Liu, W. C. Willett, and F. B. Hu. 2002. Nut and peanut butter consumption and risk of type 2 diabetes in women. *JAMA* 288:2554–60.

Kaufman, William I. 1964. *The nut cookbook*. Garden City, NY: Doubleday.

Kiple, Kenneth F., and Kriemhild Conee Ornelas, eds. 2000. *The Cambridge world history of food*. Cambridge, UK: Cambridge Univ. Press.

Klevay, L. 1993. Copper in nuts may lower heart disease risk. *Arch Intern Med* 153:401–2.

Kritchevsky, D., S. A. Tepper, S. K. Czarnecki, and D. M. Klurfeld. 1982. Atherogenicity of animal and vegetable protein influence of the lysine to arginine ratio. *Atherosclerosis* 41:429.

Kushi, L. H., A. R. Folsom, R. J. Prineas, P. J. Mink, Y. Wu, and R. M. Bostick. 1996. Dietary antioxidant vitamins and death from coronary heart disease in postmenopausal women. *N Engl J Med* 334:1156–62.

Lehner, Ernst, and Johanna Lehner. 1962. *Folklore and odysseys of food and medicinal plants*. New York: Tudor.

Margen, Sheldon, ed., and Editors of the University of California at Berkeley Wellness Letter. 1992. *The wellness encyclopedia of food and nutrition*. New York: Rebus.

McGee, Harold. 1984. *On food and cooking*. New York: Scribner.

Melina, Vesanto, and Brenda Davis. 2003. *The new becoming vegetarian*. Summertown, TN: Healthy Living Publications.

Midgley, John. 1993. *The goodness of nuts and seeds*. London: Pavilion Books Limited.

Mindell, Earl R. 1994. *Food as medicine*. New York: Simon & Schuster, Inc.

Oregon Filbert Commission. 1973. *A treasury of prize winning filbert recipes*. 3rd ed. Tigard, OR: Oregon Filbert Commission.

Rogers, Ford. 1997. *Nuts: A cookbook*. Edison, NJ: Chartwell.

Root, Waverly. 1980. *Food*. New York: Simon & Schuster, Inc.

Salter, Tina, and Steve Siegelman. 2001. *Nuts: Sweet and savory recipes from Diamond of California*. Berkeley: Ten Speed.

Sanders, T., and R. McMichael. 2000. Occurrence of resveratrol in edible peanuts. *J Agric Food Chem* 48(4):1243–46.

Shannon, Nomi. 1999. *The raw gourmet*. Burnaby, BC: Alive Books.

Spiller, Gene. 2000. *Healthy nuts*. Garden City Park, NY: Avery.

Spiller, G. A., D. A. Jenkins, O. Bosello, J. E. Gates, L. N. Cragen, and B. Bruce. 1998. Nuts and plasma lipids: An almond-based diet lowers LDL-C while preserving HDL-C. *J Am Col Nutr* 17:285–90.

Tannahill, Reay. 1988. *Food in history*. New York: Crown.

Tsai, C. J., M. F. Leitzman, F. B. Hu, W. C. Willett, and E. L. Giovanucci. 2004. A prospective cohort study of nut consumption and the risk of gallstone disease in men. *Am J Epid* 160:961–68.

Vaughan, John Griffith, and Catherine Allison Geissler. 1997. *The new Oxford book of food plants*. Oxford: Oxford Univ. Press.

Index

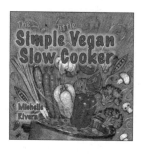